COLD WAR CROSSINGS

NUMBER FORTY-FIVE

Walter Prescott Webb Memorial Lectures

A list of other titles in this series appears at the back of the book.

COLD WAR CROSSINGS

International Travel and Exchange across the Soviet Bloc, 1940s–1960s

EDITED BY PATRYK BABIRACKI AND KENYON ZIMMER

INTRODUCTION BY VLADISLAV ZUBOK

CONTRIBUTORS:
Michael David-Fox
Patryk Babiracki
Nick Rutter
Elidor Mëhilli
Constantin Katsakioris
Marsha Siefert

Published for the University of Texas at Arlington
by Texas A&M University Press
College Station

First edition
This paper meets the requirements of ANSI/NISO Z39.48–1992 (Permanence of Paper).
Binding materials have been chosen for durability.
∞

Library of Congress Cataloging-in-Publication Data

Cold War crossings : international travel and exchange across the Soviet bloc, 1940s–1960s / edited by Patryk Babiracki and Kenyon Zimmer ; introduction by Vladislav Zubok ; contributors: Michael David-Fox, Patryk Babiracki, Nick Rutter, Elidor Mkhilli, Constantin Katsakioris, Marsha Siefert. — First edition.
pages cm — (Walter Prescott Webb memorial lectures ; number forty-five)
Includes bibliographical references and index.
ISBN 978-1-62349-030-0 (cloth : alk. paper) — ISBN 978-1-62349-142-0 (e-book)
1. Soviet Union—Relations. 2. Communist countries—Relations. 3. Exchange of persons programs, Soviet—History. I. Babiracki, Patryk, 1978– editor of compilation. II. Zimmer, Kenyon, 1980– editor of compilation. III. David-Fox, Michael, 1965– author. IV. Series: Walter Prescott Webb memorial lectures ; no. 45.
DK266.45.C65 2014
327.47—dc23
2013040307

To Robert Fairbanks

CONTENTS

PREFACE

This volume is an outcome of two related initiatives. On March 10, 2011, the Department of History at the University of Texas at Arlington hosted the annual Walter Prescott Webb Memorial Lectures, entitled "Transnational Perspectives on the Soviet Bloc, 1944–1991." Michael David-Fox, then of the University of Maryland–College Park, delivered the keynote address; the other participants were Marsha Siefert (Central European University, Budapest), Constantin Katsakioris (Hellenic Archives, Athens), and Patryk Babiracki (University of Texas at Arlington). This collection features the expanded versions of their lectures. Contributing to this volume are also the two co-winners of the accompanying international essay competition, Elidor Mëhilli and Nick Rutter, who were in the final stages of their doctoral work at Princeton and Yale Universities at the time. Vladislav Zubok (London School of Economics) kindly agreed to write the introduction. The essays follow two parallel orders: they are organized chronologically and proceed from general-theoretical overviews to case studies that are more detailed. We wish to thank all the authors for their patience and gracious cooperation during the volume's long gestation phase. We are grateful to the Department of History and our university for sponsoring and organizing the Webb Lectures and for the assistance of Jennifer Lawrence in particular. This support left us with the sole responsibility—indeed, the distinct pleasure—of coordinating the event's intellectual dimensions and ensuring that this volume would see the light of day. In editing the final versions of the manuscript, Patryk Babiracki benefitted from the Junior Research Fellowship at the Institute for Advanced Study of the Central European University in Budapest in 2012–13. Following a long tradition, and with enthusiastic appreciation, we dedicate this book to our colleague Robert Fairbanks, who served as Chair of our Department of History before stepping down in the summer of 2011.

Patryk Babiracki
Kenyon Zimmer

COLD WAR CROSSINGS

INTRODUCTION

Vladislav Zubok

The power-centered and ideology-driven debates that affected the historiography of the Cold War have given way to wider interdisciplinary projects. Historians began to rethink the boundaries of international history between 1950 and 1990 beyond the well-known narratives of the US-Soviet confrontation, divided Europe, and the Western and Soviet blocs. Attention shifted to studies of lesser-known developments in Africa, Asia, and Latin America, the nonaligned movement, and other alternatives to bipolarity. With this, the central structures of the Cold War—the divide between the blocs and the blocs themselves—went out of scholarly fashion.[1]

This volume returns to such unfashionable topics as the Soviet bloc, the Iron Curtain, and East-West relations. All the authors raise novel questions linking traditional political questions about the Cold War with transnational experiences. What was the effect of the cross-border transfers of people, technologies, and culture on the fate of the Soviet Union and the whole Soviet bloc? What were the consequences of attempts to homogenize the bloc and to export its "soft power"? How did the gap between the realities and expectations about "real socialism" affect both pilgrims from outside and the people inside? Particularly appealing is a renewed focus on individuals, as opposed to the emphasis on the state and state structures with the almost inevitable simplifications and clichés that follow from such emphasis.[2]

When I read the contributions to this volume, my scholarly curiosity was blended with an acute sense of remembrance. It is difficult to explain to younger people the mighty psychological and cultural effects that the crossings of the Iron Curtain produced. Polish journalist Ryszard Kapuściński famously described the effect of "crossing the frontier" for the first time in his autobiographical travelogue.[3] Yet crossing the border of

Poland as a journalist of *Sztandar Młodych* in 1956 was easier than crossing the Iron Curtain from the Soviet Union in 1986, when I did it for the first time. As a young Soviet-trained intellectual, specializing in the political history of the United States, I belonged to the generation that my colleague Sergei I. Zhuk called "the Beatles generation." We watched imported movies in Soviet movie theaters, read the illustrated magazine *Amerika,* and crossed the frontier thousands of times in our dreams.[4] Yet it was quite improbable in real life. The Soviet regime erected what Michael David-Fox calls the "semipermeable membrane"—i.e., regulated exchanges and contacts with the West. The membrane was double: one valve allowed exit to East European members of the Soviet bloc; and only the next valve regulated access to the "capitalist world."

Getting an external passport and "*valiuta*" (hard currency) to travel abroad from the Soviet Union until 1989–90 required a cascade of permissions and authorizations: first the triangle of the Komsomol or the party local secretary, the head of the local trade union, and the head of the working unit; then the "commission of Old Bolsheviks" that tested your loyalty and political correctness, then the clearance of the higher-ups, including the KGB and the special sector at the party central apparatus. A denial or refusal could occur in any part of this cumbersome and mostly secretive pyramid. Scientists, artists, dancers, entire symphonic orchestras, and of course many Soviet Jews had to bid farewell to their dreams of crossing frontiers because they could not obtain clearance, often without any apparent reason, just because somebody "up there" did not like something about them and did not trust their loyalty—as in the case of ballet dancer Maya Plisetskaia, who wrote an angry testimony of her experiences.[5]

This volume reminds us that, these fierce obstacles notwithstanding, hundreds of thousands, if not millions, of Soviet citizens crossed the Iron Curtain. Their ability to work, travel, and teach in "socialist" and "nonsocialist" countries created a transnational movement that the authors put in the center of their studies.

What was the impact of the movement through "the membrane"—for the people who went through it and those who did not? Broader historical frameworks can impart new meanings to old personal experiences. First, they help to understand how much the identity, one can even say patriotism, of the "Soviet" and the "East European" individual depended on external factors, such as encounters with foreign tourists, Western movies, songs, and, of course, the ability to travel outside one's country.[6] Second, new frameworks help connect the movement of people between the blocs to the unequal spread of mass consumerism and consumerist culture—an increasingly important topic for the Cold War period. The select access to the outside world transformed the Soviet and East European visitors into impromptu merchants: those Marco Polos brought back home the trophies of their travel, which generated a new powerful status hierarchy in their societies, a renegotiation of the division between the "haves" and the "have-nots." In the USSR of the 1970s and 1980s, this dependence grew phenomenally among the elites, particularly cultural elites.

Russian political thinker Dmitrii Furman observed: "For all Soviet people, including the higher echelons of the party the West has always been an object of longing. Trips to the West were the most important status symbol. There is nothing you can do about this; it is 'in the blood,' in the culture." In this statement the word "always" can clearly be contested. The longing for the West was a historical phenomenon that was "constructed"—above all, by the movements through the Iron Curtain and the observed contrast in consumerist capacities between the West and the East. Millions of Soviets (and Chinese, Albanians, and North Koreans) who did not travel outside their encapsulated societies could not have any longing for or envy of the West.[7]

The contribution of Michael David-Fox in this volume helps to address these broader framework issues in the light of rich new evidence. He analyzes the demise of the Soviet superiority complex, developed in the 1930s at the height of Stalin's terror, and suggests that the "overextension" of this superiority complex may have started at its inception, as early as during Stalin's rule. Even the officials of the VOKS (All-Union Society for Cultural Relations with Foreign Countries), employed to advertize "achievements of socialism," could not totally suppress a cognitive disjunction between the noisy "superiority" propaganda and dismal Soviet realities on the ground.[8] And the cumulative experience of the millions of Soviet people who crossed the western borders of the Soviet Union during World War II was of great historic significance—if less well studied than the later exposure of educated Soviet youth to Western ideas and cultural influences from the 1950s through the 1970s.

David-Fox reminds us that border-crossing capacities enhanced individual status in Soviet hierarchies long before the Cold War. The Stalinist system of consumption was hierarchically organized: privileged elites had the right of special access to consumer goods that the masses did not, and were not even aware of. This meant that Stalinist elites had a dispensation for *primae noctis* right to all foreign goods. There were no exceptions: even the American "donations" during the years of Lend-Lease went first of all to the elite functionaries; the same was true of the carloads and planeloads of "trophy goods" pillaged from conquered Germany.

Another important aspect of the Soviet superiority myth, David-Fox explains, was the state-supported Soviet intelligentsia and the role of "Russian culture." He adds a new wrinkle to the familiar story of collaboration between the Stalinist state and the surviving intelligentsia. For the state the emphasis on high culture provided "the best barrier" against Western technological and economic superiority. For the privileged elite of the Soviet intelligentsia this ensured state funding for cultural production and a high status that Western intellectuals could only dream about.

The discussion about the transnational functions of the Soviet intelligentsia, however, begs for a follow-up exploration: about the transnational functions of European Western intellectuals in Soviet attempts to assert their superiority. The research of David-Fox demonstrates that the Soviet Union as the "vanguard of progressive humanity" came to depend on the plaudits of the "world intelligentsia"—regularly remunerated by carefully orchestrated visits and honoraria. This worked during the 1930s, when the Soviet Union could present itself as the last bulwark against the march of Nazism and fascism. It even worked after 1945 with the Stockholm Appeal, backed by the prestige of Western friends of the peripatetic public intellectual Ilya Ehrenburg. Gradually, however, the collaboration of Western intellectuals and the effectiveness of the Soviet intelligentsia (and Soviet culture) in maintaining the Soviet superiority complex eroded, and at some point crumbled completely.

David-Fox's essay is a good start for discussing how this happened. He gives consumerism, not ideas, the central stage. The new cohorts of the Soviet intelligentsia, after a brief flirtation with asceticism, became vulnerable to Western consumerism. Instead of asserting the primacy of Soviet culture over the "soulless" West, many Soviet artists and intellectuals abroad felt intensely inferior to their Western colleagues because abroad they became the slaves of *valiuta*—dollars, Deutschmarks, and even liras. The Soviet ruble was worthless abroad, and the Soviet bank exchanged only a limited number of rubles into *valiuta*—as a meager per-diem. The resulting feeling of humiliation bred anti-Soviet sentiments more effectively than the reading of Aleksandr Solzhenitsyn and Andrei Sakharov.[9]

Finally, as Aleksei Yurchak and Sergei Zhuk demonstrate, the Soviet educated youth of the 1970s eagerly embraced Western rock culture that for many became more important than Soviet "high culture."[10]

And, again, it would be worthwhile to broaden the scope of discussion to include the "world intelligentsia," particularly its leftist part. During the 1960s increasing numbers of intellectual pilgrims to the Soviet Union preferred to deal with the Thaw writers and poets like Evgenii Evtushenko and Andrei Voznesenskii and were no longer impressed by Soviet economic and social policies. Finally, after the Soviet invasion of Czechoslovakia in 1968 the "world intelligentsia"—even the French communist intellectuals!—became disillusioned with the Soviet experiment. Some switched to China in search of a genuine revolutionary flavor; others practiced Third Worldism, etc. The Soviet Union during the Brezhnevite *zastoi* (stagnation) became boring and futureless for Western intellectuals—a verdict more terrible and damning than the verdicts of the historian Robert Conquest and the dissident writer Aleksandr Solzhenitsyn.

Patryk Babiracki recently reminded us that the movements of people across the Soviet bloc were of more than just two kinds: Soviet "occupiers" coming to Eastern Europe and the victims of Sovietization going to the Soviet gulag.[11] Here Babiracki explores a little-known case of the Soviet Union bringing in Poles not as prisoners, but as observers on tours of Ukrainian collective farms—who were then to promote the Soviet-style collectivization of Polish agriculture upon returning home. The story is bizarre—an exercise in futility—but raises a broader concern: why did Soviet communists advertise even the most dubious of their "achievements," despite many failures and the diminishing effect of advertising? Babiracki rightfully "resists easy characterizations" of this phenomenon. At the same time he mentions a Russian tradition of "Potemkin villages"—e.g., elaborate efforts to deceive foreigners. I would be more cautious in using the "Potemkinist" discourse: nothing the Russian tsars and their favorites had offered to foreigners can be compared to *pokazukha* (window dressing) and *tufta* (baloney) of Soviet officials. Even more importantly, the tsarist empire was open to foreigners and thousands of them lived and worked there permanently—in sharp contrast to the Soviet Union after the 1930s. Some sources indicate that Soviet *pokazukha* originated in the gulag and was guided more by the desire to impress and deceive higher authorities than the habit to deceive foreigners.

The myth of Soviet superiority over "liberated Poland" would be another approach to explore in this context. This myth presumed an unequal relationship that served the needs of Soviet domination and Cold War policies. It also demanded forgetting the recent history of Soviet-Polish relations, concerning Katyń, the Soviet-Polish War of 1920, the Warsaw uprising in 1944, and the repression of Polish resistance. Yet at the same time this relationship pushed Soviet officials to tirelessly persuade the Poles of the superiority of "everything Soviet": not only cultural productions—which annoyed Polish intellectuals like Czesław Miłosz—but also collectivized agriculture. And what about the Polish sense of cultural superiority over the Russians, Ukrainians, and Belorussians? I would be curious to learn if Polish peasants, on tours of Ukraine, were influenced by this mentality, prominent among Polish intellectuals. Babiracki's data has little to say about it. Much more important for peasants seemed to be the stories of the disastrous Ukrainian famine of 1932–33—and other horror stories they could learn during World War II—from Ukrainian forced laborers and even Soviet soldiers.

The cross-border traffic of peasants to promote collectivization in Poland was bound to fail. Instead, another type of cross-border traffic between Poland and the Soviet Union succeeded remarkably—the traffic of Western ideas and consumer goods to Soviet society via the Polish press, cinema, and tourists. This Polish-Soviet traffic was destabilizing enough for Soviet authorities to close the membrane valve twice, after the Polish October of 1956 and during Solidarity's heyday of 1980–81.

Nick Rutter in his chapter explores a forgotten cross-border development that was a success for the Soviet cause. In 1951 the Free German Youth's leader Erich Honecker and his friend Erich Mielke hosted the third World Youth Festival in East Berlin. Rutter explains why communist-promoted youth festivals could become a serious challenge to the Western discourse of the Iron Curtain. It was a spectacular demonstration of *pokazukha* on an international scale. In a premonition of the similar festival in Moscow in July–August 1957, communist police states suspended for a few weeks their border controls and domestic monitoring of foreigners. In defiance of Western expectations, the GDR regime allowed thousands of foreigners to experience something akin to "direct democracy." Rutter's piece complicates the assumed divide between the period of late Stalinism and the post-Stalin period. He shows how a regulated breach of the Iron Curtain could be possible at the height of the Korean War. One should also recall that 1951 was the time of spy mania in the Soviet bloc, when the communist parties in Eastern Europe were purged of "Titoists"; when "anti-cosmopolitanism" and the xenophobic campaigns in the USSR were about to reach their menacing crescendo.

Rutter also documents the Western official response—fearful and fierce attempts to stop Western youth from attending the communist-sponsored festival. Such a response was prodded by rigid anti-communist policies, combined with the McCarthyist politics of the United States. Their effect, however, was immediately harmful to Western Cold War efforts. Going to the festival not only acquired the taste of forbidden fruit, but Western travelers also—to the delight of communist propagandists—began to raise the question: whose iron curtain is it—the East's or the West's?

Rutter views this "suspension" of the Iron Curtain as part of the propagandistic contestation of the Iron Curtain metaphor. Yet 1951 was also a crucial time of diplomatic battles for the GDR's international legitimacy. Rutter mentions the role of Nikolai Mikhailov, head of the Soviet Komsomol (the Communist Youth League), in organizing the Berlin Youth Festival. Mikhailov reported to Georgii Malenkov. Considering the complexity of the temporary opening of the Iron Curtain in *several countries* of the Soviet bloc, the line of command no doubt went all the way to Stalin. Soviet interest in boosting the GDR's international legitimacy in 1951 should be placed in a larger context: in March 1952 Stalin would orchestrate the proposal of German unification to the Western powers. The East Berlin festival was followed by a propaganda campaign by the GDR's leadership to prove they were ready for reunification with West Germany. In reality, the GDR's communist leaders were desperate to gain more sovereignty and legitimacy: organizing a large and open international event was an ideal way to tell the Soviets and the world that the East German state was mature enough to cope with big tasks.[12]

The East Berlin festival can be viewed as an outcome of various factors: intentions, capacities, and timing. We have already discussed the intentions of the GDR's leaders and their Soviet backers. The diffusion and federalization of authority during the festival was perhaps only intended in part; it was also the result of lack of capacities. Because of "the primitive state of surveillance technology in 1951" Stasi just could not maintain surveillance of tens of thousands of youth. The same problem faced the Soviets in the summer of 1957. With the growth of police capacities, the desire of the secret police to control and isolate became irresistible—even though it greatly diminished the propagandist effects of the festival and its atmosphere of spontaneity and universal amity. In other words, Stasi in 1959 probably would have not allowed what happened in 1951. And this leads to the factor of timing. Seven or eight years later the risk of "suspension" of the Iron Curtain, still tolerable for the communist authorities in 1951, would become prohibitively high. One obvious reason was the growth of Western consumerism and West German *Wirtschaftswunder*. Another reason was the diminishing optimism of the postwar Eastern youth. In 1951 tens of thousands of East Germans who visited West Berlin during the festival said: "Admittedly, you've got it better. What matters, though, is that while you're going down, we're building up." In 1959–61 these same East Germans would take an U-Bahn westward without looking back.

Constantin Katsakioris pioneered transnational research about Africans in Soviet cities and in this volume explores the broader implications of the Soviet romance with African decolonization. During the Khrushchev era, Africa became a powerful booster to the Soviet sense of *moral* superiority—in comparison to all Western powers, the Soviets viewed themselves as completely free of the crimes of colonialism. Until recently, some of us wrote that African anti-colonial leaders of in the late 1950s saw the Soviet Union not as a totalitarian state, but as a beacon of progress, an alternative to much-hated capitalist ways. Katsakioris, however, supplies evidence that theirs was a much more clear-headed and critical attitude. He documents tensions between the Soviets and the assortment of governments and peoples he calls "Southerners"—presumably those from the global South. Words like "frustrated" and "disillusioned" are scattered throughout the text.

What were the sources of tensions? The most obvious source was the difference of interests between the Soviet Union and the leaders and intellectuals of the decolonization movement. There was also inequality in their relationship, what Katsakioris calls the "Orientalist" and "paternalistic approach" of Soviet officials to the "Southerners." African postcolonial leaders, most of them Western-educated intellectuals, did not get along easily with Soviet officials of Stalinist vintage. The Soviet communist apparatchiks were quite frustrated by the outcome of the Soviet romance with African leaders in 1959–64. The Polianskii report of October 1964, prepared by the Presidium member Dmitrii Polianskii to attack Nikita Khrushchev's policies, concluded: "We often lack any practical knowledge of those countries, yet provide them across-the-board financial, technical-economic, military and other assistance." Soviet generosity in Africa in many cases "led to deplorable results: the leaders of those countries ate what we gave them, and then turned away from us. Capitalists laugh at us and they have reason to do so."[13]

Still, there were those on the Soviet side who viewed Africa through ideological and even romantic lenses. Katsakioris mentions the friendship between Senghor and Russian poet Evgenii Evtushenko and the latter's invitation to the first Festival of Negro Arts in Dakar in 1966. During the 1960s Evtushenko, Andrei Voznesenskii, and other creative artists of the Thaw vintage represented Soviet "soft power" much more effectively than the host of Soviet diplomats, trade representatives, and the military. I would only encourage researchers to further explore this aspect of border crossings.

Still another source of dissatisfaction was the living experience of Africans in the Soviet Union and tension between them and the Soviet population: in Georgia and Azerbaijan, yet also in Moscow and Leningrad. Some caveats are appropriate here: generalizations can be too facile, particularly such notions as "South" and "Southerners." And the degree of tension and frustration can be better understood within various contexts: Katsakioris's evidence on the African demonstration in Moscow is new and important, yet the reactions on the African and Soviet side to this demonstration cannot be analyzed outside of the broader international context, including the rise of the Civil Rights movement in the United States. Still, the chapter has fascinating insights.

What about the issue of race and racism? Certainly, some encounters between the Soviets and the "Southerners" produced racist reactions. Katsakioris, however, finds more in the growing irritation of the Soviet population against the African and Arab students who came to study in the Soviet Union in the 1960s. These students were usually much better off than the average Soviet citizen, and their freedom to cross borders not only evoked envy, but also provided them additional income (via black market activities) and privileged status (among young Soviet women). Again, as in other contributions to this volume, the growing centrality of consumerism and economic considerations leaps forth.

The paradoxes and problems of "socialist exchange" as practiced in backward Albania by more advanced "socialist" countries is the theme of Elidor Mëhilli's contribution to this volume. Albania became a member of the East European Soviet bloc, and yet in an economic and social sense it was closer to the postcolonial countries of Africa. Mëhilli writes that socialist exchange cannot be reduced to scavenging practices by the Soviet Union. The Soviets (and the East Germans, the Poles, and the Czechoslovaks) had a give-and-take type of cooperation even under Stalin, not to mention in later periods. Inspired by Stephen Kotkin,[14] Mëhilli writes about this cooperation as a genuinely ideological enterprise that created a "vast comparative field stretching from the Balkans to Siberia." Comparisons within this field, however, also produced envy, misunderstandings, and tensions. The chapter reveals that the communist authorities resisted and remained unprepared to make realistic assessments of these problems—ideological blinkers most surely augmented incomprehension.

The Albanian case reveals strikingly common issues for different parts of the Soviet bloc. In particular, the material conditions of the state-dictated economy challenged and often defeated better intentions of "proletarian solidarity." The absence of a real estate market or other kinds of "markets," and the state distribution of food and goods, ensured that any foreign specialists, "fraternal" or not, would be settled in privileged ghettoes. Such was the case of foreign specialists in Magnitogorsk in the 1930s, and the same happened to the specialists from Czechoslovakia, the GDR, and the Soviet Union in Albania in the 1950s. Equally, the absolute centralization of international relations in the communist countries ensured that even a minor scuffle between the specialists and the locals, as well as problems with their pay and performance, automatically became a matter of high politics. It could be interpreted as a sign of disrespect, probably deliberate, toward the country that sent the specialists and toward the leader of that country. The Soviet-Yugoslav split in 1948 and the Sino-Soviet split of 1960 were linked to the problems, real or imagined, with Soviet specialists stationed in Yugoslavia and China.

Last but not least, socialist exchange exposed and abetted the feelings of superiority and inferiority we have already discussed. The Albanian communist hosts parried the complaints of East German specialists about Albania's backwardness by complaining that East Germans did not work hard enough! One wonders how the same dynamics, practices, and problems can also be found on a much greater scale in the case of Soviet assistance to the People's Republic of China during the same time. The current archival boom in China is spurring new fields of research that may soon enable us to make this comparison as well.

Marsha Siefert's chapter follows another unhappy cross-boundary initiative, a cinematic project that was never consummated. An initiative to produce a joint Soviet-American film based on the 1961 novel by American sci-fi writer Mitchell Wilson led to years and years of frustration and procrastination on both sides. Siefert views this not so much as a history of failure, but as a fascinating process: she tracks two-level negotiations on both the US and Soviet side, involving the State Department, Mosfilm, and other Soviet ministeries.

Still, it is difficult not to ask: why did *this particular* encounter end in failure? The verdict is ambiguous. The Soviet bureaucracy actually was not the main obstacle, at least not always. Other joint productions between the Goskino and foreign cinema companies succeeded, many of them with filmmakers in France and Italy. The project was certainly hurt by the fact that it did not have a versatile cultural intermediary on the US side, similar to Sol Hurok in the ballet world. Lester Cowan, the American producer, was experienced and persistent, but he was not the Hollywood heavyweight that the Soviet cinema bosses might have expected as their partner. This mismatch in the 1960s may ironically be the result of the McCarthyist purge of Hollywood during the previous decade.

Another major reason may be the timing and political context: the turbulance in US-Soviet relations during the 1960s hurt the chances of collaboration; the Cuban missile crisis of 1962, and then the Vietnam War, derailed the maiden film project with the Americans. Producer Cowen continued to push and, as Siefert shows, even became "a willing interpreter" of Soviet-US cooperation—he invested too much in it to let it fail. His Soviet counterparts, however, left the stage one by one. Siefert's contribution demonstrates that even failed projects, like this film, created a web of new relationships, becoming part of the learning curve for individuals from two very different business cultures.

In conclusion, let us fast-forward to the end of the Soviet Union: this period should provide the ultimate playground for the accumulated results of the transnational experiences this volume explores. Did the Soviets feel fatigue and overextension regarding the enormous space from East Berlin to Mozambique and Cuba in which they practiced "socialist exchange" and performed "proletarian solidarity"? And how much were they affected by the realities of their empire, within which they felt much poorer on the periphery and had to behave like the paupers outside of the "Second World"? Did the dismantling of the Iron Curtain prove as fateful for

Soviet society as for the society of East Germany? In what ways did the time bomb of an overstretched superiority myth blow up in the late years of Mikhail Gorbachev? And did this myth affect Gorbachev and his advisers? I sincerely hope the outstanding contributions in this volume will help to explore and answer these crucial questions.

I also hope that the methodologies tested in this volume will reverse nationalist denials and one-sided distortions of the "common past"—the emotional and politicized reactions that precluded for a long time the possibility of writing histories of the former "Second World." As years go by, however, the memories of how we all "survived communism and even laughed"[15]—the tragic, but also absurd, sad, ambiguous, and instructive encounters—would provide a tapestry for a less fractured and nationalist history of Eastern Europe. They may even provide the ground for future reconciliations.

NOTES

1. See, for instance, Melvyn Leffler and Odd Arne Westad, eds., *Cambridge History of the Cold War,* vols. 1–3 (New York: Cambridge University Press, 2010).

2. See Austin Jersild, "The Soviet State as Imperial Scavenger: 'Catch Up and Surpass' in the Transnational Socialist Bloc, 1950–1960," *American Historical Review* 116, no. 1 (February 2011): 109–32.

3. Ryszard Kapuściński, *Travels with Herodotus* (New York: Random House, 2007).

4. See Sergei I. Zhuk, *Rock and Roll in the Rocket City. The West, Identity, and Ideology in Svoit Dniepropetrovsk, 1960–1985* (Washington, DC, and Baltimore: Woodrow Wilson Center Press and Johns Hopkins University Press, 2010).

5. Maya Plisetskaia, *Ia, Maia Plisetskaia* (Moscow: Novosti, 1994).

6. Aside from Zhuk's study, see my *Zhivago's Children. The Last Russian Intelligentsia* (Cambridge, MA: Belknap Press, 2009).

7. Dmitry Furman, "Fenomen Gorbacheva," *Svobodnaia mysl'* 11 (1995): 68, 70–71. For the crucial role of isolation in Soviet regime's stability, see Walter D. Connor, "Soviet Society, Public Attitudes, and the Perils of Gorbachev's Reforms," *Journal of Cold War Studies* 5, no. 5 (2003): 43–80. For the role of consumerism in the Cold War context, see Emily Rosenberg, "Consumer Capitalism and the End of the Cold War," in *The Cambridge History of the Cold War,* vol. 3, *Endings,* ed. Melvyn Leffler and Odd Arne Westad (New York: Cambridge University Press, 2010), 489–512.

8. See Michael David-Fox, *Showcasing the Great Experiment. Cultural Diplomacy and Western Visitors to the Soviet Union, 1921–1941* (New York: Oxford University Press, 2011).

9. Read the descriptions of shopping in the West by Soviet dancers and filmmakers: Plisetskaia, *Ia, Maia,* and G. Danelia, *Bezbiletnyi passazhir: baiki kinorezhissera* (Moscow: Eksmo, 2005).

10. Alexei Yurchak, *Everything Was Forever Until It Was No More: The Last Soviet Generation* (Princeton, NJ: Princeton University Press, 2005).

11. Patryk Babiracki, "Interfacing the Soviet Bloc: Recent Literature and New Paradigms," *Ab Imperio* 4 (2011): 379–80.

12. The latest on the old debate about Stalin's diplomacy in 1951–52 is Peter Ruggenthaler, *Stalins großer Bluff. Die Geschichte der Stalin-Note in Dokumenten der sowjetischen Führung* (Munich: Oldenbourg Wissenschaftsverlag, 2007).

13. *Istochnik* 2 (1998): 114–20.

14. Stephen Kotkin, "Mongol Commonwealth? Exchange and Governance across the Post-Mongol Space," *Kritika* 8, no. 3 (Summer 2007): 487–531.

15. Slavenka Drakulić, *How We Survived Communism and Even Laughed* (New York: Vintage, 1992).

1

THE IRON CURTAIN AS SEMIPERMEABLE MEMBRANE

Origins and Demise of the Stalinist Superiority Complex

Michael David-Fox

Perhaps the most famous words ever uttered about the postwar division of Europe belong to Winston Churchill. In what is commonly called the Iron Curtain speech, delivered in Fulton, Missouri, on March 5, 1946, he declared: "From Stettin in the Baltic to Trieste in the Adriatic an iron curtain has descended across the Continent. Behind that line lie all the capitals of the ancient states of Central and Eastern Europe. Warsaw, Berlin, Prague, Vienna, Budapest, Belgrade, Bucharest and Sofia; all these famous cities and the populations around them lie in what I must call the Soviet sphere. . . ."[1] Churchill's speech came just days after the transmission of another of the most influential texts of the Cold War, George F. Kennan's "Long Telegram" of February 22, 1946. "At bottom of Kremlin's neurotic view of world affairs," Kennan telegraphed from Moscow to Washington, "is traditional and instinctive Russian sense of insecurity . . . isolation of Russian population from outside world and constant pressure to extend limits of Russian police power . . . are together the natural and instinctive urges of Russian rulers."[2] Both Churchill's public prophecy and Kennan's classified policy manifesto were, each in its own way, warnings that an ideological divide was premised on an even deeper civilizational rift between Russia and the West.

At Westminster College in Fulton, Churchill did not invent the term "Iron Curtain," just as Kennan did not invent the containment doctrine that was premised on his text. But Churchill did make the concept world famous at the very outset of the Cold War. In so doing, he was enshrining a metaphor that would not only rally his contemporaries but retrospectively structure historians' understanding of communism and the Eastern bloc. There are, in fact, excellent reasons why Churchill's metaphor of an Iron Curtain has survived down until the present day. It captured an important truth or, perhaps better to say, a striking part of the truth. In 1946 Churchill was eloquent in warning about communist takeovers in Eastern Europe, which in the course of only the next two years were transformed from Soviet-influenced "people's democracies" to fully Sovietized satellites of the USSR with their own brands of Stalinism. The Iron Curtain vividly evoked the salient fact that the Stalinist Soviet Union and the Stalinist regimes of Eastern Europe had become radically isolated from the outside world.

The Bolshevik new regime had aspired to regulate relations and contacts with foreigners throughout the 1920s, but the inauguration of the Stalin period at the end of that decade coincided, as is well known, with a new level of isolationist policies predicated on security and ideological "vigilance."[3] Restrictions on travel abroad, the import of foreign publications, and many kinds of professional and cultural contacts were heightened during Stalin's "Great Break" of 1928–32 and then again in the course of the 1930s. The xenophobia and spy mania of the Great Purges of the late 1930s connected foreign contacts to a wave of terror. This was followed, a decade later, by what was undoubtedly the most isolationist phase of Soviet history, the anti-Western and anti-cosmopolitan campaigns closely linked to the Cold War.

Churchill coined the metaphor of the Iron Curtain on the very eve of the launch of the militant ideological campaign known as the Zhdanovshchina, or the time of Zhdanov, which reversed the relative relaxation of policies during World War II. In April 1946, the month before Churchill's speech, Andrei Zhdanov took over as head of the Central Committee's Agitprop directorate and launched a new campaign for ideological orthodoxy that quickly included Stalin's condemnation of cultural figures guilty of "fawning before the West."[4] In the years of late Stalinism that followed, the small numbers of foreign visitors allowed into the USSR could not help noticing that Soviet citizens were afraid to talk to them or even crossed to the other side of the street. The construction of the Berlin Wall in 1961 in the heart of Cold War Europe seemed to confirm Churchill's metaphor as a kind of prophecy.

But the Iron Curtain was not only a prescient encapsulation of an important truth; it was a concept that closed off recognition of certain cross-border interactions that were crucial even under the most isolationist phases of the Stalin period. It is worth pausing, therefore, to consider the symbolic implications of Churchill's Iron Curtain. Although steel is harder and no less impenetrable, and in fact consists mostly of iron, Churchill could hardly have called it a Steel Curtain. The superior alloy steel would have been far more in line with the Soviet self-image of a modern, superior system that would leap over the advanced industrialized countries of the West. Stalin, the revolutionary pseudonym of Iosif Dzugashvili, derives from the Russian word for steel, *stal.'* The Iron Curtain recalls far more the prehistoric Iron Age, strong and brutal yet very primitive. This was the sense used by the foreign correspondent and historian William Henry Chamberlin in his 1934 book on Stalinist industrialization, *Russia's Iron Age.*[5]

Churchill's formulation thus implicitly based itself on an evocation of images about barbarism in Russia and the East that long predated the Bolshevik Revolution.[6] These fit in with his much less quoted references at Fulton to religion ("Communist parties or fifth columns constitute a growing challenge and peril to Christian civilization") and race (his offhand assumption about the predominance of the "strong parent races" of Europe).[7] The little-known Soviet response to Churchill's Iron Curtain speech, the main outline of which was summarized in *Pravda,* was to dismiss the British statesman as irrelevant and relegate him to the dustbin of history. *Pravda* recalled that Churchill, the former secretary of the British war office, had been an ardent supporter of Western military intervention against Bolshevism during the Russian Civil War of 1918–20 and predicted that this time he would be equally ineffectual. Stalin himself, a few days later, mocked his "Don Quixote-like antics."[8] Churchill, in other words, was tilting at windmills; the current Conservative Leader of the Opposition in Parliament could not stop the inevitable forward march of a superior communist civilization. Over the longer term, as Nick Rutter discusses in this volume, the Soviet and East bloc response was not to reject the reality of the *zheleznyi zanaves* (iron curtain) but to conceive a "counter-curtain": Churchill's dark line across the map of Europe was redefined as a bourgeois barricade against communist truths and, later, a defensive wall against Western aggression.[9]

For his part, Kennan, a professional student of Russian and Soviet history and politics, drew the roots of contemporary Soviet positions back to areas in which, historians today would agree, there were genuine continuities across the 1917 divide: the imperial Russian state's insecurity about border regions and the Russian ruling elite's longstanding doubts and fears about competitiveness with the West. Yet, in so doing, he echoed Churchill by drawing on hoary tropes about Russian backwardness, referring to Russians' "natural and instinctive urges," immutable fears, archaic nature, and "oriental secretiveness."[10] As in the case of Churchill, Kennan's salvo provoked an immediate response. Stalin read the widely disseminated telegram after it was acquired by Soviet intelligence. Not to be outdone after Kennan's initiative became a sensation in Washington, the Soviet dictator actually ordered an analogous cable about American intentions to be prepared and sent by his ambassador to the United States, Nikolai Novikov. After this was ghost-written by Foreign Minister Viacheslav Molotov, who emphasized the American imperialistic striving for world supremacy, it was transmitted to Moscow on September 27, 1946.[11]

As both the content of the Iron Curtain speech and the Long Telegram and the twin Soviet responses to them suggest, the incipient Cold War involved far more than a geopolitical clash. It was centrally concerned about competing claims of cultural, systemic, and civilizational superiority. Churchill's warnings about the Iron Curtain were part of a defense of Western civilization through the prism of the Anglo-American alliance. The Soviets after World War II began declaring (with justification) that Soviet power had saved the world from the Nazis, but not only that: the claim was also advanced that a Russian scientist had invented the light bulb and that Soviet culture incorporated all the best traditions of Western civilization as well. In this sense, communism presented itself as the true West.[12] Historians for some time now have been investigating this symbiotic competition over the mantel of civilization under the rubric of the "cultural Cold War." David Caute, opening his book on the topic, observed that this conflict was more than a traditional political-military confrontation. It was "at the same time an ideological and cultural contest on a global scale and without historical precedent."[13] The important element of symbiosis in the Cold War cultural or civilizational conflict between East and West is beautifully evoked by the Soviet responses to the Iron Curtain speech and the Long Telegram.

If investigating the cultural Cold War as a symbiotic relationship across the East-West divide has become a growth industry, a second line of investigation that transcends the Iron Curtain is only now becoming a serious component of historical agendas. This is the notion that even Stalinism, one of the most isolationist and autarkic regimes of the twentieth century, was shaped and influenced by border-crossings, borrowings, and constant if often covert and skewed observation of the outside world. In other words, taking the imagery of the Iron Curtain too literally can obscure an important avenue of historical investigation.

In this chapter I will make the case that Stalin's Soviet Union erected less an Iron Curtain than a semipermeable membrane. Biologists can also call this cellular barrier a selectively permeable or differentially permeable membrane. This is very much what I am trying to suggest: some goods, people, knowledge, and models from the outside world selectively and in different ways crossed the borders of communist countries. Beyond that, the image of the "West"—which was of course crucial to the dream of surpassing it—played a fundamental role in the domestic order of communist societies even at the height of Stalinist isolationism.

There are good reasons why the international and transnational dimensions in the history of communism were long hidden in the shadows of the Iron Curtain. The two successive foundational schools of Soviet history after World War II, the totalitarian and the revisionist, were both constructed around a largely domestic grand narrative about the development of Soviet communism. Diplomacy and external crises were thrown into the mix only when they were so obtrusive that they could not be ignored in the making of the Soviet system. The almost exclusively domestic focus of the first two generations of Soviet studies was bolstered by its Cold War exceptionality and driven by the conceptual keys of the totalitarian and revisionist paradigms—the primacy of ideology and political control, in the first instance, and social forces from below, in the second. Partly as a result, the study of Soviet foreign policy and international communism developed as largely segregated subfields; only rarely was international history integrally connected with the formation of Soviet communism at home.[14] To be sure, debates about the balance between particularity and comparability have in one way or another animated the Russian and Soviet field throughout its history. But the weight of the Cold War–era stress on the unique and sui generis nature of the Soviet system has been modified by post-Soviet debates about the concept of Soviet modernity and a wave of comparative and transnational studies that include Soviet material.[15]

This chapter attempts to develop one overarching interpretation that makes sense of several kinds of border crossings and international interactions in the context of communism as they had an impact on very different periods, from the early years of the Soviet regime through the post-Stalinist 1950s. It makes two interrelated claims. First, numerous border crossings had a crucial impact not just before and after, but throughout the history of Stalinism. They assumed special importance in two European contexts: both in relationship to the West, that is to say across the division of Europe, and between the Soviet Union and its new, postwar "outer empire" in Eastern Europe. Second, these border crossings are integral to understanding the rise and fall of the Stalin-era declaration that communism was a superior civilization. As this implies, these encounters were fundamental to self-understandings throughout the communist second world.

ORIGINS OF THE SOVIET SUPERIORITY COMPLEX

Prewar Soviet communism is the necessary starting point for this discussion, for the 1920s and 1930s produced the system that was put to the supreme test in World War II and provided models both for late Stalinist reconstruction and for the Sovietization of Eastern Europe. The triumph of Bolshevism in 1917 greatly amplified the nineteenth-century Russian competition with the "West" that was at the heart of the great debates over Russian national identity.[16] The West referred primarily to the great powers and advanced industrial societies of central and Western Europe. But as many people have pointed out, it was also an imaginary construct: in order to conceive of a unified "West," something much easier to do from afar, all the many differences among European countries and their historical trajectories need to be downplayed.[17] The Bolshevik Revolution, with its promise to leap into an alternative form of modernity called socialism, reconceived the West as bourgeois capitalism. This greatly heightened the competition, the threat, and ultimately the allure of what the Soviet Union measured itself against. Throughout the history of communism the "West" continued to be an ever-present measuring stick, even when it was severely misunderstood.

The Leninist orthodoxy of the 1920s was that the Soviet Union must adopt the best features of Western bourgeois societies in order go beyond them. In practice, the right kinds of foreign contacts and foreign travel, especially in the cultural and scientific realm, were prestigious for the political and intellectual elite.[18] Old Bolshevik intellectuals who had lived in Europe, when they talked about cultural revolution, wanted not only to politicize but to civilize and enlighten their own people, whom Lenin famously called semi-Asiatic. Internationally, the Soviets touted their achievements, but it was assumed that in many areas, culturally and economically, the Soviet Union still needed, to use the slogan, to "catch up and overtake" (*dognat' i peregnat'*) the advanced Western countries. This slogan, originally Lenin's, was rearticulated by the Fifteenth Party Congress in late 1926 and quickly emerged to play a central role in the ideology of the First Five-Year Plan.[19]

What came next, the Stalinist declaration of superiority over the West in all realms, became the new orthodoxy by the mid-1930s. This, it can be argued, was the ideological equivalent of the collectivization of agriculture or the forced industrialization of the Five-Year Plans. With global capitalism barely recovering from its moment of greatest crisis during the Great Depression, socialism was declared built at the "Congress of Victors," the Seventeenth Party Congress in 1934. During the mid-1930s, at the height of the Popular Front cooperation abroad, Soviet domestic audiences were constantly told that their country was the best in the world in all respects—that is, not only in terms of the political system and social order but also in cultural and even economic affairs.

As Raisa Orlova, the dissident, recalled in her memoirs about her youth in the 1930s: "If one were to do a statistical analysis of newspaper language of these years, phrases like 'the very best [whatever] in the world,' 'for the first time in the history of mankind,' and 'only in our country' would prove to be among the most frequent."[20] By the late 1930s, the party's agitators were instructed to report gushing praise from foreign delegations to underscore the leading place of "the country of victorious socialism" not only in culture and science, but in economics as well. "In machine-building the USSR holds *first place* in Europe and *second place* in the world. . . . In excavation of gold, in production of superphosphate the Soviet Union has *overtaken all the countries of Europe.*"[21]

The French writer André Gide, who in 1936 famously became the most prominent Western fellow traveler to publicly criticize Stalinism, was startled to learn that the Soviet citizen "has been persuaded that everything abroad and in every department is far less prosperous than in the U.S.S.R." When Gide suggested that people in France knew more about the Soviet Union than the other way around, he was met with a "lyrical exclamation" from the crowd: "'In order to describe all the new and splendid and great things that are being done in the Soviet Union, there would not be paper enough in the whole world.'"[22]

I call this new ideological orthodoxy the Stalinist superiority complex. It would not be hard to maintain that it became as fundamental to Stalinism as the military-industrial complex.[23] The interesting thing, however, is that this declaration of superiority in prewar Stalinism did not—at least until the xenophobic spy mania of the Great Terror of 1937–39—lead to the kind of radical isolationism that came under late Stalinism in the late 1940s and early 1950s. For the vast bulk of the population, of course, foreign travel and access to foreign publications had already become far more difficult. But especially during the Popular Front of the mid-1930s a crucial group of party intellectuals and officials flitted across Europe, organized a pan-European anti-fascist culture, and had extensive ties to sympathetic European and American figures during the height of Western admiration for the Soviet experiment. Selective or differentiated cultural and ideological engagement, and not only isolation, had profound domestic consequences. At the heart of Katerina Clark's book on cosmopolitanism and Stalinist culture in the 1930s is the fact that leading Soviet intellectuals with extensive European ties eagerly signed on to the project of making Moscow into a dominant, international capital of a new culture, especially during the Popular Front. Soviet culture was depicted as the culmination of world civilization, so selected Russian and world classics were widely published. A flood of literary translations into Russian peaked in 1937—the year the vast bulk of these intellectuals and Old Bolsheviks with extensive foreign connections were decimated.[24]

The onset of the Great Purges of 1937 marked a new era of ideological xenophobia and the height of prewar isolationism. Internal and external enemies were inextricably linked during the Great Terror: hostile capitalist and fascist states and their security services supposedly lay behind all those purged as enemies of the people, whether those enemies were socially or ethnically defined. As a result, in the words of Jörg Baberowski, xenophobia was raised to the "level of a state ideology."[25] The incitement of fear and hatred of foreigners and everything foreign became a permanent feature of Stalinism during and after the Great Purges. It is therefore all the more striking that a secret respect and desire for things Western was rampant even at the two peaks of Stalinist xenophobia and isolationism: the Terror of the 1937–39 and the anti-cosmopolitan campaign of the late 1940s. This, in turn, points to the concealed, oblique, or camouflaged border crossings that continued even under the extreme circumstances of Stalinist ideological xenophobia.

For example, when secret police chief Genrikh Iagoda was arrested during the Great Terror the NKVD inventory listed the discovery of the following items: 1,120 bottles of foreign wine, 31 pairs of foreign female shoes and 95 bottles of foreign perfume, 17 pairs of foreign pajamas, 22 foreign-made suits, and 3,904 pornographic photographs.[26] There were also three bicycles. Although it was a typical Stalinist legend of the 1940s that a Russian craftsman had invented the bicycle in 1801,[27] most Soviet bicycles before and during World War II had military applications, and Iagoda's possessions were later much in demand by Soviet soldiers in Germany in 1945. Lists of Western goods and luxury items in the possession of the Soviet elite in both the 1930s and 1940s could easily be extended. It shows that the Soviet elite was addicted to the far-from-forbidden fruits of Western material culture—acquiring them, treasuring them, and clearly, given the quantities in Iagoda's possession, distributing them at the very moment that it was cementing the orthodoxy that everything Soviet was superior.

In other words, the Stalinist superiority complex was not just a nefarious part of ideological indoctrination or part and parcel of the enforced optimism of Stalin-era Socialist Realism, the official doctrine in the arts, which depicted the present as if it were an idealized future. It also reflected a secret sense of inferiority. This, it is important to note, did not have to do merely with a deficit of luxury items or material goods. It was broader, a potentially ingrained part of the mentality of many Soviet elites who asserted Soviet superiority. The historian of East European communism, György Péteri, has referred to "the inevitable oscillation between two diametrically opposite states of mind among the Leninist modernizing elite of a relatively backward country: the hubris of systemic superiority on the one hand, and the admission of the developmental (economic, social, and cultural) inferiority. . . ."[28] The crucial fact was that under Stalinism it became heretical to talk openly of any aspect of inferiority. But that did not mean that the sentiment disappeared.

Perhaps no one was better equipped to see these dialectical features of Stalinist aggrandizement, how superiority and inferiority were intertwined, than the writer and Soviet Jewish intellectual Ilya Ehrenburg. Ehrenburg was a cultural amphibian, equally at home and equally savvy in Europe and the USSR, able to navigate among leading European intellectuals and in the treacherous waters of Bolshevik cultural politics. A Bolshevik revolutionary in his youth, he befriended Pablo Picasso and Diego Rivera in prewar Parisian cafes but, long after his decisive break with Bolshevism, remained close to party theoretician Nikolai Bukharin. In the 1920s, fending off attacks by proletarianizers and cultural militants, he continued to live mostly in Paris but continued to publish as a Soviet writer. Forced to make a choice after Stalin came to power, he subordinated himself to the demands of the Stalin Revolution. By so doing, he continued to be able to move with almost unique frequency and ease between the Soviet and the European worlds. In the 1930s he became a much-traveled cultural ambassador to Europe and a major figure of anti-fascist culture. This was emblematic of the continuing engagement of pre-purge Stalinist culture with the European anti-fascist Left. Devastated by the Nazi-Soviet Pact, Ehrenburg regained his footing during World War II, reinventing himself as a wildly popular war journalist.[29] Millions of Soviet soldiers treasured his articles at the front to the point that Molotov once said that Ehrenburg alone was worth several divisions.

In the 1950s, having miraculously survived Stalinism, Ehrenburg was able to further Soviet-European cultural ties once more as a major figure of the Thaw—and a legendary link to prewar European culture for a younger generation of Soviet intellectuals.[30] Ehrenburg understood very well the insecurities that underlay the loud, Stalinist declarations of superiority. It was at the height of the Thaw when he wrote these words: "Unending talk about one's superiority is linked with groveling before things foreign—they are but different aspects of an inferiority complex."[31]

THE SOVIET UNION MARCHES WEST

It is in the context of the Stalinist superiority complex, seemingly so durable and widespread yet so predicated on isolation and concealed concerns about inferiority, that I would propose viewing the Soviet march West during World War II and in the postwar creation of the Soviet bloc. The 1930s cross-border exchanges in the increasingly closed-off country were most pronounced among elites or, if not, involved imports and exports (such as cultural, scientific, or ideological phenomena) that were not predicated upon physical travel. By contrast, the wartime and postwar contacts with the outside world began to assume a mass character, but their effects continued to be camouflaged by the persistence of Stalinism into the 1950s.

The first, often overlooked step in this process came with the Nazi-Soviet Pact in 1939–41. The once and future mortal enemies carved up the territories between them after signing the secret protocol of the pact. The Red Army moved into eastern Poland and western Belorussia in September 1939, and Soviet troops were stationed in the Baltics. This was a first, short-lived experiment with exporting the Soviet model west. The coercive aspects of this, such as mass deportation and extermination of local elites—priests, landlords, and nobles, among others—have received much attention. But what has been far less observed is the official Soviet civilizing mission in the new territories. Soviet occupation forces and the Soviet press alike talked about raising the newly conquered new territories up from backwardness and eliminating the vestiges (*perezhitki*) of capitalism. This was the same language used toward the non-Russian peoples inside the Soviet Union.[32]

The only problem was that the Soviets who actually saw these newly acquired territories could not perceive them as backward or inferior at all, at least in crucial respects. In his book *Revolution from Abroad* Jan Gross gave unforgettable descriptions of how Red Army troops, officers, and Soviet officials alike reacted to life in the most rural backwater of eastern Poland—a land of indescribable plenty to the Soviets. The stores were rushed; watches, clothing, food were snapped up. Soviet citizens could not believe that the stores placed no limits on purchases. Coming into contact with Soviets for the first time, a young leftist sympathizer of communism, a Polish Jew, noted the irony: "We waited for them to ask how was life under capitalism and to tell us what it was like in Russia. But all they wanted was to buy a watch. I noticed that they were preoccupied with worldly goods, and we were waiting for ideals." As this suggests, while standards of living and material goods were but one of many key nodes of comparison and exchange between the communist and noncommunist world, the economy of extreme shortages under Stalinism made this an overriding issue that colored many others. If asked about Soviet life while in eastern Poland during 1939 and 1941, the Soviets, evidently instructed in how to defend the superiority of their homeland, invariably replied with the same words: "*U nas vse est*'"—We have everything. Taunting them for an ignorance born of isolation and waiting to trap them into an affirmative response, local youths rejoined: "Do you have Amsterdam, or Greta Garbo?" But if ridiculed, the Soviets often snapped back rather effectively: "we have tanks, guns, and airplanes."[33] Not for the first time, pride in military might and pride in empire became a necessary substitute for domestic privation.

The Eastern Front in World War II, a cataclysm of scarcely conceivable proportions, was the decisive theater of the entire world war. The scale of the human and social destruction almost defies imagination: the estimates of 24–27 million Soviet casualties, the horrors of Nazi occupation and genocide, the brutalization of total, ideological warfare, and the massive destruction of cities, infrastructure, and housing. The size of the Soviet population in 1941, some 200 million, was not regained until 1956. The war was also a trial by fire for a new generation of Soviets who survived, especially the "front generation" to which the party by necessity granted new authority and autonomy. Millions of Soviet citizens saw Europe, and even after the war's end hundreds of thousands of Soviet military personnel stationed abroad continued to have direct contact with the non-Soviet world.[34]

The shock and often rage of these Soviet citizens at the indescribable prosperity and unheard-of luxury they witnessed—even in war-torn and defeated Germany—cannot be underestimated. Pillaging and looting ensued on a mass scale, especially after Stalin's so-called package decree of 1944 allowed for sending items home. The celebrated Soviet writer Konstantin Simonov, the poet and war correspondent who was a prominent participant in both Stalinism and the Thaw, expressed the weight of the sense of shock felt even by privileged elites: "The contrast between the standard of living in Europe and among us, a contrast which millions of military people encountered, was an emotional and psychological blow."[35] It was telling indeed that as the Red Army moved into Europe toward the end of the war, Soviet political and security ruling circles, reportedly from Stalin on down, evoked the historical ghost of "Decembrism."[36] This referred to the 1825 Decembrist uprising against tsarism by army officers who had experienced life in Paris during the Russian victory in the Napoleonic wars. Decembrism emerged out of a milieu of young Westward-looking cultural and intellectual figures and was later radicalized in secret societies. With his paranoia about a new Decembrism, the old revolutionary Stalin took on the uncanny guise of a twentieth-century tsar Nicholas I.

If Stalin was suspicious about Red Army officers, he was ruthless about Soviet POWs and displaced persons, or indeed any Soviet person who had spent unsupervised time abroad. The more than five million Soviet displaced persons in German-occupied Europe—POWs, forced laborers, and voluntary exiles, including some two million sometimes forcibly repatriated by Britain and the United States from the Western parts of Germany under their control—were "filtered" upon return to the USSR. Their most common fate was forced labor in the Gulag or execution. Only one-fifth of those five million were allowed to return to their homes and families.[37] Even Soviet citizens liberated by the Red Army at Auschwitz in January 1945 found themselves interrogated by the military counterintelligence agency SMERSH in the same buildings from which they had just been freed.[38]

Despite all preventative measures and the postwar ideological crackdown under Zhdanov, the aftereffects of the Soviet presence in Europe at the war's end were profound. As we have seen, even the isolationist Stalinist 1930s maintained crucial interactions with the outside world for cultural and political elites, and these helped foster cultural and ideological engagements that affected core aspects of Stalinism. The war, however, opened up a taste of the outside world for a highly closed society and greater familiarity with its material culture on a wider scale. One historian has coined the phrase "trophy Westernization": in 1950 one-third of all cars in Moscow were foreign, trophies from abroad. By the same token, in 1951, during what Martin Malia (with clear reference to the later Thaw) called the ice age of Sovietism, only one-fourth of films in distribution in the Soviet Union were Soviet; the rest were foreign trophy films taken from abroad.[39] Deep under the frozen surface of orthodoxy far-reaching currents were moving, changing the nature of the society. Finally, the kind of initiative and de facto autonomy that the war of extermination in the East inevitably fostered had far-reaching effects, at first more cultural or psychological than political. "The war alone," as Elena Zubkova puts it, "did not on the whole change people's relationship to the regime":

> Those who believed in it earlier just came to believe in it even more, especially after the victory. Those who had no illusions remained unconverted. The psychological impact of the war took a different form. The war awoke in people the capacity to think in unaccustomed ways, to evaluate a situation

critically, and never again to accept uncritically any exclusive version of the truth.[40]

The conditions of European material and economic superiority witnessed abroad circa 1945 alone did not and could not destroy the Stalinist superiority complex. Oleg Budnitskii's study of the war diaries and memoirs of Soviet officers and intellectuals in Europe in 1945 shows a striking unanimity: all of them criticized the low intellectual culture they saw in defeated Germany, the absence of books, weak knowledge of literature, and scorn for the addiction to petty knickknacks among the German burghers.[41] The stress on higher culture as a key indicator of Soviet superiority was first forged on a mass scale in the mid-1930s campaign for *kul'turnost'*, meaning "culturedness" or enlightened behavior and outlooks. Culturedness implied disdain for "backward" (by implication non-European, non-Russian, or non-intelligentsia) habits and nonedifying or low-brow cultural forms.[42] It incorporated an early form of Soviet consumerism, in that certain kinds of possessions were deemed part of a cultured lifestyle.[43] Despite the crudeness of the initial Stalinist campaign, which included political literacy under the rubric of culturedness, the long-lasting effects of the concept were so great because it resonated at once with the long-established values of the Russian-Soviet intelligentsia and the aspirations of the new Stalinist elite. Ehrenburg wrote the day after the Nazi surrender: "We have saved not only our homeland, we have saved universal culture."[44] The same defense of higher culture was later prominent in the Cold War contest with the materially and technologically advanced consumer society of the United States. It reflected pride in the huge gains in mass literacy brought about in the first three Soviet decades, the significant achievements of the educational system and Soviet science, and a genuinely mass Soviet cult of literature and high culture.

Ironically, this stress on higher culture and values, forged out of the sometimes hostile marriage between the Soviet intelligentsia and the Bolshevik leadership and then inscribed into the culture of 1930s Stalinism, came to recapitulate the old, prerevolutionary Slavophile notion that greater Russian spirituality offset the economic or technological prowess of European societies. The fact that cultural superiority became the last, best defense against consumer capitalism was also ironic given the centrality of materialism in Marxism-Leninism, the doctrine that the economic base determined a superstructure that included the realm of culture.

A DOUBLE-EDGED SWORD: THE SOVIET ENCOUNTER WITH EASTERN EUROPE

If the Stalinist superiority complex sustained significant but as of yet glancing blows in World War II, the postwar establishment of a Soviet bloc in Eastern Europe in certain ways reinforced or reinvented it. The Soviet press depicted the people's democracies of Eastern Europe as indebted and necessarily grateful to the Soviet Union for their new, better way of life. This was an extension into new territory of what Jeffrey Brooks has called the "culture of the gift," an inculcated sense of gratitude in Soviet public culture that was closely integrated into the cult of Stalin. More broadly, Soviet citizens were invited to take pride in the Soviet Union's new superpower stature, encouraging, in Brooks's words, "a sense of superiority that proved hard to suppress."[45]

How else to explain the remarkable and seemingly irrepressible arrogance of representatives of the Soviet Union in Eastern Europe, such as advisers, propagandists, and lecturers? As Norman Naimark wrote in his study of the postwar Soviet zone of occupation in Germany, "All over the zone, they lectured about the advantages of Makarenko's system of pedagogy (and the weaknesses of the German), about Pavlov's brilliant experiments (and nothing of Freud). . . . In the land of Volkswagen, BMW, and Mercedes . . . they lauded exclusively the Soviet automobile and aircraft industries." However, the Soviet commitment to demonstrating the superiority of victorious Soviet culture also led to a flurry of activity in the Soviet zone in book publishing, art, and music. Precisely because East German cultural figures remained skeptical of Soviet claims, the postwar Soviet struggle for the allegiance of the German intelligentsia in East Germany turned into a very high priority.[46] In other words, although the Soviet superiority complex was an ideological postulate that affected attitudes and perceptions, it produced very concrete, real-world consequences.

At the same time as Soviet representatives in Eastern Europe were talking about the superiority of all things Soviet, a huge program of reparations was occurring that involved dismantling and transporting factories and property east. This was of course dictated by Soviet devastation during the war. But the sheer scale of appropriations by the USSR's managerial and administrative elite undermined the Soviet claims to superiority. As Austin Jersild has recently argued, the Soviets systematically canvassed

Eastern Europe for "forms of knowledge, industrial technology, and machinery that would help them in their effort to address their own backwardness and their grand plans of competition with distant America." At the same time, the power of the Soviet managers to commandeer resources also imparted a sense of their right to command. Elidor Mëhilli's work on the socialist bloc as a zone of exchange is an important supplement to Jersild's focus on Soviet interests and intentions because it points to the far-reaching dynamics of circulation within and among the newly socialist East European countries themselves. A corollary of Mëhilli's argument is that the Soviets could also be influenced by their participation in this zone. In other words, the basic fact of Soviet dominance, which Jersild highlights and Mëhilli acknowledges, did not mean that influence within the bloc flowed only from East to West. Thus, by 1956 Soviet officials were voicing notions that east-central Europeans had been saying to themselves for years: Soviet engineers should go to places like Czechoslovakia to improve their training and qualifications, and not the other way around.[47]

What is fascinating about postwar Soviet–East European interactions is that some Soviet advisers, scientists, and scholars refused to follow the logic of the Soviet superiority complex in the new, "outer empire." To be sure, numerous Soviet mediocrities, as John Connelly has described, did seize the chance to lord it over their most distinguished East European counterparts. But other Soviet representatives were strongly supportive and admired their East European colleagues.[48] One example was the leading Soviet medievalist B. D. Grekov in Poland. Grekov, director of the Soviet Academy of Sciences' Institute for Slavic Studies, had a healthy respect for Polish scholarship. He warned the academy's presidium in Moscow about Polish knowledge of "our experience with vulgarization" in the 1920s and 1930s, the time of the forcible "Bolshevization" of the academy and general persecution of nonparty scholarly elites. This open recognition of Soviet errors in the not-so-distant past was hardly consistent with instructing a new pupil faithfully to follow the Soviet road to socialism in all respects. His stance, moreover, was part of a broader effort involving Grekov and others to stave off a "frontal attack" on Polish historiography in 1947–48.[49] As this suggests, a number of Soviet representatives and advisers in Eastern Europe warned others about repeating Soviet mistakes or excesses, including the persecution of the intelligentsia during the first phase of Stalinism in the early 1930s.[50] Future studies will find rich material—in fact, a virtual laboratory—for exploring Soviets' attitudes toward their own revolution's historical trajectory as they contemplated the road to socialism in East European countries.

THE THAW AS HEYDAY AND DECLINE OF THE SUPERIORITY COMPLEX

"The key to sustaining utopian drives," Amir Weiner has observed, "is the belief that the gap between the official claims and reality is bridgeable." This belief was plausible during the 1930s, when control over information about the outside world and terror combined with the Depression-era crisis of the Western world. The war, in Weiner's formulation, "changed it all" by creating a "time bomb" in the form of the newly acquired empire in Eastern Europe. As Weiner encapsulates the shift, "the influx of destabilizing information and reformist ideas in the form of tourism and print media from Poland, Hungary and Czechoslovakia, American and British radio broadcasts, and Finnish television, locked the Soviets in a catch-up struggle to block the influx and a losing battle over the eyes and ears of their own audience."[51]

While the critical long-term importance of the war can scarcely be overstated, as already argued above, the creation of the Soviet bloc in and of itself as a result of the war was only the precondition for a consequential opening to the outside world—which now included a communist "second world" as well as Western and developing countries. The sudden end to Stalinist isolationism, it is also crucial to recall, was largely initiated and pursued by the Soviet regime itself during the Khrushchev Thaw beginning in the mid-1950s. There was an equally momentous domestic decision that took place simultaneously—to empty the Gulag camps of some four million incarcerated prisoners.[52] These included even Baltic and Ukrainian nationalists, which (as Weiner has shown elsewhere) directly fueled crises in the Soviet Baltics and western Ukraine by jump-starting a destabilizing cross-border synergy with the major 1956 rebellions in Hungary and Poland. What produced these unexpected consequences was the striking "confidence" on the part of Stalin's successors that they could "conquer the opposition without resorting to mass terror."[53]

This newly manifested Khrushchev-era confidence marked an extraordinary shift from the suspiciousness and implicit pessimism that fueled so many Stalinist policies. In Miriam Dobson's words, Khrushchev's political vision was "full of optimism" even if it was "riddled with complexities and ambiguities."[54] This optimism had far-reaching ramifications, both externally and internally. Indeed, the end of extreme Soviet isolationism from the outside world deserves to be directly juxtaposed with the end of the internal isolation of millions of Gulag inmates. After all, the intimate link between internal and external enemies was a core component of Stalinist ideology; both major Thaw-era developments were predicated on the notion that external and internal enemies alike did not pose such a radical threat, and perhaps were not even enemies at all. Even the term *izoliatsiia,* while not used in a negative sense in relation to the outside world, was the standard synonym for incarceration in Soviet penal policy. The drastic curtailment of both forms of external and internal isolation were initiated at the top because the decisions flowed from a remarkably optimistic sense in the mid-1950s that the Soviet way of life could now withstand such contacts.

As this suggests, one core feature of the Stalinist superiority complex, which was the view that Khrushchev and his leadership grew up with and imbibed for decades, survived to fuel this 1950s Soviet confidence: the certainty that Soviet socialism was inherently superior and would outlive capitalism. This is what Khrushchev meant when he declared to an alarmed group of Western ambassadors at a November 18, 1956, reception at the Polish embassy in Moscow: "We will bury you" (*My vas pokhoronim*). This was not a threat, but expressed the notion, as he prefaced the famous remark, that "history is on our side."[55] At the same time, the Thaw overturned a second key pillar of the Stalinist superiority complex: catching up with and overtaking the West, the slogan of the early 1930s era of forced industrialization, returned as the new orthodoxy and replaced the mid- to late 1930s official declaration of outright superiority in all realms. In this sense, the Thaw marked, at one and the same time, the heyday and demise of the superiority complex ratified under Stalin. Or put another way, the Stalinist superiority complex was modified and metamorphosed into a Soviet one.

But even this modified, Khrushchev-era version of the superiority complex was undermined by forces initiated by the leadership but well beyond their control. The effect of the Soviet opening to the outside world starting in the mid-1950s was nothing less than revelatory. If most travel outside Soviet borders had been prohibited during late Stalinism, by 1956 no less than 560,000 Soviets traveled abroad, and this reached 1.5 million in 1958. Eastern Europe, the new Soviet bloc, was the most common destination; whereas Western countries were largely available only to elites, nonparty members and non-white-collar workers could travel within the socialist camp. Decades later, Soviet travelers vividly remembered their first impressions, admiration, and even shock to their world views on seeing conditions in Eastern Europe. At the same time, high Soviet officials, ever concerned with international prestige, worried repeatedly that Soviet travelers abroad created the impression of being "uncultured," that is to say, embarrassingly backward.[56]

In published Soviet travel accounts, Eastern Europe was, in the words of Anne Gorsuch, "presented as a younger and less advanced version of the Soviet self." But this official depiction was challenged by a sense of shock among Soviet travelers and tourists to the newly-Sovietized lands that was similar to what Soviet troops had experienced in 1939 and 1945. East Europeans also found ways to reinforce their status vis-à-vis visiting Soviets, for it was the national tourist agencies and guides in the bloc countries that often set itineraries and wrote texts for the Soviet visitors.[57] Soviet visitors to Eastern Europe often perceived not less experienced, socialist younger brothers but, in a striking inversion of the official orthodoxy, what they hoped the Soviet Union might become. Here there is an analogy with Thaw-era Soviet films that often depicted Soviet conditions as modern, clean, and somehow more like the West.[58]

Foreigners also went east on a far greater scale, and this also led to some far-reaching shocks. A series of remarkable international openings took place in Moscow, demonstrating the confidence, even overconfidence, of the Khrushchev leadership. These included the sensational Picasso exhibit in 1956, the mass exhilaration of the World Youth Festival in 1957, and the unprecedented American National Exhibition at Sokol'niki Park in the summer of 1959.[59] By 1973, almost three million foreign tourists visited the USSR annually.[60]

Khrushchev's declaration that the USSR would "catch up and overtake" the United States in consumer goods directly linked his domestic effort to boost the retail sector and his mass housing campaign to the international superpower competition of the Cold War.[61] In other words, Cold War competition was extended to the realm of material and consumer culture. Of course, the United States and West European countries had from the start of the cultural Cold War recognized that consumption and standards of living were among their most potent weapons.[62]

Because of the centrality of consumerism to the cultural Cold War, György Péteri has coined the phrase the Nylon Curtain—an alternative to the Iron Curtain as a marker of the systemic divide. It was nylon rather than pig iron or steel that became a marker of advanced industrial modernity after World War II. Nylon also serves as a metaphor for the desirable consumer goods from the West that over the postwar decades became not just luxury items for the communist elites but potentially available to a broader population. Finally, in Péteri's discussion, nylon serves as a permeable rather than unbridgeable demarcation between two systems: "The curtain was made of Nylon, not Iron. It was not only transparent but it also yielded to strong osmotic tendencies that were globalizing knowledge across the systemic divide about culture, goods, and services." Péteri's Nylon Curtain deliberately evokes the title of David Riesman's 1951 fictional work "The Nylon War," a mock journalistic account of "Operation Abundance" in which the USSR was subject to an all-out bombardment of consumer goods. In Riesman's fictional reportage, the operation was based on an idea that before long took on a prophetic ring: "if allowed to sample the riches of America, the Russian people would not long tolerate masters who gave them tanks and spies instead of vacuum cleaners and beauty parlours. The Russian rulers would thereupon be forced to turn out consumers' goods, or face mass discontent on an increasing scale."[63] Many of Riesman's readers apparently believed that Operation Abundance was indeed taking place.

However, in the 1950s the Soviet Union did have one powerful cultural-ideological weapon to fend off the allure both of Western consumer societies and the shock of relative East European prosperity. This was the notion, which was not at all mere propaganda but in fact shared by many Soviet citizens, that Soviet culture, values, and lifestyle trumped advances in technology or goods. In other words, there is a line of continuity, completely unexplored in the literature, stretching from the early Soviet cultural revolution to the Stalinist culturedness campaign and veritable cult of high culture in the 1930s to the Khrushchev-era competitive opening to the outside world.

This meant that at the post-Stalinist moment when communist countries (including the newly Sovietized states of East Europe) deliberately embarked on a competition with the West in the realm of consumer goods and the retail sector, they brought this sense of exceptionalism, of difference and superiority, in culture and lifestyle. This is a crucial point.

It would be an oversimplification to see the very fact of this competition as an immediate, inevitable defeat for post-Stalinist societies. For example, the British historian Susan Reid has analyzed the comments that Soviet citizens made in visitors' books at the US National Exhibition in Sokol'niki Park in 1959, the site of the famous Nixon-Khrushchev Kitchen Debate. Why were there so few books, many Soviets wanted to know?[64] For many Soviet observers, high-tech kitchenware was no replacement for culture or a convincing representation of the good life.

The notion that consumer goods would be used in a collectivist, socialist lifestyle, and not simply in aping the West, was at its height in the 1950s and early 1960s in both the USSR and in communist east-central Europe. For example, Khrushchev proposed that automobiles would be used in collectivist carpools to a far greater extent. But when Communist Party functionaries in Hungary quickly took over the carpool cars for their own individual purposes, the original collectivist plan was undermined long before it was officially repudiated during the Hungarian new economic course.[65] In terms of popular perceptions of those elites and their superior socialist lifestyle, it didn't help that the cars in question were Mercedes; East German party elites, for obvious reasons, used Audis. In other words, the nomenklatura elite's long-established addiction to Western goods and luxuries had symbolic significance and undermined the attempt to create a collectivist, socialist lifestyle and alternative consumerism.[66]

Future historians will have to explain how notions of exceptionalism and an alternative modernity in the Soviet bloc were gradually yet ultimately fatally undermined. This story is not yet fully written, but when it is, concrete transnational contacts and cross-cultural exchange will play a central role.[67] Along with the ongoing competition with the "West," Soviet travel and interaction with the bloc countries became a major factor in Soviet history. The dynamics of "socialist" transnational exchange, or cross-border influences in a communist second world that in the 1950s stretched from Eastern Europe to China, was less restricted and more extensive, and ultimately involved a different set of dynamics, than interactions with capitalist Western Europe and the United States.[68] Soviet involvement in the bloc was also significant in that Eastern Europe inevitably had more contacts with the other side of the European continent, thus creating two sets of transnational exchange between East and West.[69] The Iron Curtain was very real, in the sense that the divisions and barriers between the Soviet-dominated socialist camp and the rest of the world cannot be downplayed. At the same time, new scholarly investigations will be enabled by the recognition that the partition it marked was not airtight but semipermeable.

The Stalinist superiority complex, in sum, created an ideological time bomb for the Soviet Union. Paul Kennedy talked about imperial overstretch, meaning military and economic overcommitment, as a prime reason for the decline and fall of empires.[70] The Stalinist superiority complex was an example of ideological overstretch. Its most unsustainable claims were modified under Khrushchev's Thaw when once again the task became to catch up and surpass, but the overconfidence of the Khrushchev leadership—expressed both in the sudden end of isolationism and the plunge into a formidably challenging competition in the realm of mass consumption and lifestyle—was predicated on its premises. The Stalinist superiority complex had evolved into a Soviet one. But because the original version was so heavily dependent on everyday isolationism to undergird its claims, the Soviet superiority complex after Stalin faced what became a dual and ultimately insuperable challenge: coping with the effects of intimate Soviet contact with the newly communist countries of Eastern Europe and the fateful post-Stalinist opening to the outside world.

NOTES

1. The March 5, 1946, speech, reprinted many times, may be found in Winston S. Churchill, "The Sinews of Peace," in *Churchill's Iron Curtain Speech Fifty Years Later,* ed. James W. Muller (Columbia: University of Missouri Press, 1999): 1–14, quotation on 8. For context, see Martin Gilbert, "The Origins of the Iron Curtain Speech," in *Churchill: Resolution, Defiance, Magnanimity, Good Will,* ed. R. Crosby Kemper (Columbia: University of Missouri Press, 1996): 34–61.

2. George F. Kennan, "'Long Telegram' on the Soviet Union, 1946," in *American Foreign Relations Since 1898: A Documentary Reader* (Malden, MA: Blackwell Publishing, 2010): 85–90, quotation on 86–87.

3. For an overview, see A. V. Golubev et al., *Rossiia i Zapad: Formirovanie vneshnepoliticheskikh stereotipov v soznanii rossiiskogo obshehestva pervoi poloviny XX veka* (Moscow: Instiut rossiiskoi istorii RAN, 1998): 69–167.

4. Kees Boterbloem, *The Life and Times of Andrei Zhdanov, 1896–1948* (Montreal: McGill-Queen's University Press, 2004), 269–83, quotation on 279. For a recent archival study of the Zhdanovshchina in one cultural field, see Kiril Tomoff, *Creative Union: The Professional Organization of Soviet Composers, 1939–1953* (Ithaca: Cornell University Press, 2006), chs. 4–5.

5. William Henry Chamberlin, *Russia's Iron Age* (Boston: Little, Brown, 1934).

6. See, inter alia, Marshall T. Poe, *"A People Born to Slavery": Russia in Early Modern European Ethnography, 1476–1748* (Ithaca: Cornell University Press, 2000); Martin Malia, *Russia under Western Eyes: From the Bronze Horseman to the Lenin Mausoleum* (Cambridge:

Harvard University Press, 1999); Larry Wolff, *Inventing Eastern Europe: The Map of Civilization on the Mind of the Enlightenment* (Stanford: Stanford University Press, 1994); Ezequiel Adamovsky, *Euro-Orientalism: Liberal Ideology and the Image of Russia in France (c. 1740–1880)* (Bern: Peter Lang, 2006); Lev Kopelev et al., eds., *Russen und Russland aus deutscher Sicht,* 5 vols., Wuppertaler Projekt zur Erforschung der Geschichte Deutsch-Russischer Fremdenbilder (Munich: W. Fink, 1985–2000).

7. Churchill, "The Sinews of Peace," 9, 10.

8. Quoted in Jeffrey Brooks, *Thank You, Comrade Stalin! Soviet Public Culture from Revolution to Cold War* (Princeton: Princeton University Press, 2000), 207.

9. Nick Rutter, "The Western Wall: The Iron Curtain Redirected, 1951," in this volume.

10. Kennan, "Long Telegram," 87.

11. John Lewis Gaddis, *The Cold War: A New History* (New York: Penguin Books, 2006), 30.

12. Greg Castillo, "East as True West: Redeeming Bourgeois Culture, from Socialist Realism to *Ostalgie,*" ch. 4 of *Imagining the West in Eastern Europe and the Soviet Union,* ed. György Péteri (Pittsburgh: University of Pittsburgh Press, 2010).

13. David Caute, *The Dancer Defects: The Struggle for Cultural Supremacy during the Cold War* (Oxford: Oxford University Press, 2003), 1.

14. An important exception is Jon Jacobson, *When the Soviet Union Entered World Politics* (Berkeley: University of California, 1994).

15. For an extended historiographical interpretation, see Michael David-Fox, "The Implications of Transnationalism," *Kritika* 11, no. 4 (Fall 2011): 885–904.

16. A classic study is Nicholas V. Riasanovsky, *Russia and the West in the Teaching of the Slavophiles: A Study of Romantic Ideology* (Cambridge: Harvard University Press, 1952). See also "The Scythian Rome: Russia," ch. 3 of Liah Greenfeld, *Nationalism: Five Roads to Modernity* (Cambridge: Harvard University Press, 1992).

17. For example, see Michael Confino, "The New Russian Historiography and the Old—Some Considerations," *History and Memory* 21, no. 2 (2009): 7–33. Major studies of Russian views of the "West" include Iver B. Neumann, *Russia and the Idea of Europe: A Study in Identity and International Relations* (London and New York: Routledge, 1996), and Catriona Kelly, *Refining Russia: Advice Literature, Polite Culture, and Gender from Catherine to Yeltsin* (Oxford: Oxford University Press, 2001).

18. For a significant transnational study, see Susan Solomon, ed., *Doing Medicine Together: Germany and Russia between the Wars* (Toronto: University of Toronto Press, 2006).

19. Jacobson, *When the Soviet Union Entered,* 207. As we shall see, the slogan was effectively shelved in the mid-1930s with the declaration of Soviet superiority, but reappeared in the context of Khrushchev's Cold War competition with the United States.

20. Raisa Orlova, *Memoirs,* trans. Samueli Cioran (New York: Random House, 1983), 81.

21. "SSSR—moguchaia industrial'naia derzhava," "Pod znamenem internatsional'noi solidarnosti," and "Nasha rodina," in *Sputnik agitatora,* no. 19 (October 1938): 38–39, 45–47, and no. 13 (July 1938): 13, respectively.

22. André Gide, *Return from the U.S.S.R.,* trans. Dorothy Bussy (New York: Alfred A. Knopf, 1937), 31–33.

23. For an extended discussion, see Michael David-Fox, "Rise of the Stalinist Superiority Complex," ch. 8 of *Showcasing the Great Experiment: Cultural Diplomacy and Western Visitors to Soviet Russia, 1921–1941* (New York: Oxford University Press, 2011).

24. Katerina Clark, *Moscow, the Fourth Rome: Stalinism, Cosmopolitanism, and the Evolution of Soviet Culture, 1931–1941* (Cambridge: Harvard University Press, 2011).

25. Baberowski and Anselm Doering-Manteuffel, "The Quest for Order and the Pur-

suit of Terror: National Socialist Germany and the Stalinist Soviet Union as Multi-Ethnic Empires," ch. 5 of *Beyond Totalitarianism: Stalinism and Nazism Compared,* ed. Michael Geyer and Sheila Fitzpatrick (Cambridge: Cambridge University Press, 2009).

26. This is a very partial enumeration of the list in Karl Schlögel, *Terror und Traum: Moskau 1937* (Munich: Carl Hanser Verlag, 2008), 480–81.

27. Slava Gerovitch, "Perestroika of the History of Technology and Science in the USSR: Changes in the Discourse," *Technology and Culture* 37, no. 1 (1996): 107–108.

28. György Péteri, "Nylon Curtain: Transnational and Transsystemic Tendencies in the Cultural Life of State-Socialist Russia and East-Central Europe," *Slavonica* 10, no. 2 (2004): 113–23, quotation on 119.

29. The best biography of Ehrenburg remains Joshua Rubenstein, *Tangled Loyalties: The Life and Times of Ilya Ehrenburg* (New York: Basic Books, 1996); see also Katerina Clark, "Ehrenburg and Grossman: Two Cosmopolitan Jewish Writers Reflect on Nazi Germany at War," *Kritika* 10, no. 3 (Summer 2009): 607–28.

30. Vladislav Zubok, *Zhivago's Children: The Last Russian Intelligentsia* (Cambridge: Harvard University Press, 2009), 166.

31. Ilya Ehrenburg, *Memoirs: 1921–1941,* trans. Tatiana Shebunina (New York: Grosset and Dunlap, 1966), 26.

32. Tarik Cyril Amar, "Sovietization as a Civilizing Mission in the West," in *The Sovietization of Eastern Europe,* ed. Balázs Apor, Péter Apor, and E. A. Rees (Washington, DC: New Academia Publishing, 2008): 29–46. For those peoples that had never experienced capitalism, the *perezhitki* were those of colonialism and feudalism. On the origins of the term among Soviet ethnographers, see Francine Hirsch, *Empire of Nations: Ethnographic Knowledge and the Creation of the Soviet Union* (Ithaca: Cornell University Press, 2005), 190, 218.

33. Jan Gross, *Revolution from Abroad: The Soviet Conquest of Poland's Western Ukraine and Western Belorussia* (Princeton: Princeton University Press, 2002), 48–50.

34. The overview above is based upon Stephen Lovell, *The Shadow of War: Russia and the USSR, 1941 to Present* (Malden, MA, and Oxford: Wiley-Blackwell, 2010), 2–6.

35. Quoted and discussed in ibid., 298, and Elena Zubkova, *Russia after the War: Hopes, Illusions, and Disappointments,* trans. Hugh Ragsdale (Armonk, NY: M. E. Sharpe, 1998), 18.

36. Zubkova, *Russia after the War,* 25; Vladislav Zubok and Constantine Pleshakov, *Inside the Kremlin's Cold War: From Stalin to Khrushchev* (Cambridge: Harvard University Press, 1996), 36, 51; Antony Beevor, *The Fall of Berlin, 1945* (New York: Penguin Books, 2003), 446.

37. William Hitchcock, *The Struggle for Europe: The Turbulent History of a Divided Continent, 1945 to Present* (New York: Anchor Books, 2004), 17.

38. Richard Overy, *Russia's War: A History of the Soviet Effort* (New York: Penguin Books, 1998), 309.

39. Lovell, *Shadow of War,* 294; Martin Malia, *The Soviet Tragedy: A History of Socialism in Russia, 1917–1991* (New York: Free Press, 1994), 292.

40. Zubkova, *Russia after the War,* 18.

41. Oleg Budnitskii, "The Intelligentsia Meets the Enemy: Educated Soviet Officers in Defeated Germany, 1945," *Kritika* 10, no. 3 (Summer 2009): 629–82, quotation on 676.

42. Vadim Volkov, "The Concept of *Kul'turnost'*: Notes on the Stalinist Civilizing Process," in *Stalinism: New Directions,* ed. Sheila Fitzpatrick (New York: Routledge, 2000), 210–30; Steve Smith and Catriona Kelly, "Commercial Culture and Consumerism," ch. 2 of *Constructing Russian Culture in the Age of Revolution: 1881–1941* (Oxford: Oxford University Press, 1998), esp. 113, 152; Timo Vikhavainen, *Vnutrennyi vrag: Bor'ba s meshchanstvom kak moral'naia missiia russkoi intelligentsii* (St. Petersburg: Kolo, 2004); Richard

Stites, *Russian Popular Culture: Entertainment and Society since 1900* (Cambridge: Cambridge University Press, 1992), esp. 12.

43. David Hoffman, *Stalinist Values: The Cultural Norms of Soviet Modernity, 1917–1941* (Ithaca: Cornell University Press, 2003), 118–45.

44. Quoted in Brooks, *Thank You,* 206.

45. Ibid., 242, 207.

46. Norman Naimark, *The Russians in Germany: A History of the Soviet Zone of Occupation, 1945–1949* (Cambridge: Harvard University Press, 1995), 418.

47. Austin Jersild, "The Soviet State as Imperial Scavenger: 'Catch Up and Surpass' in the Transnational Socialist Bloc, 1950–1960," *American Historical Review* 116, no. 1 (February 2011): 109–32, quotation on 130; Elidor Mëhilli, "Socialist Encounters: Albania and the Transnational Eastern Bloc in the 1950s," in this volume.

48. John Connelly, *Captive University: The Sovietization of East German, Czech, and Polish Higher Education, 1945–1956* (Chapel Hill: University of North Carolina Press, 2000), 44, 51–52.

49. Elizabeth Valkenier, "Stalinizing Polish Historiography: What the Soviet Archives Disclose," *East European Politics and Societies* 7, no. 1 (1993): 114–18, 128–31. On the broader significance of this episode, see Michael David-Fox and György Péteri, "On the Origins and Demise of the Communist Academic Regime," in *Academia in Upheaval: Origins, Transfers, and Transformations of the Communist Academic Regime in Russia and East Central Europe* (Westport, CT: Bergin & Garvey, 2000), 3–38.

50. Connelly, *Captive University,* 44, 51, 52, 69, 191–92.

51. Amir Weiner, "Robust Revolution to Retiring Revolution: The Life Cycle of the Soviet Revolution, 1945–1968," *Slavic and East European Journal* 86, no. 2 (2008): 208–31, quotation on 226.

52. Here see Miriam Dobson, *Khrushchev's Cold Summer: Gulag Returnees, Crime, and the Fate of Reform after Stalin* (Ithaca: Cornell University Press, 2009).

53. Amir Weiner, "The Empires Pay a Visit: Gulag Returnees, East European Rebellions, and Soviet Frontier Politics," *Journal of Modern History* 78 (June 2006): 333–76, quotation on 339.

54. Dobson, *Khrushchev's Cold Summer,* 14.

55. "We Will Bury You," *Time,* November 26, 1956.

56. Anne E. Gorsuch, "Time Travelers: Soviet Tourists to Eastern Europe," in *Turizm: The Russian and East European Tourist under Capitalism and Socialism,* ed. Gorsuch and Diane P. Koenker (Ithaca: Cornell University Press, 2006), 205–26.

57. Ibid., 209, 215.

58. Anne E. Gorsuch, "From Iron Curtain to Silver Screen: Imagining the West in the Khrushchev Era," ch. 7 of *Imagining the West,* ed. Péteri.

59. Eleonory Gilburd, "Picasso in Thaw Culture," *Cahiers du monde russe* 47, nos. 1–2 (2006): 65–108; Pia Koivunen, "The 1957 Moscow Youth Festival: Propagating a New, Peaceful Image of the Soviet Union," in *Soviet State and Society under Nikita Khrushchev,* ed. Melanie Ilic and Jeremy Smith (London: Routledge, 2009): 45–65. On July 23, 2009, on the fiftieth anniversary of the Sokol'niki exhibition, I attended the conference at George Washington University, "Face-off to Facebook: From the Nixon-Khrushchev Kitchen Debate to Public Diplomacy in the 21st Century," whose participants included dozens of former exhibit guides and staff.

60. B. E. Bagdasarian et al., *Sovetskoe zazerkal'e: Inostrannyi turizm v SSSR v 1930–1980-e gody* (Moscow: Forum, 2007), 92.

61. On mass housing under Khrushchev, see Steven E. Harris, *Communism on Tomorrow Street: Mass Housing and Everyday Life after Stalin* (Washington, DC, and Baltimore, MD: Woodrow Wilson Center Press / Johns Hopkins University Press, 2013).

62. See, inter alia, Greg Castillo, *Cold War on the Home Front: The Soft Power of Midcentury Design* (Minneapolis: University of Minnesota Press, 2010).

63. Péteri, "Nylon Curtain," 114–16, quotations on 115, and citing David Riesman, "The Nylon War," in *Abundance for What? And Other Essays* (New York: Doubleday, 1964), 67. The work was originally published in *Common Cause* 4, no. 6 (1951): 379–85.

64. Susan E. Reid, "Who Will Beat Whom? Soviet Popular Reception of the American National Exhibition in Moscow, 1959," ch. 9 of *Imagining the West,* ed. Péteri.

65. György Péteri, "Alternative Modernity? Everyday Practices of Elite Mobility in Communist Hungary, 1956–1980," ch. 3 of *The Socialist Car: Automobility in the Eastern Bloc,* ed. Lewis Siegelbaum (Ithaca: Cornell University Press, 2011); see also Péteri, "Streetcars of Desire: Cars and Automobilism in Communist Hungary (1958–70)," *Social History* 34, no. 1 (February 2009): 1–28; on Khrushchev, see 8.

66. For a broader consideration of luxuries under state socialism, see the collection of essays by David Crowley and Susan E. Reid, eds., *Pleasures in Socialism: Leisure and Luxury in the Eastern Bloc* (Evanston, IL: Northwestern University Press, 2009).

67. For a new work containing much material on concrete cross-border contacts outside the capital cities during the Brezhnev period, see Sergei I. Zhuk, *Rock and Roll in the Rocket City: The West, Identity, and Ideology in Soviet Dniepropetrovsk, 1960–1985* (Baltimore: Johns Hopkins University Press, 2010). In the Czechoslovak context, see the important work by Paulina Bren, *The Greengrocer and his TV: The Culture of Communism after the 1968 Prague Spring* (Ithaca: Cornell University Press, 2010).

68. In the words of Mëhilli in this volume, socialist exchange "was both enabled and constrained by radical centralization, output-focused economies, the parallel structure of the party-state, and the formal and informal channels maintained between socialist states." Mëhilli, "Socialist Encounters," 128.

69. On these points, see Jersild, "The Soviet State as Imperial Scavenger"; Elidor Mëhilli, "The Socialist Design: Urban Dilemmas in Postwar Europe and the Soviet Union," *Kritika* 13, no. 3 (Summer 2012): 635–65.

70. Paul Kennedy, *The Rise and Fall of the Great Powers: Economic Change and Military Conflict from 1500 to 2000* (New York: Random House, 1987).

2

THE TASTE OF RED WATERMELON

Polish Peasants Visit Soviet Collective Farms, 1949–1952

PATRYK BABIRACKI

"Well then," he said, "if this melon is called a 'collective farm girl,' why isn't it red?"

"It may not be red, Mr. Witos, but you'll find it's very sweet-smelling and delicious. I think you'll learn to like it."

—Nikita Khrushchev's recollection of his conversation with Wincenty Witos in the late summer of 1944[1]

The notion that during the Cold War culture, ideas, and perceptions mattered no less than traditional weapons is hardly new.[2] In a veritable public relations race, both superpowers invested lavish resources in selling their ideologies both among allies and in the enemy "camp." World War II had created a new need for international propaganda in both the United States and the USSR. By the end of World War II, the Soviet authorities boasted a rich experience in wooing international public opinion. Scores of Westerners in particular arrived in the USSR in the 1920s and 1930s, many upon invitation. The Soviet state was then young and insecure, and Soviet authorities had hoped that these visiting intellectuals, activists, and workers would validate the legitimacy of the fledgling

---

Research funding for this chapter was provided by the Fulbright-Hays Program of the US Department of Education in 2006. The author wishes to thank Jeffrey Brooks and the participants of the Webb Memorial Lectures series for constructive criticisms at different stages of writing.

regime by producing upbeat eyewitness accounts of life in that country upon returning home.[3]

Courting of foreign public opinion became even more important during the Soviet Union's westward expansion after World War II. The launch of the new, informal empire, of which these soft-power initiatives were part, resulted in contradictions that begged for explanation. The new satellite states provided the USSR with a buffer zone against the West, a new source of raw materials for the devastated economy, and grounds for triumphalism—after all, it appeared as though exporting communism westward validated the efficiency of the Soviet system and its international appeal. Yet the Soviets also had to face up to the fact that despite the significant leftward shift in the political commitments of East European populations during the preceding years, the Soviet version of communism had few enthusiasts in the region. Captive East European publics included individuals whose minds were freer than contemporary commentators and later scholars acknowledged. It was in Moscow's interest to win over the hearts and minds of the local workers, peasants, intellectuals, and often even the half-committed political elites. This turned out to be a challenge, particularly in the period 1948–54. In these years, the pressure to transplant Soviet political, economic, and cultural models onto East European soil, driven by Stalin's need to manage a more uniform set of institutions more easily, was the strongest. Perhaps the most remarkable story that emerges from recent histories is that of how often the Soviets failed to achieve their goals.[4]

Collectivization of agriculture was something that East European peasants feared and resented the most.[5] This was especially true of Poland, a country that shared a border and a long history of mutual distrust with its powerful neighbor to the east. Russia had annexed large parts of Poland at the end of the eighteenth century and increasingly subjected these lands to aggressive Russification. The more recent Soviet invasion in 1939, killings of thousands of Polish officers in the Katyn' Forest, and the arrests of Polish opposition leaders by the NKVD (Soviet security police) after World War II caused widespread resentments that blunted the positive resonance of the Red Army's liberation of Poland from the Nazis. Besides suspicions grounded in Russophobic bias, Poles in the border regions or those who traveled to the USSR knew better than most Westerners about the devastating consequences of collectivization. The bickering of Polish peasant movement leader Wincenty Witos with the secretary of the Ukrainian Communist Party, Nikita Khrushchev, over the color and taste of a watermelon during a meeting in Lublin in the summer of 1944—a year in which Ukraine produced an abundance of these fruits—was really about the value of collective farming and of the Soviet system more generally.[6] The two statesmen's playful exchange of double-entendres, cited in the epigraph, foreshadowed a tension that would be no laughing matter to anyone involved in the years to come. This is because only four years later, in the summer of 1948, Stalin demanded the collectivization of agriculture in the Soviet Union's newly formed East European satellite states. The local communists quickly set out to implement the new directives, and in their attempts to develop the East European countryside on the Soviet model they unleashed a wave of state coercion and peasant resistance in rural areas throughout the region.

This essay tells a story of how Soviet and Polish communists tried but failed to enlist the support of the distrustful Polish peasantry for collectivization. I focus on a little-known but important aspect of this project, the state-sponsored trips of nearly 1,500 Polish delegates to Soviet collective farms during the apex of Polish Stalinism between 1949 and 1952.

By the standards of the Stalinist era, characterized by extreme isolationism not just from the West but also within the countries of the Soviet bloc, the excursions were quite exceptional. The beginning of peasant exchanges coincided with the consolidation of Poland's harsh border regime. As Dariusz Stola observed, in 1952, between Poland and the outside world stood more than 2,000 kilometers of barbed wire, 1,300 kilometers of watch towers, and a 3,000-kilometer-long strip of plowed, smoothly raked earth, which facilitated tracking down instances of illegal entries or exits from the country. The borders were guarded by 30,000 soldiers, "with orders to shoot anyone who would try to escape."[7] That same year, only 12,000 people received passports for one-time international travel; most of these individuals consisted of "carefully selected and tested party functionaries and activists traveling to other countries of the Soviet bloc on official business."[8] Though the communist regimes purported to rule in the name of the toiling classes, workers and peasants were, somewhat paradoxically, subjected to the harshest restrictions on travel. The trips of hundreds of peasants to the USSR were, therefore, doubly unusual. From the historical point of view, they reveal larger, systemic difficulties that both Soviet and Polish communists confronted as they cooperated to mobilize the broader Polish masses for this imperial project. They also put into relief another major problem communists faced of having to weigh the potential benefits and increasingly obvious disadvantages of border crossings within the Soviet bloc.

COOPERATIVE FARMING: A PREHISTORY

The concept of cooperative farming had always been controversial for European socialists. Karl Marx and Friedrich Engels (and many of their contemporaries) saw it as the best way to combine large-scale agricultural production with sound labor practices. For them, cooperative farms were a just alternative to the big enterprises of European landowners whereby peasants worked long hours for menial wages while the enterprises prospered—in part, thanks to owners' ability to combine advanced industrial technology with economies of scale. Cooperatives also seemed like a viable alternative to individual peasant farms whose owners, unable to compete with the capitalist giants, were gradually sliding into ruin. However, by the beginning of the twentieth century, the rationale behind cooperatives had lost its appeal to some thinkers. As a result of industrialization, the lot of the individual farmer had begun to improve. Peasants eventually also benefited from technological advances, began employing better tools, and obtained better crops. Prices of natural products generally went up, and pressure on land also relaxed as more of the rural population left their homes to work in the cities.[9]

Cooperative farming was one of many of Marx's ideas that enjoyed an unexpectedly gratifying afterlife in Soviet Russia. After the October Revolution of 1917, Vladimir Lenin revived the concept (by then considered anachronistic in socialist circles) and tried to use collectivization as a remedy for the devastating effects of World War I and the ongoing civil war. He assumed that poor and middle peasants would revitalize Soviet agricultural production by adding their newly acquired land and scarce property to a common pool. It was Lenin's expectation that under the leadership of the Bolsheviks the two groups would marginalize the prosperous peasants known as the "kulaks," who were presumed to be the "capitalist element" in the village. But events took a completely different course. Collectivization brigades from the cities often resorted to violence as they tried to expropriate not only the richest peasants but also the middle and the poor.

The peasant resistance that followed forced the Bolsheviks to forgo the idea by 1920. Instead, Lenin decided to rebuild the national economy by relying on private agriculture. This strategy assumed that once individual farmers started producing enough food, the cities could industrialize, and eventually, as these more favorable conditions stimulated the prosperity of the peasants, the latter would turn to cooperative farming voluntarily. In the late 1920s, however, Joseph Stalin inverted Lenin's conclusions: he ordered a rapid forced collectivization meant to secure a surplus that could be used to help the cities industrialize. But the ruthless expropriations, grain procurements from peasants, and deportations and executions of real and imagined "kulaks" had disastrous effects. They paralyzed the economy by reducing available labor power and depriving the remaining peasants of the incentive to work. Eventually, Stalin's policies led to a famine on a national scale and left the Soviet countryside poor and broken for decades to come.[10]

In the years that immediately followed World War II, despite their commitment to orthodox Marxism and Stalinism, Polish communists refrained from restructuring the Polish countryside on the Soviet model. Although there was some talk of cooperatives among party members, generally tactical considerations prevailed since Polish leaders feared that even the smallest hints to that effect would buttress rumors about the Sovietization of Poland. Stalin himself, aware of the unpopularity of such measures, was said to discourage such plans; the keenest Soviet observers of Polish public life seconded him in dissuading Soviet news organizations from planting articles about collectivization in the Polish press.[11] Besides, some communists, especially party secretary Władysław Gomułka, championed the concept of a "Polish road to socialism." To peasant ears, this was a reassuring promise to preserve private land ownership and individual production. The solution made particular sense to the Poles, due to the political capital they had earned from the land reforms of 1944—which redistributed land from the former gentry estates among the poorest peasants.

Officials from the Soviet International Department (the Central Committee's body responsible for managing the party's activities abroad, and something of an institutional successor to the disbanded Communist International) were dismayed by the lack of a decisive program for the transformation of agriculture on the part of the Polish communists.[12] In the climate of the impending Cold War, the perceived threat from the United States, and the maturing conflict with Yugoslavia's Josip Broz-Tito, Stalin changed tactics and pushed for institutional uniformity in the Soviet bloc. The Communist Information Bureau (henceforth the Cominform) finally issued a directive for collectivization in European People's Democracies during its second meeting in Bucharest in June of 1948. During the plenum of the Central Committee of the Polish Workers' Party (Polska Partia Robotnicza, or PPR), the chief communist economist Hilary Minc accepted "production cooperatives" as the new form of cooperative work in the countryside.[13] The other Polish communists responded with mixed signals to the Soviet initiative. Jakub Berman was the party's main ideologue also responsible for culture and security in the Politburo. He later claimed to have tried changing the language of the resolution by suggesting the word "cooperativization" (*uspołecznienie*) instead of "collectivization," which apparently irritated Stalin.[14] Gomułka's support was even more halfhearted. Although he now described the idea as "strategically correct" and performed a thorough self-criticism for his previous views, he continued to see it as "tactically harmful."[15] His stand earned him much criticism and served as one of the pretexts to exclude him from the Central Committee soon thereafter in November 1949.

In striking resemblance to Lenin's domestic plans, the Polish collectivization program as it emerged in 1949 was to be gradual and voluntary for the peasants.[16] The communists really wanted to make the superiority of collective farming a self-evident truth to the Polish peasant. It was also in their interest to avoid violent popular protests against this initiative. The Polish leaders knew from security police reports that the expression "collective farm" had the worst associations among rural inhabitants. Many peasants had heard about the hunger and poverty of the Soviet *kolkhozy* from Soviet soldiers during World War II, and after the Soviet invasion of eastern Poland in 1939 many Poles saw for themselves the collective farms that were being quickly set up by the new administration. While some peasants later spread outlandish tales of shared food and women in the Soviet collective farms, much of the information that passed from mouth to mouth was true.[17] Some sections of the population knew about the terror and victims of Soviet collectivization. Others saw it through the prism of their own experiences in unfree labor systems, either on prewar Polish landed estates or wartime *ligenschaften* set up during the Nazi occupation.[18]

For all these reasons, the top Polish communists at first tended to encourage, not force, Polish peasants to join the cooperatives. They created three types of cooperative farms—with a fourth added in 1950—based on different degrees of property sharing and income distribution among farm members. In this scheme, type I allowed peasants to cultivate their own plots independently, type III resembled Soviet collective farms, and types Ib and II constituted intermediate forms.[19] Peasants who joined the cooperatives also enjoyed significant tax breaks and advantageous credit.[20] Minc, who otherwise planned to collectivize only 1 percent of all Polish farms in 1949, also expected that based on these incentives peasants would line up to join the cooperatives in such numbers that many would have to wait before being able to do so.

Long lines indeed became the order of the day in Stalinist Poland, but the desire to join a cooperative was hardly what drove the people who stood in them. As in the USSR earlier, peasants were hostile to the idea; hence the socialist transformation of agriculture proceeded much more slowly than in other satellite states.[21] The outcome was also more meager than originally planned, since only 0.1 percent of farms became collectivized by the end of the year.[22] The Soviet ambassador to Poland, Viktor Z. Lebedev, expressed his concern with this state of affairs in his letter to Stalin dated February 26, 1950. "In Poland, collectivization is taking place mainly in the new territories, which had been detached from Germany," wrote Lebedev, referring to the country's newly acquired western provinces, adding that the process "barely touched" the core Polish territories. "This is even understandable," he editorialized, "since nobody is really overseeing these efforts on the excuse that haste is uncalled for, [and even] harmful." Lebedev further accused the leadership of the Polish United Workers' Party (Polska Zjednoczona Partia Robotnicza, or PZPR, a largely reincarnated PPR) of explicitly forbidding the Polish peasants to share their allegedly favorable impressions from the USSR with their peers, because "much of what they had seen does not fit into the Polish conditions."[23] As in other similar instances, such foot-dragging by the Polish authorities raised suspicions among zealous Soviet observers.

One scholar speculates that Stalin's subsequent intervention with Bolesław Bierut, Poland's president, PZPR's First Secretary, and the leader of the ruling triumvirate, may have been the reason behind the latter's decision to accelerate the pace of collectivization. During the IV Plenum of the PZPR's Central Committee, the party's leader ordered the creation of 2,000 agricultural cooperatives by the end of the year and specified a minimum quota of 120–150 collective farms per each of the country's voivodships (an administrative unit).[24] From that point on, collectivization was voluntary only in theory. Local party officials frequently resorted to force or subterfuge as they tried to meet the demands from above while facing widespread hostility and resistance from the peasants.[25]

ON THE ROAD

Hoping to sway the Polish peasants in favor of collective farming, the communists gave some of them the opportunity to see for themselves the purported advantages of this system. Like their comrades in other East European countries, they thus relied on teaching by example, or mimesis, to complement other forms of propaganda about collectivization.[26] At least six delegations of Polish peasants went to the Soviet Union between 1949 and 1952. At least one delegation of forty-five Soviet peasants and activists visited Poland in 1950. All peasant exchanges were organized by the Communist Parties' International Departments, several government agencies (notably the Ministries of Foreign Affairs, Ministries of Agriculture, and respective security organs) as well as local peasant organizations. Candidates had to apply for passports, undergo political screenings with the security police, and obtain entry visas from the Soviet Ministry of Foreign Affairs. A typical delegation was composed of rank-and-file peasants from different regions of the country (mostly male), party activists, several journalists, and a few members of youth organizations. Upon arrival in the USSR, the delegation, ordinarily several hundred people strong, split up into smaller units. These, led by Polish directors and Soviet guides and accompanied by journalists and security officers, then ventured into the field, in both a figurative and a literal sense.

Scores of Western intellectuals who visited the Soviet Union between the 1930s and the 1970s were hoping to find solutions to grand social problems that plagued their own societies. It is clear now that hardly all guests were impressed and not every Western pro-Soviet panagyric reflected its author's often miserable experience in the USSR; some travelers, too, simply kept silent after their return. Still, for many reasons, most of these returnees became cheerleaders for the Soviet experiment; in so doing, they rewarded their former hosts and responded to political pressures in their home countries. Those who enthused about the Soviet Union were seeking social justice, equality, a general sense of purpose, and genuine humanistic values: "Most of them were idealistic, hopeful, and ready to believe that radically new departures were possible in remodeling the organization of society and its social policies and personal needs could be fully harmonized."[27] These predispositions became a crucial element in creating a positive image of the USSR abroad. On the one hand, they allowed the travelers to rationalize or ignore the negative aspects of the Soviet reality that they were witnessing due to an omission on the part of their hosts. On the other hand, they permitted the hosts themselves to avoid potentially awkward challenges from their guests.

The Polish peasants shared none of these utopian longings; if they erred, it was on the side of suspicion. For most future delegates, the adventure began in their native villages. Like the French workers between the wars, candidates for trips to the Soviet Union had been preselected by the local party organizations; like them, too, they were then "elected" during formal assemblies.[28] Peasants who participated in these meetings usually instructed the selected travelers about the things to which they should be paying attention. They also gave the delegates a list of questions to ask once on the spot, about such issues as the average yields per hectare of land, the amount of daily wages, production of animal husbandry, and so forth.

Some of the questions passed on to the village representatives were quite specific—e.g., "Is that true that one sheep can give twenty-two kilograms of wool; or, can one cow give 9,000 liters of the milk per year?" Others specifically requested that the delegates pay attention en route "to the general economic conditions, since on the spot everything will be prepared." Upon arrival, they were asked to engage in informal conversations with the collective farmers, especially the old ones in order to get the most accurate information, as well as "to pay more attention to those places that are not being shown."[29] Evidently, the village communities saw such delegations as opportunities to confront the hyperbolic descriptions of model farms that they had heard from collectivization brigades and from the press. Beginning in 1949, these official scenarios portrayed the typical Soviet collective farm as an agricultural cornucopia and social paradise in which people worked hard, but also earned high wages, lived prosperously, and generally enjoyed themselves.[30] But the communist authorities correctly concluded that the questions addressed to the traveling peasants suggested that "the peasants do not believe in the achievements of the Soviet collective farms about which they hear on the radio and read about in the press."[31]

Tensions between Polish wariness of the Soviet system and the Soviets' ability to dispel it occurred early, during the journey to the USSR. The train ride to (but also from and within) the Soviet Union afforded peasant visitors extended opportunities to confront the abundant official propaganda about Soviet agriculture and the country in general.[32] For their part, the Soviet authorities made a tremendous effort to ensure that these first impressions were good. As in the case of Western intellectuals who came to the USSR, Soviet authorities assumed that making their guests feel good during their stay would help create a positive impression of the entire experience. For example, the Soviet ambassador Lebedev requested that the Ukrainian Ministry of Foreign Affairs arrange for a first-class train car and a restaurant car to meet the delegates on the Soviet-Polish border. While the former was sent immediately, it took the ministry no small effort to locate a suitable restaurant car. After the official meeting in the border town of Brest (Brześć), the delegates were to make a few more stops on their way to Kiev in order to take part in official rallies and festivities. To ensure that they were in a good mood, the Soviet authorities issued instructions to supply the peasant travelers with vodka and cigarettes upon their arrival at each station.[33] Nor did the hosting officials spare any efforts to craft their guests' final impressions, trying to eliminate any undesirable incidents that could imperil future propaganda efforts. To ensure that everything went smoothly, the Ukrainian Central Committee ordered that special train engineers should be selected to drive the first Polish delegation in 1949 back to the border. Despite these precautions, the engineer lost his hat on the way and stopped the train to go look for it. Instead, he was arrested by the Ukrainian security police after a brief scuffle.[34]

For Western political pilgrims, the VIP treatment (which was much more intense and much more personalized) created a sense of obligation to their hosts: "they were not bribed, but they could not help feeling that it is not nice to turn around and be harshly critical of those who showered them with kindness, who took such good care of them."[35] In addition, the idea that they were being cynically deceived was particularly difficult for visiting intellectuals to accept because they took particular "pride in their ability to see through sham."[36] The potential impulse to criticize Soviet reality was further dampened by the complex relationships within their own social and intellectual milieus. They resented the seemingly chaotic and unequal Western capitalist system; their grand visions of a just society seemed to match the generosity, order, and lack of economic extremes they thought they had witnessed in the USSR. As intellectuals, they often felt isolated in their own societies, and the generosity of their hosts satisfied their longings for a more welcoming community. They had a sense that if they wrote anything negative about the Soviet Union upon coming home, the very intellectual community to which they belonged would turn upon them. One can easily imagine that the majority of Polish peasants were free of such anxieties. In criticizing the Soviet collective farms to fellow farmers in Poland they would be preaching to the choir; it was by praising them that they would risk a loss of social status and prestige.[37]

Indeed, evidence suggests that the VIP treatment left some Polish peasants undeterred from their own investigative missions. During their long train journeys, the delegates had time to look around and observe their Soviet hosts and the passing landscapes outside the window. What they saw made them uneasy. During the first delegation in 1950 the peasants were "particularly surprised" to see that the houses of Ukrainian peasants were built from clay. What they saw from the train windows while riding through the war-ravaged territories of Belarus and especially the Smolensk region tended to exacerbate this negative impression. In moments such as this, the guides had to explain that peasants had lived in even worse conditions before the revolution. During guided tours of the USSR, the tsarist legacy traditionally "absolved" the Soviet system of "all the defects and errors which the propaganda was unable to pass over in silence," and these tours were no exception.[38] It is unclear whether the guide for the 1950 delegation succeeded in convincing the peasants, as he claimed he did.[39] Hollander observed that the Western intellectuals' positive predispositions toward the Soviet system drove them to generalize from their relatively narrow experiences into a broader, flattering picture of the USSR. Given that the Polish peasants' initial attitudes were exactly contrary, one is led to believe that the guide was too optimistic in his evaluations. On the train, and later in the collective farms, Polish peasants were likely to generalize the negative experiences from their trip. Here the Soviet hosts were at a disadvantage because masses of peasants were so much harder to control than a handful of intellectuals. In the end, the possibility that peasants would get a glimpse of the "unofficial" Soviet reality was greater.

Occasionally, the Soviet hosts themselves unwittingly created situations that were bound to raise eyebrows among the guests and left a dubious picture of the system they were promoting. To many peasants, the train ride was an opportunity to evaluate to what extent their hosts represented the high standards they promoted. In June 1950, Vagan Grigor'ian from the Soviet International Department learned from an accompanying TASS (Soviet telegraph agency) correspondent that a couple of his compatriots had attracted the attention of the peasant delegates with their unsavory appearance. For two weeks, he reported, everyone slept in common train cars without separate compartments. On one occasion, the Poles noticed the "torn underwear" of another traveler. Moreover, a certain Khodzevskii charged by the USSR Ministry of Agriculture with taking care of the delegation attracted a lot of attention because for the whole two weeks he had been walking around in rumpled clothes and occasionally even walked barefoot around the train platform.[40] Given that material prosperity was an important aspect of Soviet self-promotion, lack of basic consumer products such as underwear may have posed a problem for the distrustful peasants. In addition, rumpled clothes and shoeless strolls along the train station contrasted with the image of civic respectability that the Soviet state tried to project. The Polish officials' estimates suggested that only 10–15 percent of their traveling protégés retained a negative impression from the trips to the USSR, but incidents such as the ones described suggest that the percentage of the unconvinced was likely higher.

BUILDING A POTEMKIN VILLAGE

Negotiations about the meaning and credibility of the collective farms as well as about Soviet life in general reached their climax among the barns and pigsties of the imperial center. In 1949 the sole destination for visiting Polish peasants was the Soviet Socialist Republic of Ukraine. Despite the calamities of collectivization, Nazi robberies, and destruction caused by war, not to mention the postwar drought, Ukraine continued to feed the entire Union by providing the best crops. In 1950 the delegates were invited to the Russian Republic as well. Visits to Moscow were added to the itineraries, and the decision to highlight the capital may well have been the main reason why the visitors also got to see collective farms in the Russian Republic.

The Soviet countryside beckoned, and the Polish delegates wanted to see as much as they could. Split up into smaller groups, members of the 1949 delegation, the third to visit the USSR since the war, visited 127 collective farms, i.e., farms in which peasants co-owned and collectively cultivated a parcel of land, raised animals, etc. The Poles also toured 34 state farms (*sovkhozy*) where animals and equipment as well as the land belonged to the state and where conditions were generally much better because of the fixed income the peasants received. The members of the Polish delegations also had the opportunity to see 27 Machine-Tractor Stations (MTSs), state institutions that rented out tractors and other equipment to the collective farms.[41] Staffed by former enforcers of collectivization often brought from the cities, they were also powerful instruments of political control of the countryside—"islands of party activism among a sea of peasants unsympathetic to the Communist regime."[42] The first delegation in 1950 was able to see over 40 collective farms, more than 10 MTSs and state farms, about a dozen scientific institutes and experimental stations, as well as several industrial centers including the tractor factory in Kharkov, the metallurgical plant Azovstal, and Dnieprogos, the newly rebuilt hydroelectric power station.[43] The delegates also had the opportunity to peek into the private dwellings, pantries, and farm buildings of the Soviet collective farmers.[44]

"Potemkinist" discourse, to use Sheila Fitzpatrick's term, presented an idealized image of collectivized countryside to Soviet domestic publics, thereby further affirming the Stalinist regime.[45] "Potemkin villages" trace their origin to late eighteenth-century Russia. The concept refers to the anecdotal settlements erected by Grigorii Potemkin, Catherine the Great's viceroy of the Crimea. It is said that the field marshal was so eager to impress the tsarina with a picture of prosperity in the newly conquered lands under his care that he ordered the building of a series of cardboard, painted villages, which Catherine could admire from afar during her grand tour of the empire's southern domains. The story was, in fact, a malicious rumor spread by the more spiteful foreign dignitaries who accompanied Catherine. By emphasizing the real hastiness with which various sites on the empress's route were receiving their facelifts, they minimized Russia's unquestioned accomplishments in developing the area.[46] To Westerners, "Potemkin villages" had stood for false facades and alleged Russian deceitfulness ever since, an impression that early twentieth-century Soviet guides eagerly tried to dispel by taking the Western visitors to as many "model" collective farms as possible.[47]

Yet in the Soviet case, tours of prosperous collective farms really were part of an elaborate system designed to deceive.[48] Foreigners constituted the main public for these staged tours. One instance in 1952, when the visitors were inadvertently shown a dilapidated collective farm, illustrates the artifice of the entire process. The group visiting Voronezh was able to see only one unimpressive collective farm. Startled, its members learned that the wage per workday (*trudoden'*, a unit of labor that measured contributions through different kinds of activity on a farm) was about one kilogram of wheat and 0.85 to two rubles in cash. This left them unimpressed; after all, members of Poland's nascent collective farms at that time received at least 4.8 kilograms of wheat per workday in addition to potatoes and a much higher cash payment.[49] The farm's manager faltered in responding to the delegates' questions and thus further fueled their suspicions. Lastly, it turned out that this was the most successful collective farm in the Voronezh oblast, a region that already lay in the most fertile area of the USSR, the Black Earth belt. In many ways the farm was therefore better than a typical one in the USSR, since according to data from 1946, 75.8 percent of collective farms paid their members less than one kilogram of wheat per one day of labor.[50] In 1950 an average resident of the collective farm in the Russian Republic obtained for their work 164 kilograms of grain per year. Nearly one-third of the collective farmers received no monetary compensation at all for the labor.[51] To save face, the Soviet organizers of course had to prevaricate by presenting the farm as grossly substandard. To prevent further mishaps during this carelessly planned excursion, they decided to cancel the remaining visits and showed the Poles only the fields of two other collective farms.

So despite the cancellation of visits to the remaining collective farms, the members of the Polish delegation nevertheless had managed to visit a *kolkhoz* that belied the boastful assertions of Soviet propaganda. Undoubtedly, in the eyes of many Poles the experience reinforced what they had expected to see from the beginning. The discovery of this incident came as an unwelcome surprise to the Soviet authorities in Moscow. An International Department employee, Ian Dzerzhinskii (the son of the infamous Feliks Dzierżyński, the Polish-born founder of the Cheka, the first Soviet security police), had a chat with one of the delegation's participants during a reception organized by the Ministry of Agriculture on June 2. The Polish peasant struck the Soviet official as an enthusiastic supporter of cooperative farming, but also as someone who seemed, nevertheless, oddly restrained when asked about his impressions from the most recent trip. Only through further inquiries with an official from the Ministry of

Agriculture did Dzerzhinskii learn that the Poles had been taken to a non-"model" collective farm.[52] The Soviet official's entirely accidental discovery of this omission on the part of the local authorities raises the question of how many similar incidents remain unknown. Consequently, it further suggests that the Polish peasants may have had many more opportunities to form a negative impression about the Soviet Union, or to confirm existing ones, than is given in the official Soviet estimates.

Dzerzhinskii quickly initiated measures meant to prevent another embarrassment. Within the next three days he must have informed somebody in the International Department about the incident, because on June 6 Nikolai Pukhlov forwarded the information to Grigor'ian. He wrote: "With regard to the group of Polish peasants who visited the Voronezh province, the main task—familiarizing themselves with the Soviet experience in collective farms—has not been fulfilled."[53] On June 7 the Ministry of Agriculture received an official reprimand from the Central Committee.[54] On June 12 and with the green light from Mikhail Suslov, the Soviet Union's main ideologue and the chief of the International Department, two officials left Moscow for the Voronezh province in order to inspect the objects to be shown to the second delegation of Polish peasants, expected to arrive on June 10.[55] In the meantime, after consultations with local party officials and collective farm management in the Voronezh region, the Ministry of Agriculture revised the itinerary of the third trip of Polish peasants (expected on June 25) and submitted the draft to the Central Committee for approval on June 21.[56] The speed with which the entire response was carried out testifies to the importance of the issue. And indeed on numerous occasions the charades yielded the desired results, and the model villages genuinely impressed the Polish peasants.[57]

Yet despite the efforts of the Soviet guides and Polish group directors, local Soviet authorities frequently found themselves having to explain the seemingly less appealing aspects of collective farming. During the first trip in 1950, for example, the delegates encountered farmers paid four to five kilograms of wheat and three to five rubles in cash per workday. They compared this with the wages they received in their own cooperatives, which in Poland's western voivodships were much higher. In response, the organizers told the peasants that in Soviet collective farms there was a relatively large quantity of working days per member of the cooperative. They thus suggested that the norms per workday were lower, and the farmers received the payments more frequently. This explanation may have struck the guest as credible, since even local officials in various parts of Poland at the time calculated daily norms and "workdays" according to different criteria.[58] But it fell on deaf ears nonetheless: according to the report, the peasants in this group found more convincing the hosts' emphasis on a widespread system of additional bonuses for exceeding the plan, as well as on the necessity to work more in the Soviet context, given the scope and scale of postwar destruction.[59]

In 1952 the dwellings of the collective farm workers severely disappointed some Polish peasants, especially those coming from the country's western and economically more prosperous voivodships. For the first time, officials began to suspect that to some degree such disappointments had to do with the "one-sidedness" of Polish propaganda about the booming and glamorous "agro-towns," or large-scale consolidation projects initiated by Khrushchev a year earlier.[60] Such propaganda, cautioned one Polish official, focused on the final product instead of on the gradual process of building such sites. Again, the excursion's political directors concluded on an optimistic note. They observed that doubtful attitudes changed after the Soviet collective farmers themselves discussed the progress of the Soviet village during the preceding several decades and "impressing the Polish peasants with the enormous needs, the scale and the cost of rural development."[61] But even the officials concluded that some delegates under their care remained unconvinced by these explanations. The report from the unfortunate trip to Voronezh in 1952 noted that "many others" remained skeptical about the conditions for raising livestock, the allegedly free health care, and other social services. Even though the document's author admitted that "relatively fewer" delegates than in the past tried to explain Soviet agricultural successes by reference to the fertility of the soil alone, some continued to do so, thereby minimizing the significance of the Soviet agricultural techniques.[62] Finally, the Polish official also acknowledged that the majority of the delegation members had been positively predisposed toward collective farming before setting foot on Soviet soil.[63] The seemingly offhanded nature of these remarks obscured their profound significance: the fact that by recruiting the already committed members of newly established Polish collective farms (73 of the 114 individual farmers on the trip belonged to cooperatives), the communists were losing the battle for the hearts and minds of potential converts to the idea of collectivization.

Similarly, selected collective farmers in the toured villages also refused to play the official game. Sometimes such people complicated the work of the guides by contesting the official view of the Soviet village. During the first trip in 1952, for instance, the participants encountered the Ukrainian population that had been resettled from Poland in 1946–47. According to the communist officials, some of these people "seemed unsympathetic to the Polish excursion." Elsewhere, the peasants ran into a collective farmer who was clearly "sarcastic" when he discussed his present life only in superlatives. Another time, an elderly woman started talking about poverty and lack of bread. The party activists were quick to intervene: after a few questions for the woman they set out to prove that she was resentful of the Soviet Union because her son had been killed as a member of a "fascist band."[64]

Some scenes from the Soviet collective farms clearly struck the Polish delegates as bogus. In 1949 a female farmer who was visiting a preschool in the Ukraine publicly commented on the contrast between the brand-new attire of the village children and the crisp white bed linens on the one hand and the kids' grimy hands and feet on the other. The delegate read this scene as though the children had been hastily dressed for the arrival of the delegates. She implied that despite the hosts' efforts, the unwashed bodies of the children betrayed signs of longtime neglect, thus revealing the true nature of child care on collective farms. She was probably largely correct. As one scholar pointed out, "Although the walls of the restaurant cars and the festive mood were meant to separate the Polish delegates from the severe reality of life," reality "got through to them, ruining the illusory barriers that have been built by the communists."[65]

FINDING THE PEASANT PILGRIMS

Ever since they began inviting foreigners for guided tours of collective farms, the Soviet authorities had been facing what Michael David-Fox called a "Potemkin Village dilemma." Showing their guests a maximum of sites strengthened the credentials of the Soviet system, but it also raised the chances of unwittingly exposing its multifarious weaknesses.[66] As they were preparing the peasant trips, the Polish communists also confronted a paradox. In order to produce the most convincing testimonies from the USSR, they had to send there the most trustworthy members of the village communities. Yet frequently these were also the staunchest enemies of

Figure 2.1. "'How can one grow such beautiful beets?' asks the Polish delegate." Reprinted by permission from *Co widzieliśmy na Ukrainie radzieckiej* (Warsaw: Ludowa Spółdzielnia Wydawnicza, 1950), 58.

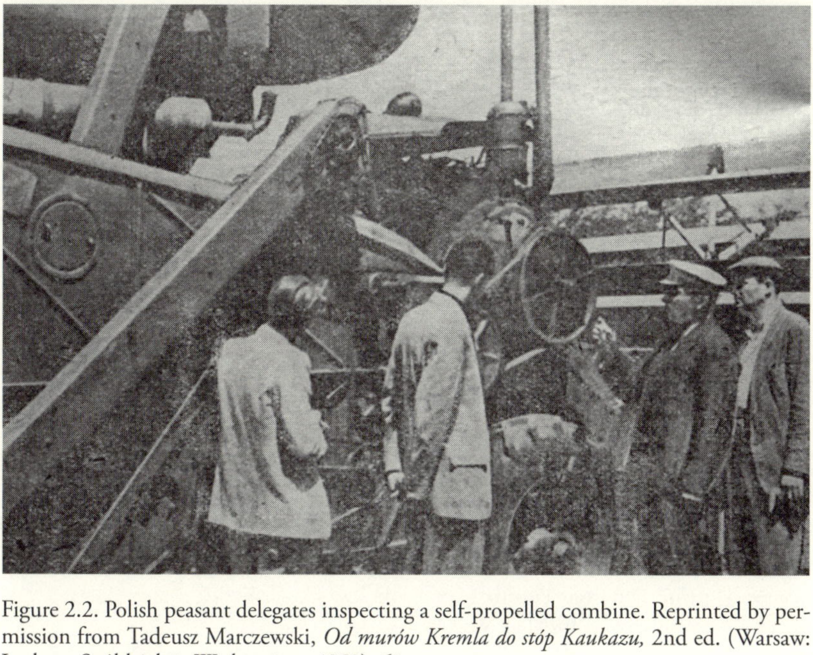

Figure 2.2. Polish peasant delegates inspecting a self-propelled combine. Reprinted by permission from Tadeusz Marczewski, *Od murów Kremla do stóp Kaukazu,* 2nd ed. (Warsaw: Ludowa Spółdzielnia Wydawnicza, 1953), 61.

Figure 2.3. Children at a Ukraine nursery. Reprinted by permission from Tadeusz Marczewski, *Od murów Kremla do stóp Kaukazu,* 2nd ed. (Warsaw: Ludowa Spółdzielnia Wydawnicza, 1953), 114.

Figure 2.4. Polish guests taking notes after a visit to the Machine Tractor Station. Reprinted by permission from Tadeusz Marczewski, *Od murów Kremla do stóp Kaukazu,* 2nd ed. (Warsaw: Ludowa Spółdzielnia Wydawnicza, 1953), 43.

collectivization of agriculture and the most critical commentators of the excursions. The Polish authorities' constant effort to ensure the success of such initiatives can be seen as an attempt to resolve this conundrum. These efforts ended in a failure, I suggest, since in order to produce nominally positive results, the Polish authorities began choosing only those peasants for the trips who, like the earlier Western travelers, had already been favorably predisposed toward the Soviet system. They gave up on potential converts, whom they deemed out of reach, and wagered on pilgrims, to use Hollander's term. These peasant pilgrims ultimately made little difference, since they did not enjoy the trust of their village communities.

To the Polish communists, the three-year experiment with peasant excursions constituted a sharp learning curve.[67] They relied on trial and error to fine-tune the selection criteria in picking out the candidates for such trips. The first and second groups, both visiting Ukraine from late February to early March of 1949 consisted of 24 and 165 people respectively (see Table 2.1). The pilot visit was unusual: it included 13 administrative employees of the Peasant Mutual Aid Society (Samopomoc Chłopska), only 3 individual farmers, 2 senior PZPR officials, 1 official from the moribund Polish Peasant Party (Polskie Stronnictwo Ludowe, or PSL), 2 representatives of youth organizations, and 3 journalists.[68] In the second group, the majority was composed of rank-and-file peasants (117 people). Eighty-three members of the delegation belonged to the PZPR, 9 to the PSL, and 24 to the Peasant Party (Stronnictwo Ludowe, or SL).[69] Both delegations received good marks from Ukrainian and Polish officials, including the Ukrainian party secretary, Nikita Khrushchev, who openly encouraged organizing more such events.[70] Still, a number of incidents with negative political overtones (mostly snide comments and provocative questions coming from the participants) or simple displays of indifference toward the Soviet collective farms made the officials think about how to avoid these in the future.

Based on these experiences, the Polish vice-consul in Kiev, Paweł Włoński, made several recommendations about the makeup of future delegations in his report to the International Department of the PZPR's Central Committee dated March 17, 1949. He suggested including more peasants who actually "work in the field" (presumably in contrast to activists) as well as more specialists, such as "agronomists, tractor drivers, etc. who could popularize the Soviet experiences in practical capacities." The

Table 2.1. Polish peasants in the USSR, 1949–52 (*total excludes group III–1950 and groups II and III–1952)

Year of Departure	*Group No.*	*Month*	*Total Participants*	*Members of Cooperatives*	*Individual Peasants*	*POM Employees*
1949	I	February–March	24		3	
1949	II	February–March	165	117		
1949	III	June–July	395			
1950	I	May–June	241	115	63	20
1950	II	June 8–29	233	98	62	19
1950	III					
1952	I	May–June	180	167		
1952	II					
1952	III					
Total*			1,076	625		

Sources: AAN, syg. 237/XXII-120; AAN, syg. 237/V-134; AAN, syg. 237/XXII-651; Jarosz, *Polityki*, Tkaczow, "Propaganda."

consul wanted to see more women since they played a big role in Polish agriculture. The Polish communists also generally considered peasant women to be "backward" and vulnerable to enemy propaganda. This was another reason why they strove so hard to get them involved in the collectivization campaign.[71] In Włoński's reckoning women made up only 25 percent of the total (i.e., 6 people) during the first trip, whereas the second time around they composed only 11 percent (18 people). Włoński suggested that the organizers should try to aim at 30–40 percent next time. The diplomat also wished to see more "representatives of village amateur theaters, village clubs, folk choirs and village reading rooms." He also recommended that more nonparty members be included. This was to be done at the expense of the now-discredited PSL members, who were, in the consul's view, "influenced by the shady ideology" of the party's previous leadership.[72] In sum, a dual mechanism was at play: the govern-

PZPR Members	*PSL / SL / ZSL Members*	*Nonparty Members*	*Activists and Administrative Employees*	*Women*	*Others*	*Hostile / Indifferent*
2	1		13	6 (25%)	5	
83	9/24			18 (11%)		
199	2/49	131		153		10–15%
173	34	34	67	45	14	10% hostile
165	42	22	31		19	10–14%
						4% negative

ment official wanted to maximize the benefits of such visits not only by eliminating potentially hostile elements, but also by including a diverse mixture of the most credible, visible, and articulate members of the village community. The task was contradictory, since such individuals were most likely to be critical of Soviet reality.

The officials in the PZPR's Central Committee must have taken the consul's recommendations to heart. On May 5, 1949, they sent a letter to all party provincial committees emphasizing that the purpose of the peasant delegations was to help organize agricultural cooperatives. This was to be done by transforming the already existing "founding committees" into executive boards of production cooperatives.[73] Based on the party's decision, such committees had been created at the end of March 1949, but only in regions of the country that met two specific criteria. According to one of them, the local peasantry had to be poor, so that joining a cooperative would appear as a solution to their economic problems and not as their cause. The second criterion involved a guarantee that the future collective farms in the given region had the potential to become model institutions of their kind within a relatively brief period of time.[74] Out of 164 villages that met these criteria, only 115 established "founding committees." But out of those, only forty cooperatives materialized, because the inhabitants of other villages requested more time to think it over.[75] It seems that these hesitant peasants became the preferred candidates for visits to the USSR, as the Central Committee's letter specifically pointed out that "they should be picked from villages where the founding committees already exist or [one] is about to be created."[76]

The communists' criteria suggested a concern with the credibility of the candidates in their communities. The letter from the Central Committee further specified that candidates for such trips should be "carefully chosen." The authors admonished that the selection should be made according to three additional principles. According to the first, two candidates should be picked from each village and include a man and a woman. Undoubtedly, the communists' concern with gender parity resonated with their official support of women's equality. One suspects, though, that in this case the desire to include a fair percentage of women had more to do with the latter's pivotal roles in peasant households and, consequently, within the village communities—no doubt augmented by the demographic imbalance caused by World War II. The other criteria confirm this interpretation. The authorities emphasized that the people chosen for the trips be those who enjoyed the trust of their villages. They must be "people that we can be sure other people in their villages will believe to correspond with reality." Finally, they wrote, "priority should be given to report things that members of 'Peasant Self-Help' and not just members of political parties. It is important that among the delegates there would be a significant number of nonparty member peasants who enjoy the trust of those who are still hesitant."[77]

In the end, the third delegation of Polish peasants in 1949 who visited Ukraine between June 20 and July 4 turned out to be much smaller than planned: it included only 199 PZPR members, 49 SL members, 2 PSL members, and 131 nonparty members.[78] According to another report, it included a total of 395 people, including 153 women. Originally, the trip was to include 483 people, but many selected candidates for the trip were ultimately unable to go because they did not get their entry visas on time.[79]

This illustrates how centralized control coupled with inefficiency tended to undercut the communist propaganda initiatives on the Polish side. In the final cut, the participants represented over 300 Polish villages from all regions of Poland. In addition, a certain number of people—15 percent of the total number—gained a place by circumventing the officially prescribed screening channels such as local peasant organizations, the government, or the party.[80]

This time around, the groups' directors streamlined their political analyses and translated the successes and failures of agricultural sightseeing into specific figures. According to the reports that were forwarded to Warsaw, 240 delegates from the entire trip came back as "well-disposed activists who will be good agitators." Additionally, 100 participants had "positive attitudes," but seemed passive and would not make good agitators. There were also people who either could not care less about the collective farm or who were unimpressed with them. At least 50 people from the group (including party members) were said to have come back negatively disposed.[81] These included individuals who had been resettled from western Ukraine and western Belarus after World War II. The vice-consul further explained that in every group of twelve people 10 percent were "absolutely hostile and negatively predisposed to the problems of the new countryside and Soviet reality." In his view, this was bound to have negative consequences for the entire collectivization campaign.[82] To the dismay of political directors, a steady number of participants continued to explain the impressive crops with reference to the natural fertility of the soil, and not to the beneficial influence of collective farming.[83] While 85 percent of the delegation had been generally convinced about the usefulness of cooperative agriculture, "40 people upon coming home will conduct mendacious, slanderous and hostile agitation against the Soviet Union, and 5% of the total will comprise a useless passive element."[84] These estimates were rather optimistic, as many peasants were likely to keep mum about their critical impressions from the USSR in order to avoid harassment by the authorities.

In their search for the perfect peasant, the officials continued to adjust the filtering techniques for visits to the USSR. As before, recommendations for future occasions followed in their report. One was that candidates need not be "believers in collective farms" so long as they were influential people. The group directors further suggested medical examinations of delegation members to exclude women in late stages of pregnancy and people with heart or lung problems, as well as those carrying venereal diseases. Especially the latter caused the Polish side some embarrassment.[85] The Polish consul in Kiev expressed his wish to see more intelligentsia during future trips. The number of women, he added, could also be increased to 50 percent.[86] The diplomat likewise expressed his satisfaction with the percentage of "working peasantry" during the third excursion, except for settlers from the East who should not be allowed to go next time on account of their particular prejudices.

The impulse to replace potential converts with existing believers came from mid-level functionaries who were directly responsible for the results. This trend would continue in later years. A brief look at the two subsequent excursions that took place in 1950 (in May and in June) shows that the local party officials effectively ignored the recommendations from the center. Out of the 241 people in the first delegation, there were 173 PZPR members, 34 ZSL members, and only 34 nonparty members; 115 travelers were members of agricultural cooperatives, including 38 chairmen of cooperatives, 63 individual peasants, 20 POM employees (Państwowe Ośrodki Maszynowe, or State Machine Centers, similar to the Soviet Machine-Tractor Stations), 29 party activists, and 14 others. In addition, there were only 45 women in the delegation.[87] Therefore, in every possible way, the composition of the delegation turned out to be the exact opposite of the directives sent out by the Central Committee. It included a vast majority of Communist Party members and de facto members of cooperatives—in other words, people who were neither the most credible from the point of view of the average peasant nor those who needed convincing. It is likely that the local officials took the easy path and chose either people who were likely to retain a positive view or simply those who wanted to go.

This discrepancy between the directives from the Polish Central Committee and the actual composition of the delegation remained pronounced during the second trip, which tells us that the composition of the earlier group may not have been accidental. Local authorities found it easier to produce the desired results by picking the well-disposed peasants rather than by converting the most credible ones. The second trip in 1950 consisted of 233 people, including 98 peasants from cooperatives, 62 individual peasants, 19 POM employees, 13 journalists and writers, 6 village teachers, and 31 party activists from all party levels. It included as many as 165 PZPR members, 42 ZSL members, and only 22 nonparty members.

This time around, the officials in the Central Committee took note of the mid-level insubordination.[88]

Some voivodship committees did an especially poor job in choosing the candidates. The Białystok committee selected thirty people, but as many as twenty-one were chosen on the very day of the departure.[89] It is not clear from the report, but this last-minute improvisation may have been caused by a lack of volunteers—after all, parts of the Białystok region, located in eastern Poland, had been under Soviet occupation between 1939 and 1941. Among those who joined the excursion were seven "opponents of cooperative farming," one syphilitic, and "a complete illiterate." The Warsaw committee sent six people who were "hostile to cooperative farming."[90] It may be that the poor results had to do with the fact that the local authorities did not take the propaganda project seriously. But this is unlikely, given that it was precisely local authorities who tended to exceed the Central Committee's directives during the Polish collectivization campaign in an attempt to impress their superiors.[91] It would be more plausible to suspect that on the one hand, the organizers had a preference for obedience in conformity, and on the other, they were short of willing candidates among those who were trusted and influential.

It is therefore interesting to observe that despite their ostensible advantage as sole rulers of the country, communist officials were ineffective in reducing, much less eliminating, the "dissent" among the Polish delegates. The dissenters included those who were hopelessly prejudiced, antagonistic, provocative, or ostensibly indifferent toward collective farming. The report examined the opinions of 205 members of the first delegation, including cooperative members, individual peasants, and POM employees. The authors noted that 60 individuals could be classified as active participants, "distinguished by general good form and maturity;" 70 could be described as "absolutely positive and showing great interest during the trip, but requiring a degree of assistance and care before they can be used in a propaganda initiative; about fifty others, are classed as inactive, mainly people who did not speak up much during the trip" and could be used for propaganda only under direct supervision of the party; finally, 19 individuals (or 10 percent) were people "who should not have gone to the USSR, distrustful, alien, and even hostile to the USSR and to propaganda work, they cannot be utilized."[92] The tally of the second delegation in 1950 was remarkably similar. Out of 233 members as many as 23 (10 percent) "arrived in the Soviet Union and left with 'unfriendly or hostile attitudes.'"

According to the report, another 10 people could also bring harm since their low political level "prevented them from understanding" what they had seen in the Soviet Union.[93]

The outcome was slightly better for the delegation that visited in May and June of 1952. Most of the 167 peasant participants apparently came back convinced of the superiority of the cooperative over individual agriculture.[94] However, the author of the report also noted that most of the peasants who went to the USSR had left Poland already convinced about the utility of collective farming. Based on the feedback from the group directors, only 7 individuals (4 percent) came with preexisting negative attitude toward the socialist system. In addition, 19 individuals (11 percent) were perceived as dubious and "inhibited" and therefore "spelled little hope" that they would make effective agitators for cooperative farming.[95] As before, many peasants were likely to keep their criticisms to themselves. In contrast, the local officials had an interest in underestimating the rates of dissent, since doing so would allow them to claim the credit for a potential success.

RESULTS OF THE PEASANT EXCHANGES

Overall, the results of the Poles' tours of Soviet collective farms resist easy characterizations. To most travelers, the trips probably constituted a welcome break from the day-to-day routine; some participants perhaps even understood them as an enjoyable, albeit eccentric, sort of vacation at a time when indulging in international forms of leisure was virtually impossible. Evidence suggests that, as in the case of their Western predecessors, the farmers' stays in the USSR tended to confirm their preexisting opinions about the *kolkhozy* rather than spur a radical change of perspective.[96] This was especially true of the skeptics who, upon visiting the Soviet model farms, liked them even less than before. Due to the efforts of Polish local authorities, over time, the self-avowed and suspected enthusiasts of collectivization formed a majority of trip participants. On the one hand, this constituted but a nominal success, since by embracing collectivization these individuals ostracized themselves from the peasant community and were regarded by the latter with distrust and hostility. "You are not allowed to speak differently, you must say that everything is good, no matter what you saw," one woman was reported as saying to a delegate who returned from the USSR praising Soviet agricultural achievements. This was a typical response.[97] On the other hand, the remarkably high percentage (10–15 percent) of those who were ostensibly "hostile and useless elements" upon their return (and in all likelihood, the proportion was twice or three times that) was sure to undermine communist efforts by casting aspersions on the Soviet collective farm system. The communists punished the most ostentatious acts of such whispered propaganda with arrests and imprisonment. In March of 1950, for instance, peasant Jan Dąbrowski, a veteran of the tours, was sentenced to three years in a labor camp. His crime was stating during a village meeting that in "that collective farm paradise," people were dying from hunger. "They want to do the same in Poland, so that people work but have nothing from it." Dąbrowski ended up in prison and was ultimately released after serving one year, which suggests the authorities had a halfhearted approach to such crimes.[98] In any event, they were hardly in the position to track down all such cases.

Perhaps the greatest success of the communists was that these international journeys provided them with an eye-catching and partly factual framework on which they could build broader propaganda campaigns. The spin began at the Polish train station where top-level officials, orchestras, and local residents welcomed the travelers with great pomp.[99] By covering the events, the press provided broader publicity. Belying the facts, testimonies structured as conversion experiences formed the core of articles in weekly periodicals and the daily press.[100] In Poland several pamphlets appeared under such titles as *We Saw It with Our Own Eyes*, *The Land of Good News*, etc.[101] In addition, each visit gave birth to dozens of village meetings and even press conferences with the returnees.[102] But even then, as with other propaganda initiatives, the effectiveness of these stories was rather limited. The propaganda was uneven. In 1949 and 1950 the Soviet Information Bureau representative (of Polish extraction), Vladislav Sokolovskii, complained that the Polish press was giving little attention to the former delegates.[103] Some of the literature that appeared in Poland after the excursions was laced with sarcasm about the "Soviet reality." The job of some officials was to fish out such potentially subversive content. For instance, the same Jerzy Wasilewski who in the summer of 1949 led a group of peasant delegates to the USSR only a few months later published a pamphlet in which he "tried to smuggle fragments that represent the Soviet reality in a crooked mirror." According to the Polish consul in Kiev, Wasilewski was guilty of commenting on the limited choices of candy,

Figure 2.5. A group of trip participants under the Lermontov statue in Piatigorsk. Reprinted by permission from Tadeusz Marczewski, *Od murów Kremla do stóp Kaukazu,* 2nd ed. (Warsaw: Ludowa Spółdzielnia Wydawnicza, 1953), 87.

Figure 2.6. Cover of a Polish 1950 propaganda pamphlet entitled *What We Saw in the Soviet Ukraine.* Reprinted by permission from *Co widzieliśmy na Ukrainie radzieckiej* (Warsaw: Ludowa Spółdzielnia Wydawnicza, 1950).

the slow speed of Soviet trains, the unappealing looks of Soviet consumer items, and the humorous sight of a collective farm orchestra.[104]

Perhaps the hardest question has to do with the peasant trips' impact on the Soviet parties involved. Stalin had once said that imposing the Soviet system on Poland would be like saddling a cow.[105] No other initiative from Moscow came closer to this fantastic scenario than the call to collectivize the Polish countryside. Stalin's decision originated in his overarching geopolitical considerations; the Polish authorities themselves ended up saddled with the ungrateful task of implementing it. But Soviet officials on all levels contributed to the ambitious project too, not the least through co-organizing the guided tours of the collective farms. How did they understand their roles in these initiatives and the grand imperial project of which they were part?

To the extent that the work of the officials in the International Department depended on being well versed in Polish affairs, we can assume that they appreciated the enormity of the challenge they were up against. They had access to reports about the trends in public opinion from various Soviet organizations working abroad, such as the Soviet Information Bureau. Anonymous letters to *Wolność* (*Freedom*), a Soviet newspaper for the Polish population, reached them in 1950–51. Written by self-described disillusioned Polish Sovietophiles and enthusiasts of collectivization, probably peasant activists, they painted a bleak picture of fierce peasant resistance against and disappointment with the existing cooperatives.[106] Did such officials as Dzerzhinskii, like some of his compatriots at the time, see it as Soviet history redux? Such a view would dictate the need to stay on course with the stick-and-carrot strategy, and imply the eventual victory of empire-cum-socialism over noncompliant, though malleable peasant masses. Or did they feel exasperated, overwhelmed by the daunting task, taken hostage by another "exercise in frustration," so typical of late-Stalinist institutions geared at molding foreign public opinion?[107] More research is required to answer these questions; until the answers become clearer, our understanding of the Soviet empire after World War II will be incomplete.

Exactly what lower-level Soviet activists and peasants thought about Poland's collectivization is equally difficult to tell. Unsurprisingly, immediately after the war, Soviet peasants expressed interest in those East European developments that they saw as affecting their own living standards. During meetings with agitators, collective farm workers commonly asked why the Soviet government was shipping bread to other countries while they themselves were going hungry. "How is the harvest in the countries of East and South-Eastern Europe?" many others inquired.[108] Vladislav Zubok has remarked that intellectuals of the time had a greater chance of seeing a total solar eclipse than meeting a foreigner.[109] Perhaps then a *kolkhoznik*'s likelihood of encountering an entire group of foreigners, even one from a "near abroad" country, compared with that of seeing a flying pig—or at least a saddled cow. Certainly, the visits of Polish farmers to Soviet *kolkhozy* must have been memorable events, and following the Polish tours, the Soviet side also organized some propaganda efforts to publicize them.[110] Those who read about them in the newspapers may have perceived the imitation of the Soviet system abroad as its ultimate vindication. On that official level, the newfound prosperity of the collectivized Polish countryside resonated starkly with the image of doom and gloom in the "imperialist," interwar Poland.[111] Alternatively, perhaps they felt sorry for those Polish farmers who were about to share the misery of the Soviet *muzhik.*

A unique delegation of Soviet collective farm employees to the fledgling Polish cooperatives in September 1950 revealed another set of reactions that testified to the ambiguities of empire-in-the-making. The group consisted of forty-five people, mostly men, largely collective farm and MTS managers as well as farmers. On the one hand, a participating Soviet official was correct in observing that the Polish peasants lived more prosperously than before the war. On the other hand, he complained in his report that the large credits offered to cooperative members by the authorities as incentives for joining created an "artificial" basis for cooperative agriculture, which discouraged peasants' self-reliance. But the official overstated the impact of such credits: many Polish collective farm managers knew little about investment strategies and unwittingly squandered the state funding.[112] Moreover, his emphasis on the "excessive prosperity" that the Poles allegedly flaunted suggested that the state of Polish cooperatives rubbed the Soviet visitors the wrong way and raised questions about their own performance. Earlier, the Soviet hosts treated the Polish peasants to latter-day Potemkin villages. Ironically, now the Soviets saw only the best farms because the majority of the existing collectives turned out to be economic failures.[113] But the Poles became victims of their own success. As early as 1949, Nikita Khrushchev had encouraged Soviet peasants' trips to Polish collective farms.[114] Yet the obvious complications involved in this kind of reverse traffic help explain why the Soviet authorities chose not to repeat the experience.

CONCLUSION

An unreformed opponent of a truly red watermelon, Wincenty Witos died in October 1945, a little more than a year after meeting with Khrushchev. Like him, most Polish peasants failed to warm up to the idea of collectivization. The drive to transform Polish agriculture went ahead as planned as a result of pressure from Moscow, a push from the Polish communists, and eager participation of local officials. Like their Soviet counterparts earlier, Polish peasants put up a fierce resistance against collectivization. The case study of Polish peasant excursions helps partially explain their ferocious defiance, which, together with the blatantly catastrophic effects of collectivization on the Polish countryside, forced the communists to abandon the plan by 1956. The Soviet Union's transnational initiatives ultimately did little to convince skeptical farmers about the viability of the Soviet agricultural system. On the contrary, they backfired on the communists: instead of winning over the skeptics, they allowed suspicious peasants to personally scrutinize the Soviet collective farms at the expense of the Polish state. And even though only a minority of the trips' participants criticized what they saw, their opinions received the most sympathetic hearings from fellow villagers, families, friends, and neighbors upon returning home.

The Soviet-Polish initiatives put into relief the weaknesses of Stalin's new empire more generally. Stalinism suffered from several inherent structural flaws. First, it married short-term economic advantages afforded by centralized planning with long-term economic inefficiency; the result of this misalliance was the stupendous economic growth of the 1930s and its corollary, the devastated countryside. Second, through a combination of terror and central planning it promoted performance indicators based on quantity, not quality, in the economy and politics alike. Third, it depended on a world of self-referential stories and symbols, which required boundaries to be hermetically sealed against the potentially subversive, international traffic of people, goods, and ideas.

Unlike the thousands of Western travelers to the USSR in the interwar era, the Polish peasants were much more Sovietophobic and less inhibited from voicing their doubts upon coming home. Peasant visits unfolded in a manner that contrasted starkly with those of Western intellectuals and working classes alike. Less idealistic than most intellectuals, but more numerous and certainly more demanding; more suspicious, and, in contrast to the French working classes, unconstrained by left-wing politics, they required a special approach. It is difficult to guess how many Soviet hosts ultimately failed to recognize this fact; yet given the larger, systemic flaws of Stalinist institutions, it is also difficult to imagine what they could have done differently to put up a more convincing show. The Polish communists, divided on issues of recruitment strategy, also found that the delegations largely reinforced preexisting ideas about collective farming; as the local authorities responded by selecting delegates committed to collectivization, they also undermined the propagandistic value of the excursions.

The Soviet expansion into Eastern Europe firmly consolidated Stalin's hold on half of the continent, to be sure. But it also complicated Soviet power in crucial ways. On the one hand, after the homogenization of communist institutions across the Soviet bloc, the hardwired flaws of the Soviet state turned into shortcomings of empire. It was therefore symptomatic that the local Polish communists ultimately managed to feign the success of the peasant excursions by enlisting mostly those who had been fans of collectivization in the first place—thus defeating the goal of the entire enterprise and, in their own little way, undermining the project designed at the top. From the perspective of Polish communists, the pros of Stalinism were more offset by its cons than in the USSR. For instance, even though local Polish officials coerced peasants into joining cooperatives, there were limits to what they could do. Unlike in the USSR two decades earlier, the process was supposed to be voluntary and the top authorities refused to condone violence; "unofficial" harassment on the local level usually resulted in administrative discrimination or economic coercion, and not death, while even those formally tried for propaganda against collectivization had to face jail sentences and not the Gulag or a firing squad.[115] Therefore for the 10–15 percent of overtly skeptical Polish delegates who toured Soviet collective farms, the consequences of insubordination were always lower than they were for their Soviet hosts—whether the Poles asked ostensibly provocative questions to the manager of a *kolkhoz* or denigrated Soviet agricultural achievements upon returning to Poland. In that sense, the structural flaws of the Stalinist empire proved to be more malignant than their equivalents in the Stalinist state, particularly when cross-border traffic was involved.

Ultimately, the communists had to choose between two sets of contradictions in what we could call an "internationalist dilemma." Either they had to learn how to neutralize the undesirable, latent consequences of any transnational initiatives—a difficult task for all the reasons mentioned—or they had to resolve the tension between closed borders on the one hand, and their commitment to socialist internationalism together with institutional integration across the Soviet bloc on the other. And although Polish peasants' large-scale tours of Soviet collective farms ceased on the eve of de-Stalinization, this larger paradox they embodied plagued the party and state officials up until communism collapsed.

NOTES

1. Nikita Khrushchev, *Khrushchev Remembers: The Last Testament*, trans. and ed. Strobe Talbott (Boston: Little, Brown, 1974), 160–61.

2. For theoretical discussions of "the new Cold War history" and representative examples, see, e.g., John Lewis Gaddis, *We Now Know: Rethinking Cold War History* (New York: Oxford University Press, 197); Odd Arne Westad, "The New International History of the Cold War: Three (Possible) Paradigms," *Diplomatic History* 24, no. 4 (Fall 2000): 551–65; Vladislav Zubok and Constantine Pleshakov, *Inside the Kremlin's Cold War: From Stalin to Khrushchev* (Cambridge: Harvard University Press, 1996); David Caute, *The Dancer Defects: The Struggle for Cultural Supremacy during the Cold War* (New York: Oxford University Press, 2003).

3. Paul Hollander, *Political Pilgrims: Western Intellectuals in Search of the Good Society*, 4th ed. (New Brunswick, NJ: Transaction, 2007); Michael David-Fox, "The Fellow Travelers Revisited: The 'Cultured West' through Soviet Eyes," *Journal of Modern History* 75 (June 2003): 300–335; Rachel Mazuy, *Croire plutôt que voir. Voyages en Russie Soviétique (1919–1939)* (Paris: Odile Jacob, 2002).

4. Norman Naimark, *Russians in Germany: A History of the Soviet Zone of Occupation* (Cambridge: Harvard University Press, 1995); John Connelly, *Captive University: The Sovietization of East German, Czech, and Polish Higher Education, 1945–1956* (Chapel Hill: University of North Carolina Press, 2000); Vladislav M. Zubok, *Failed Empire: The Soviet Union in the Cold War from Stalin to Gorbachev* (Chapel Hill: University of North Carolina Press, 2007).

5. For an overview, see Mark Pittaway, *Eastern Europe 1939–2000* (London: Hodder Arnold, 2004), 55–56, 63–64, 70–72.

6. Jan Karol Wende described how Khrushchev and other Ukrainian officials brought the watermelons to the liberated Poland by airplane to sweeten the discussions of the postwar population exchanges. See *Ta ziemia od innych droższa . . .* (Warsaw: PWN, 1981), 193.

7. Dariusz Stola, *Kraj bez wyjścia? Migracje z Polski, 1949-1989* (Warsaw: IPN and ISP-PAN, 2010), 10.

8. Ibid.

9. Adolf Dobieszewski, *Kolektywizacja wsi polskiej, 1948–1956* (Warsaw: Fundacja im. Kazimierza Kelles-Krauze, 1993), 9–14.

10. See Lynne Viola, *Peasant Rebels under Stalin: Collectivization and the Culture of Peasant Resistance* (New York: Oxford University Press, 1996); Sheila Fitzpatrick, *Stalin's Peasants: Resistance and Survival in the Russian Village after Collectivization* (New York: Oxford University Press, 1994); Dobieszewski, *Kolektywizacja,* 15–23.

11. Dariusz Jarosz, *Polityka władz komunistycznych w Polsce w latach 1948–1956 a chłopi* (Warsaw, DiG, 1998), 16; Andrzej Skrzypek, *Mechanizmy uzależnienia: Stosunki polsko-radzieckie 1944–1957* (Pułtusk: WSH im. Aleksandra Gieysztora, 2002), 260; Patryk Babiracki, "Between Compromise and Distrust: The Soviet Information Bureau's Operations in Poland," *Cultural and Social History* 6, no. 3 (September 2009): 350.

12. See the famous report from L. Baranov, N. Pukhlov, and V. Ovcharov to Suslov entitled "On Anti-Marxist Orientation in the Leadership of the PPR," April 5, 1948, reprinted in Giennadij A. Bordiugow et al., eds., *Polska—ZSRR: Struktury podległości* (Warsaw: ISP-PAN, 1995), 204–17.

13. Cited in Jarosz, *Polityka władz,* 18; On the International Department, see Grant M. Adibekov, *Kominform i poslevoennaia Evropa, 1947–1956* (Moscow: Rossiia Molodaia, 1994), 1–17.

14. Teresa Torańska, *Oni* (Warsaw: Omnipress, 1989), 112; also see stenogram of the KC PZPR plenum on August 21–September 3, 1948, Archiwum Akt Nowych (Archive of Contemporary Documents, Poland, henceforth AAN), sygnatura 295/II-12, karta 273.

15. Dobieszewski's reference to Gomułka's speech from the above plenum, published in *Nowe Drogi,* cited in Dobieszewski, *Kolektywizacja,* 23.

16. Jarosz, *Polityka władz,* 20.

17. Stanisław Siekierski, "Świadomość chłopów okresu kolektywizacji w świetle pamiętników," *Przegląd humanistyczny* 4 (1990): 55–56; Wojciech Śleszyński, *Okupacja sowiecka na Białostocczyźnie 1939–1941: Propaganda i indoktrynacja* (Białystok: Benkowski and Białostockie Towarzystwo Naukowe, 2001), 195–97.

18. Jarosz, *Polityka władz,* 64–65.

19. Dobieszewski, *Kolektywizacja,* 33–34.

20. Jarosz, *Polityka władz,* 40–54.

21. In the years 1950, 1953, and 1955 Poland was the least collectivized country of the Eastern bloc. The percentage of collectivized arable land in these years was respectively 1.2, 6.7, and 11.4, and the percentage of farms that joined cooperatives was 2.2, 5.8, and 6.0. In 1955 the only exception was Yugoslavia, which had an even smaller percentage of arable land included in cooperatives. See Jarosz, *Polityka władz,* 510.

22. Dobieszewski, *Kolektywizacja,* 51.

23. He specifically mentioned Hilary Chełchowski, the director of the Central Committee's Agricultural Department and deputy member of the Political Bureau, who "'supervises' the collectivization while being an opponent of collectivization." See Aleksander Kochański et al., eds., *Polska w dokumentach z archiwów rosyjskich 1949–1953* (Warsaw: ISP Pan, 2000), 73.

24. Skrzypek, *Mechanizmy,* 260.

25. Jarosz, *Polityka władz,* 81–98.

26. Gail Kligman and Katherine Verdery discuss mimesis as one of the "pedagogies of knowledge production" within the context of Romanian collectivization in their book *Peasants under Siege: The Collectivization of Romanian Agriculture, 1949–1962* (Princeton: Princeton University Press, 2011), 248–56.

27. Hollander, *Political Pilgrims,* 104.

28. Jarosz, *Polityka władz,* 98; Mazuy, *Croire,* 68.

29. Jarosz, *Polityka władz,* 98–99.

30. Dariusz Jarosz, *Obraz chłopa w krajowej publicystyce czasopiśmienniczej, 1944–1959* (Warsaw: Stowarzyszenie Redaktorów, 1994), 103–10.

31. Jarosz, *Polityka władz,* 98.

32. On propaganda of Soviet collectivization in Poland, see Robin Gates Elliott, "Saddling the Cow: The Collectivization of Agriculture in Poland, 1948–1956" (Ph.D. diss., Georgetown University, 2007), 219–26.

33. Serhij Tkaczow, "Propaganda kolektywizacji—wycieczki polskich chłopów na Ukrainę w latach 1948–1949," *Czasy Nowożytne* 6 (1999): 188.

34. Ibid., 191.

35. Hollander, *Political Pilgrims,* 352.

36. Ibid., 154.

37. Siekierski, "Świadomość," 54–55.

38. Mazuy, *Croire,* 222.

39. AAN, syg. 237/V-135, k. 3.

40. Russkii Gosudarstvennyi Arkhiv Sotsial'no-Politicheskoi Istorii (Russian State Archive of Social and Political History, henceforth RGASPI), fond 17, opis' 137, delo 284, list 51.

41. AAN, syg. 237/XXII-651, k. 3.

42. Walter G. Moss, *A History of Russia* (New York: McGraw-Hill, 1997), 2:226.

43. AAN, syg. 237/V-135, k. 2.

44. AAN, syg. 237/V-134, k. 6.

45. Sheila Fitzpatrick, *Stalin's Peasants: Resistance and Survival in the Russian Village after Collectivization* (New York: Oxford University Press, 1994), 16–18.

46. Isabel de Madariaga, *Russia in the Age of Catherine the Great* (New Haven: Yale University Press), 370–73; David M. Griffiths, "Catherine II Discovers the Crimea," *Jahrbücher für Geschichte Osteuropas* 56, no. 3 (2008): 339–48.

47. Michael David-Fox, "The Potemkin Village Dilemma," ch. 3 of *Showcasing the Great Experiment: Cultural Diplomacy and Western Visitors to Soviet Russia, 1921–1941* (New York: Oxford University Press, 2011), 98–141.

48. Stalin and other top Soviet communists knew full well about the calamitous situation in the Soviet countryside. See Yoram Gorlitzki and Oleg Khlevniuk, *Cold Peace: Stalin and the Soviet Ruling Circle, 1945–1953* (New York: Oxford University Press, 2004), 133–42.

49. AAN, syg. 237/V-134, k. 140; Jarosz, *Polityka władz,* 148.

50. Tkaczow, "Propaganda," 185, citing E. Zubkova, "Mir mnenii sovetskogo cheloveka 1945–1948 gg," *Otechestvennaia istoriia* 3 (1998): 29.

51. Iu. N. Afanas'ev, ed. *Sud'by rossiiskogo krest'ianstva* (Moscow: RGGU, 1996), 428–31.

52. RGASPI, f. 17, op. 137, d. 874, ll. 107–108.

53. RGASPI, f. 17, op. 137, d. 874, l. 106.

54. RGASPI, f. 17, op. 137, d. 874, l. 105.

55. RGASPI, f. 17, op. 137, d. 874, ll. 106, 109.

56. RGASPI, f. 17, op. 137, d. 874, ll. 119–21.

57. E.g., a report after the first trip in 1950 reported "enormous fields of wheat, stretching over the space of hundreds of hectares, and promising the harvest of 30–35 q, completely without weeds." AAN, syg. 237/V-135, k. 2.

58. Jarosz, *Polityka władz,* 133.

59. AAN, syg. 237/V-135, k. 3.

60. On "agro-towns," see Stephen Lovell, *The Shadow of War: Russia and the USSR, 1941 to the Present* (Malden, MA: Blackwell, 2010), 78.

61. AAN, syg. 237/V-135, k. 139.

62. AAN, syg. 237/V-135, k. 140.
63. AAN, syg. 237/V-135, k. 139.
64. AAN, syg. 237/V-135, k. 141.
65. Tkaczow, "Propaganda,"198.
66. See David-Fox, *Showcasing the Great Experiment,* 98–141.
67. The archival information about the numbers and breakdown of trip participants is inconsistent and incomplete. The greatest discrepancy exists between documents from the International and Agriculture Departments of the Polish Central Committee. Here I shall rely on reports from the former—they not only were the most detailed, but also were composed right after the trips took place and therefore seem the most reliable. In his exhaustive treatment, Jarosz, for example, cites a table from the Agriculture Department and political reports from the trips without pointing out that these two sets of documents give contradictory information about the trips, including their overall numbers, dates, and numbers of participants. See his *Polityka władz,* 100.
68. Tkaczow, "Propaganda," 190. Tkaczow's data comes from Ukrainian archives.
69. Ibid., 191. His sources mentioned 166 participants. Two peasant parties existed in the summer of 1949. The PSL was formerly independent but now largely disemboweled by the communists' peasant party earlier headed by the aging Wincenty Witos and his first deputy, Stanisław Mikołajczyk. The SL was a procommunist splinter from the PSL. The communists eliminated the remaining opposition from the PSL by "unifying" parties in November 1949, thus creating PZPR's satellite party, *Zjednoczone Stronnictwo Ludowe* (the United Peasant Party, or ZSL).
70. AAN, syg. 237/XXII-120, k. 44.
71. Elliott, "Saddling the Cow," 234.
72. AAN, syg. 237/XXII-120, k. 54.
73. AAN, syg. 237/V-134, k. 3.
74. Dobieszewski, *Kolektywizacja,* 46.
75. Ibid., 47–48.
76. AAN, syg. 237/V-134, k. 3.
77. AAN, syg. 237/V-134, k. 3.
78. AAN, syg. 237/V-134, k. 5.
79. AAN, syg. 237/XXII-651, k. 1; AAN, syg. 237/XXII-120, kk. 5–7.
80. AAN, syg. 237/XXII-651, k. 1; AAN, syg. 237/XXII-120, kk. 5–7.
81. AAN, syg. 237/V-134, k. 10.
82. AAN, syg. 237/XXII-651, k. 2.
83. AAN, syg. 237/V-134, k. 54.
84. AAN, syg. 237/XXII-651, k. 2.
85. AAN, syg. 237/V-134, k. 8.
86. AAN, syg. 237/XXII-651, k. 5.
87. AAN, syg. 237/V-135, kk. 4–5. According to a document produced in 1952, cited by Jarosz, the first trip in 1950 included 224 people, and the second trip consisted of 241 participants. It is difficult to explain this discrepancy as other than a counting error somewhere along the bureaucratic chain. For the sake of consistency, I am relying on the data compiled right after the trip took place. Cf. Jarosz, *Polityka władz,* 100, and AAN, syg. 237/XII-34, k. 90.
88. AAN, syg. 237/V-135, k. 7.
89. AAN, syg. 237/V-135, k. 9.
90. AAN, syg. 237/V-135, k. 9.
91. Jarosz, *Polityka władz,* 177–82.
92. AAN, syg. 237/V-135, k. 5.
93. AAN, syg. 237/V-135, k. 9.
94. AAN, syg. 237/V-135, k. 138.

95. AAN, syg. 237/V-135, k. 139.
96. Hollander, *Political Pilgrims;* Mazuy, *Croire,* 285.
97. Jarosz, *Polityka władz,* 101; Siekierski, "Świadomość," 55.
98. Wiesław Władyka, ed., *Kartki z PRL. Ludzie, fakty, wydarzenia* (Poznań and Warsaw: Sens and Polityka, 2005), 1:153.
99. Tkaczow, "Propaganda," 202.
100. See Jarosz, *Obraz chłopa,* 105; Tkaczow, "Propaganda," 198.
101. Tkaczow, "Propaganda," 200. See also Tadeusz Marczewski, *Od murów Kremla do stóp Kaukazu. Wspomnienia uczestnika wycieczki chłopów polskich do Związku Radzieckiego,* 2nd ed. (Warsaw: Ludowa Spółdzielnia Wydawnicza, 1953); S. Piotrkowski, *Na Ukrainie szumi pszenica* (Warsaw: Książka i Wiedza, 1950); *Co widzieliśmy na Ukrainie Radzieckiej* (Warsaw: Ludowa Spółdzielnia Wydawnicza, 1950).
102. RGASPI, f. 17, op. 137, d. 78, ll. 72–84. On that same press conference, see RGASPI, f. 17, op. 137, d. 283, ll. 108–38.
103. Gosudarstvennyi Arkhiv Rossiiskoi Federatsii (State Archive of the Russian Federation, henceforth GARF), f. R-8581, op. 2, d. 277, l. 4; GARF, f. R-8581, op. 2, d. 277, l. 277.
104. AAN, syg. 237/XXII-651, k. 24; Jerzy Wasilewski, *Na Ukrainie radzieckiej* (Warsaw: Wydawnictwo Ludowe, 1949).
105. Norman Davies, *Heart of Europe: The Past in Poland's Present* (New York: Oxford University Press, 1983), 3.
106. RGASPI, f. 137, op. 17, d. 280, ll. 67–71, 135–42; RGASPI, f. 137, op. 17, d. 622, ll. 4–16.
107. See Vladimir Pechatnov, "Exercise in Frustration: Soviet Foreign Propaganda in the Early Cold War, 1945–47," *Cold War History* 1, no. 1 (2001): 1–27.
108. See the document "Informatsiia Voroshilovgradskogo obkoma VKP(b) 'O reagirovanii trudiashchikhsia voroshilovgradskoi oblasti na voprosy mezhdunarodnogo i vnutrennogo polozheniia Sovetskogo Soiuza," August 14, 1947, Secret. In E. Iu. Zubkova et al., eds., *Sovetskaia zhizn.' 1945–1953* (Moscow: Rosspen, 2003), 38–39.
109. Zubok, *Zhivago's Children,* 21.
110. Tkaczow, "Propaganda," 198–99.
111. Brooks, *Thank You,* 58.
112. Elliott, "Saddling the Cow," 384.
113. Ibid., esp. ch. 4.
114. AAN, syg. 237/XXII-120, k. 45.
115. Elliott, "Saddling the Cow," esp. ch. 5.

3

THE WESTERN WALL

The Iron Curtain Recast in Midsummer 1951

NICK RUTTER

In August 1951, the world seemed to be turning red. The Korean peninsula had suffered three invasions in five months, the last by the world's largest and most recently communized country. For the newly established *Union française*—France's postwar euphemism for its prewar empire—the candle was alight at both ends. In Indochina, arms shipments from the anticolonial United States were effective but indecisive against the Viet Minh. In France, the Communist Party won over 26 percent of the National Assembly vote in June 1951. And across central Europe the debate over whether an "Iron Curtain" in fact existed—and if it did, to which side the curtain belonged—was in full bloom.

The debate began on March 5, 1946, when former prime minister Winston Churchill borrowed a theater term to describe the barrier which had "descended across the Continent," "[f]rom Stettin in the Baltic to Trieste in the Adriatic."[1] A few days later Joseph Stalin responded nonplussed, asking *Pravda* readers: If "the Soviet Union has lost in men several times more than Britain and the United States together . . . [w]hat can be surprising in the fact that the Soviet Union, in a desire to ensure its security for the future," assists governments "loyal" to it?[2] To Stalin's subordinates, the argument was familiar. Shortly after the Yalta Conference of February 1945, Foreign Minister Viacheslav Molotov, annoyed at Western meddling in Polish politics, jotted on an internal report: "How governments

---

The author thanks the editors for outstanding suggestions as well as the Fox International Fellowship and Smith Richardson Foundation for enabling me to visit a variety of institutional archives.

are being organized in Belgium, France, Greece, etc. we do not know"; nor "[have we] interfered, because it is the Anglo-American zone of military action."[3] That April, Stalin reportedly told Yugoslav allies Josip Tito and Milovan Djilas: "This war is not as in the past; whoever occupies a territory also imposes his own system as far as his army can reach. It cannot be otherwise."[4] To communists, Churchill's objection to Soviet-modeled governments in the Soviet "sphere of influence" was not only impractical; it was hypocritical. Had Britain not banned India's Communist Party (CPI) for two full decades (from 1924 to 1943), relenting only when CPI leaders pledged to support the war? Had Churchill's and Harry Truman's democracy-builders not favored "loyal" parties along their own "iron curtain," from Kiel in the Baltic to Trieste in the Adriatic?[5] To communist ears, Churchill's roar against "police government" was late capitalism's cry of desperation.

Considering the backlash that Churchill's address triggered in the world communist press, it is reasonable to assume that Soviet propagandists disliked his metaphor. In fact, Soviet editors added "*zheleznyi zanaves*" (iron curtain) to their political lexicon and did little to change its meaning. A widely publicized September 1946 speech by Soviet Minister of Culture Andrei Zhdanov promised that "[h]owever much bourgeois politicians and literary figures . . . try to erect an iron curtain through which the truth about the Soviet Union cannot reach abroad," and "however much they try to belittle the real growth and sweep of Soviet culture—all such attempts are doomed to failure."[6] Zhdanov did not repress or redefine Churchill's term; instead, he recast it. In the East as in the West, the curtain was a barrier built to shield police-state citizens from democracy. The dispute was over which side was which.

Five years later, in midsummer 1951, the curtain followed a slightly different route (east of Yugoslavia), and the debate, though still hot, spoke more simply. Whereas Churchill had associated the curtain with political philosophy, and Zhdanov with "the truth," propaganda now showed pictures of barbed wire, mines, and watchtowers. What had been a border between rival modes of government had become a breach of Article 13 of the United Nations' 1948 Universal Declaration of Human Rights, the "right to leave any country, including [one's] own, and to return."[7] In summer 1953, the *New Yorker*'s Joseph Wechsberg recounted how in order to get to Bucharest he first had to go to Vienna's Romanian embassy (visa applications available Wednesdays and Saturdays, noon to two); next to the

Hungarian embassy (visa required for passage to the Romanian border); and finally to the headquarters of the Soviet Occupation Zone (a travel pass required to go from Vienna to the Hungarian border). When Wechsberg at last reached Bucharest, the US embassy rejoiced. They were used to three new American faces a year, each on a diplomatic passport.[8]

As difficult as travel to Eastern Europe was, Western media assured readers that outbound travel was that much worse. "Anybody who wants to see the 'free frontier' of a 'free' People's Democracy should visit the Austro-Hungarian border, which looks not so much like a frontier as the outside of a concentration camp," Britain's leading anti-communist journal asserted in September 1951.[9] However loudly the bloc touted internationalism, the Iron Curtain spoke louder of isolationism.

Communist rejoinders to this line of attack could be clever, even persuasive. Regarding the barbed wire borders, Eastern propagandists could ask: Are soldiers prisoners of the barbed wire around their bases? As for the watchtowers and mine fields that lined the "liberated" East, they were there to thwart invasion, not emigration. Given that Germany and Austria had invaded twice in the past thirty-five years, the argument made sense. So much sense that Soviet propaganda told Westerners to come and see the border for themselves.[10]

The biannual, two-week World Youth Festival had specialized in this manner of empirical propaganda since 1947. For the festival's unofficial sponsor, the USSR's Communist Youth League (Komsomol), the fact that most participants paid Communist Party dues was a sign of strength, not weakness. Noncommunist participation was welcome insofar as it validated the event's billing as a free forum for anyone aged fifteen to thirty. Still, the genius of the festival was that no matter how few nonbelievers came, the mere invitation defied Churchill's curtain. So long as journalists took notice, the original false curtain would lose its purchase on the world imagination. At the inaugural festival in Prague, sixteen months after Churchill's speech, organizers thus set out to hold an event governed by participants, not police, one that enacted world peace instead of simply saying it.

The Western press, however, foiled planners' expectations. The *New York Times*, it appears, printed just two back-page articles during the four-week 1947 Prague Festival. In Budapest two years later, a reportedly 175-member US delegation garnered only one, published six days after the festival's end.[11] Aware of the attention deficit, the festival's official sponsors,

Budapest's WFDY (World Federation of Democratic Youth) and Prague's IUS (International Union of Students), selected their next host accordingly. Berlin was buzzing with international news media in 1951. By hosting the world's largest international event six years after its near obliteration, and fifteen after the Nazi Olympics of 1936, the newborn German Democratic Republic (GDR) would put its socialist rebirth on show for the world to see.

To publicize the rebirth, WFDY invited a record 26,000 foreign delegates to Berlin, nearly three times the number that had visited Budapest two years earlier.[12] East Germany's Socialist Unity Party (SED) promised 1.4 million East German participants, nearly 8 percent of the republic's total population. Residents of "the heap of rubble outside Potsdam," as Berthold Brecht described Berlin upon his return in 1949, began a feverish campaign to house, feed, and greet the guests.[13] And in at least one respect, the campaign succeeded. The *New York Times* published thirty-six festival-related articles in seventeen days in summer 1951, despite a paltry 66-person US delegation. The attention owed in part to several thousand US, British, and French soldiers stationed in Berlin and in part to readily available press licenses. Above all else, though, the third festival's fame owed to Berlin's symbolic weight as "the divided centre of [Europe's] divided centre."[14] The fact that the International Preparatory Committee (IPC) expected 400 US delegates, but as of opening day had only 6, suggests that organizers overestimated Berlin's allure. Yet as we will see, the poor noncommunist turnout owed as much if not more to anti-communist alarm than it did to communist overconfidence.[15]

What pleased festival planners most in August 1951 was not the exaggerated press coverage, but the US action that inspired it. Faced with an open East, Washington summarily shut borders, withheld passports, arrested travelers, and called on all other "free" states to do the same. The two-week festival thus turned the tables on a five-year debate. Critical readers around the "free" world found themselves reposing a once-rhetorical question: Whose Iron Curtain is it?

NEARING THE CURTAIN

The border between East and West was a line in the imagination in summer 1951. With little personal experience or balanced news to judge by, visions of a radically different society came easily to younger minds. In material terms, the Iron Curtain was a line of barbed wire studded by border checkpoints. In immaterial terms, it was the gateway to unbounded possibilities. This is how it appeared to 600 mostly male, twenty-something passengers aboard a train covered in *Pace! Peace!* السلام*!* as they departed Vienna on August 3, 1951, singing WFDY's "World Peace Song" in a dozen languages. After long, arduous, often illegal journeys from their respective homelands, the young radicals were headed east, to a better world.

But a few hours north of Vienna, the euphoria gave way to impatience. The train's corridors had filled with cameras pointed out the window, and shouts went up at farm fences and road crossings. To the photographers' disappointment, nothing more appeared. As one passenger put it, the train had "rolled across the border without anyone except the conductor being the wiser."[16] At a Bohemian station a half hour later, a Czech telegraph operator assured a twenty-four-year-old American that the silent crossing should come as no surprise; the Czechoslovak border was open to the world. "The warmongering governments of many of your nations have been trying to keep you from entering the lands of peace and democracy," he assured. Four years earlier, at the inaugural Prague World Youth Festival, WFDY president Guy de Boisson of France had spoken similarly. Your friendships "will be used as weapons to destroy the barriers and fictive iron curtains that some people want to build between the nations," he told a giant crowd on Wenceslas Square.[17] Boisson's curtain was not Churchill's, of course, but Zhdanov's. A primary objective at all three festivals, in Prague, Budapest, and now Berlin, was to debunk notions of a xenophobic East. Another man at the Bohemian station underscored this task's urgency when he quietly disagreed with the telegraph operator. Feigning naïveté, he murmured to the twenty-four-year-old American: "Perhaps a weaker believer than you or I could find the barrier again, about half a mile or so from the tracks," put there "for the duration of the Festival in East Berlin." Aboard the train just a few minutes earlier, a young Italian had jumped up from his seat and pointed excitedly out the window. The signs were in Czech. The border was crossed. "There is no such thing as the 'Iron Curtain!'" the Italian cried. "The whole thing is an invention of the capitalist press[!]" The camouflage had succeeded.[18]

The prospect of crossing the Iron Curtain was equally fantastic to Peter Waterman, a fifteen-year-old London communist whose father managed the city's leading leftist bookstore. Standing on the pier at Dunkirk, awaiting passage to the newly Polish port of Szczecin (formerly German Stettin), Waterman joined the cheers when Poland's famed ocean liner, the *M/S Batory,* came into view. Entering the harbor, the ship blasted the Soviet football song "We Are the Leningrad Youth" from its on-deck speakers. The sight and sound were "sensational," Waterman says, and the young leftists went wild.[19] The British press and state had done their best to discourage them from attending the festival. But the travelers had stood their ground; they too were determined to see the better East.

The comradeship that arose aboard the *Batory* and the "peace train" from Vienna derived in no small part from collective risk. For a few months in early summer 1951, authorities across Italy had withheld passports for travel to communist countries. Police in Athens jailed a young man for recruiting festival delegates. In Paris, the Fourth Republic set a temporary ban on Czechoslovak charter trains. Farther west, the United States refused passports to the communist author of *Spartacus,* Howard Fast, the lawyer-turned-singer Paul Robeson, as well as to Robeson's twenty-four-year-old, Soviet-education son, Paul Jr., all three of whom hoped to attend the festival.[20] Farther east, British colonial officials in Malaysia (according to Komsomol documents) threatened festival-goers with capital punishment, while in Indonesia, Sukarno's foreign minister prohibited diplomats from expressing any "sense of sympathy" for the event. In West Africa, the French warned that returnees from Berlin would owe colonial authorities in Dakar a 20,000-franc penalty.[21]

The inspiration for these threats is not hard to guess. Throughout spring 1951, Secretary of State Dean Acheson had led a "global campaign to counteract and discredit" the Berlin Festival, the scope of which far surpassed that which had taken aim at Prague and Budapest.[22] Asked in May 1951 in the House of Commons what stance the United Kingdom would take, Foreign Secretary Herbert Morrison admitted that he felt "most reluctant to interfere with [young Britons'] freedom of action in such a matter," considering as "they are not easily duped." "[A]llies," however, had convinced him. Any "exploitation of young people to serve the aims of the Soviet Government," Morrison conceded, required restrictive measures.[23]

Outside the Soviet bloc, Western travel restrictions attracted little attention until August 3, 1951, when 280 British delegates ran into trouble in the small city of Saalfelden, Austria. They had crossed the English Channel a few days earlier, and after losing several comrades to French port authorities alerted by London, they had taken a train across Switzerland and Austria's westernmost French Occupied Zone. Now in the US Zone at Saalfelden, US military policemen (MPs) boarded and asked passengers for their "grey cards." Without the card, travelers would have to head back to Innsbruck to apply for one. Alarmed, a British trade union choir singer managed to telephone the British consulate in Innsbruck from the station platform to ask what exactly the Americans wanted. No need to worry, the consul assured; only the Russians bothered with the ash-colored "interzonal pass." Minutes later, however, the consul changed his mind. Having consulted with his American colleagues, he informed the singer, not without embarrassment, that the exception was now the rule. Without a "grey card," Berlin-bound delegates would have to buy tickets back to the Channel at seven pounds apiece.[24]

The climax of the Kafka-like ordeal came the following day, when a few dozen British delegates, fresh from a night on a gym floor in Innsbruck, resolved to outwit their captors. By dividing into small groups and boarding a north-bound train, they would slip past Saalfelden and debark at Linz, the provincial capital only twenty-five kilometers from the Czechoslovak border. To their frustration and amazement, though, the American dragnet proved too tight. At seven that evening military policemen boarded their northbound train. Sitting toward the back, the fugitives managed to jump off at an unknown stop and set out on foot for Saalfelden, confident that upon arrival they could slip onto an after-hours, Vienna-bound train. Once in Vienna, it would be a short walk to the Soviet sector, and all would be well. On Saalfelden's outskirts, however, the net tightened yet again. Walking along the unlit road, the group approached four US jeeps, headlights pointed directly at them. As one London School of Economics student recounted on paper a few days later:

> We repeated our previous statement concerning our right to pass; we warned that the consequences of the behavior of [the US officer] and his troops would be his responsibility, and finally we asked to be allowed to see the Colonel of the unit. [The officer] said "yes" to the last demand, but instead of acting upon the decision he again ordered his man forward, and they menaced us repeatedly with their rifles and bayonets. At this point, I went up to him and repeated that any harm to any person which might result from his action would be his responsibility alone, and I urged him to take us to the Colonel immediately. He made no reply but struck me across the face with his rifle butt which opened a large cut above my right eye.[25]

A letter to the *Manchester Guardian* from the mother of a Trinity College (Dublin) student was just as graphic. Her son had joined the British delegation not for love of communism, she assured, but because "the small sum involved" was an unbeatable price. In his latest letter, her son described how, upon arrival in Saalfelden, he and the other absconders were forced into

> an open barbed-wire compound with over a hundred French [delegates], and kept there in the freezing cold of 4 a.m., without food, water, sanitation or fire. The Americans promised to turn a hose on us if we lit a fire. Later they doubled the guards and took us in lorries to the station where we were again put in a train for Innsbruck. There must have been many thousands of us on that train of all nationalities, all unjustly arrested. The enormous train pulled into a tiny station at the entrance to the American zone and stopped there in the boiling sun for nearly six hours. The Americans demanded that the French [take] us under armed guard back to Innsbruck, but, apparently, the French would not agree, so we came back here [to Innsbruck] free, as our right, and were cheered all the way by sympathizing Austrians.[26]

As word of the US soldiers' breaches of free speech and free travel spread, British anger mounted. Letters to government and the press expressed outrage at English roses "ha[ving] to relieve themselves in front of young sardonical [*sic*] American guards" and "half-drunk Americans manhandl[ing] Scots lassies." To skeptics, the statements were specious, and the whole incident was overblown. According to *The Economist,* Britain's Communist Party (CPGB) had sent the 280 delegates to Austria rather than around Denmark on the *Batory* to provoke a punitive response. However true the conspiracy theory was, the public outrage drowned it out. Held at gunpoint by US soldiers between two train tracks at Saalfelden station, with only a foot of clearance on either side, a young woman was nearly killed by a passing train. When others asked for a toilet, the Americans refused. There on the platform they were "forced to improvise a shelter . . . by standing in a circle, holding up raincoats, and whilst this was going on, an officer of the US Army ordered his men to break the circle of the girls and expose them." All this for a youth jamboree? British newspaper readers asked. "Had these loutish morons been unarmed [by] our British boys," one would-be delegate's aunt wrote her government, "I assure you that my nephew could and would have knocked the stuffing from any one of them." The Americans were "not show[ing] much prowess in Korea," anyway. Whitehall, meanwhile, said nothing. By August 15, Britain's communist-backed National Civil Liberties Council had lost its patience and warned Foreign Minister Morrison, "These accounts are so grave and the issues of principle arising are of such importance that we are at a loss to understand the continued silence of the Foreign Office on this matter." Even the *Economist* editors conceded that the CPGB's provocation plot had hinged on "quite unnecessary brutality" by US forces. If Washington wished to prevent world communism from making more hay from the "Innsbruck scandal," it argued, an investigation and subsequent apology were in order.[27]

Dean Acheson, however, was not known for his apologies.[28] In a statement to Morrison's Foreign Office, US ambassador to London Walter Gifford blamed the delegates' poor treatment on their poor judgment. And when the Soviet High Commissioner in Austria joined the chorus of critics, his US counterpart replied with Acheson's approval: "Believe me, dear General Sviridov, I dislike the necessity of grey cards as much as you." If Moscow would do away with its grey cards, not only for the sake of propaganda spectacles but for "legitimate purposes of business and pleasure," then the United States "would be most happy" to follow suit.[29] In public, Morrison's Foreign Office agreed. Behind closed doors, however, its leader was furious. At an in-house meeting on August 17, Morrison asked colleagues "to what extent we should admit there had been consultation between the interested Governments with a view to curtailing attendance at the Festival," and in particular, "what we should say in defense of the United States' action at Innsbruck." To help remind Britons who the enemy really was, Morrison called for a press statement "draw[ing] attention to the fraternization which had taken place [in East Berlin] between the British and North Korean delegates."[30] The damage, however, was already done. For two widely publicized weeks, the Soviet bloc had opened its Iron Curtain to visitors, and the West had scrambled to keep it shut.

DEFENDING THE CURTAIN

Some Western delegates to the 1951 World Youth Festival grew up in bourgeois homes and turned to Marx at university.[31] Some spotted a festival advertisement in the union newsletters, and like the Trinity College student, marveled at the low price. Others were activists or party functionaries, the couriers of WFDY's global propaganda network. And still others were impostors—supposed "defenders of peace" who in reality went to Berlin to defend Churchill's Iron Curtain versus Zhdanov's fictive one. The GDR Ministry of State Security (*Stasi*) warned in late July that the West was busy recruiting young spies, collecting festival train schedules, and arming itself with an American "compound" to be "sprayed on flammable materials, then lit."[32] That nothing of the kind took place owed in part to the strategic spirit of "containment." Any overt violation of "peace and friendship" would only redound to the festival's benefit, substantiating its claims about a Western threat and, with it, a "Western curtain." But the impostors' passivity also owed to circumstance. As two Americans learned, one en route to Berlin and the other at the event itself, a wide variety of festival delegates considered Zhdanov's curtain more defensible than Churchill's.

The impediments erected by Western bureaucrats, if not by American GIs, reinforced this conviction. Inside the makeshift World Youth Festival headquarters in Vienna's Soviet sector, an American posing as an Italian reporter observed "no intermingling of delegations. Almost distrustful of each other, each of the various national groups huddled conspicuously together," awaiting the festival identification cards that would ensure passage into the bloc. Moments later, when the cards appeared, faces and identities softened simultaneously. Walking toward Vienna's North Station, national contingents shouted "Peace!" in different languages. Upon arrival, "delegates who had hitherto closely identified themselves with their own delegations began to mix a bit among others." And on the platform, Vincent Tortora, the incognito American, watched a crowd surround a young Italian writing "*PACE*" (peace) in chalk across a train:

> Following the lead of a most enthusiastic Egyptian, a few of the more intrepid individuals, seeking to overcome the language barriers between groups, hit upon a type of international Communist language. Patting the leaders of other delegations on the back, embracing them warmly and shaking their hands violently, they shouted loudly, "Stalin! Marx! Collectivism! Lenin!" etc. It was not long, indeed, before all six hundred delegates were enthusiastically employing this newly invented language . . . . [33]

The pidgin "Bolshevik" spoken on the Vienna platform and at the festival itself was a cause of special concern to Western governments. At a symposium held the day after the Chilean delegation's return to Santiago, criticism of East Germany's one-party politics was limited to "parenthetical" statements, a US diplomat noted. The returnees, not unlike the revelers in Vienna's North Station, seemed to have been "blinded by the symbolism of words."[34] The nuance and complexity of native tongues had given way to Soviet calques—absolute terms that permitted no ambiguity or irony. In festival-speak, Marxists fought for peace, and the bourgeois fought for profit.

Inasmuch as Marxist-Leninist vocabulary worried Western bureaucrats, it also emboldened Western impostors. In spring 1951, Brooklyn native Vincent Tortora heard friends talking about the "*Festival della Gioventu*" after class at the University of Padua. Next he heard them talk about sending 25,000 lira (forty 1951 dollars) to the Italian Communist Party (PCI) in hopes of securing one of Italy's 1,500 delegation seats. Then came the complaints. Nearly all who applied had received postcards from the party faulting their failure to provide "ample proof" of "good faith." When Tortora's editor at the Padua student newspaper encouraged him to try his own luck, saying, "Just tell them that you're an American Communist," the result was the same. "Of course we trust you here," explained a Padua party member, in response to Tortora's self-introduction as a refugee who had "fled the United States to escape capitalism." The trouble was that "in Rome they're afraid you might be an agent of Wall Street." Annoyed but undaunted, Tortora wheedled a blank PCI card from a communist peer while discussing world politics in the city's public garden, promising to use it in an anti-McCarthy exposé for the US press. After filling in the card and covering it in stamps, the "omnipresent symbols of legality in Italy," Tortora the faux-communist bought a train ticket to Vienna.[35]

To Tortora's surprise, the "economy of trust" in Berlin was more laissez-faire than in Italy.[36] While expulsions did occur, they were rare. Fearful of forfeiting the event's claim to impartiality, festival organizers relegated many security tasks to delegation leaders.[37] Free German Youth (FDJ) chairman Erich Honecker expected Stasi informers to be vigilant, and East German interpreters to flag possible spies.[38] Yet considering the primitive state of surveillance technology in 1951 and the mammoth size of several Western delegations—chief among them France with 3,000 and Italy with 1,500—traditional security was insufficient. Festival police, furthermore, could do nothing that might validate the "police government" models outlined by Churchill in 1946, Orwell in 1948, or Arendt's brand-new *Origins of Totalitarianism*.

In some senses, the event was typically totalitarian. True to Arendt's description, its managers were "never content to rule by external means, namely, through the state and a machinery of violence." Its target audience, meanwhile, was the "atomized, isolated individual" who preferred to collective causes to liberal cacophony.[39] Nevertheless, the diffuse power structure was distinct from that of totalitarian models.[40] At the festival the customary imbalances of power between native and foreigner, state and citizen, old and young, were turned on their heads. East Germany's Volkspolizei (People's Police) hence commanded officers in mid-July: "Don't let yourselves be provoked!"[41] Bourgeois reporters wanted nothing more than to exaggerate acts of "police government," no matter how trivial. The optimal response to delinquent delegates, in other words, was none at all. Delegation leaders could do their own policing and call the Volkspolizei, Stasi, or festival organizers if matters got out of hand.

The expulsion of twenty-one-year-old *Harvard Crimson* editor (and future US stock market oracle) George Goodman is a case in point. Goodman, like Tortora, was an undergraduate journalist who saw in the 1951 festival a chance for publication. For one week, Goodman's Harvard-leftist imposture worked perfectly. But after seven nights in close quarters with sixty-five "misguided" countrymen, the disguise wore thin. On the evening of August 12, the head of the US delegation (and vice president of Prague's International Union of Students, or IUS), a twenty-six-year-old Yale-educated doctor named Halsted Holman, gathered the US delegation together for a mid-festival meeting. Holman was the type of congenial idealist "who would ask you a question and then smile as you replied," wrote Goodman. But at the meeting that night, in a lecture on the severe consequences that awaited delegates who leaked their own or anyone else's identities to the US press, there was no smiling. After several minutes Holman paused, "pushed back his tweedy jacket and stuffed his hands into his pockets," before announcing: "This afternoon, in the Soviet exhibition, I saw Mr. Goodman take several damaging photographs." Goodman had positioned the camera under his left arm. What he was photographing Holman did not say. But considering the well-publicized nature of the exhibition and the fear of McCarthyism that pervaded the US group, we can be sure that fellow delegates featured prominently. Goodman had violated the delegation's compact and done its members great potential harm, Holman said. He must hand over the film, which Goodman did. And for the moment, the matter seemed settled.

At one in the morning on August 14, Goodman awoke to a knock on his dormitory door. He got dressed, got in a car, and sped downtown to the House of World Youth on East Berlin's central square—the home of Honecker's committee and the IPC. After two hours of "polite" interrogation, festival officials informed him that the "leadership of the American delegation has decided that you may no longer be with that delegation." Contrary to Goodman's later insinuation that it was East German "guards" who blew his cover; contrary to the *New York Times*'s report that Stasi thugs had "hauled him out of bed" and shuttled him to West Berlin; and contrary to Goodman's note to the *Crimson* that given all the "Folk police," "Maybe I'll get shot," the events of August 14, 1951, fit no Cold War cliché. Holman had caught the spy in the act and called the authorities. The authorities had asked the spy to leave. And after his "polite" hearing, George Goodman had gathered his bags, got on the subway, and exited at the West Berlin corner of his choosing.[42]

Imposture was easier for some delegates than for others, of course. Second World delegations wore state-made uniforms. They vetted delegates carefully in pre-festival competitions. Once in Berlin, they transported delegates from event to event via bus rather than sidewalk. The Romanians, according to one source, left their East Berlin dormitory for two reasons only: to perform on stage or to eat in the cafeteria. That two Romanians still managed to reach West Berlin and never return proved the schema's necessity and underscored the difficulty all East European delegation leaders faced: How to direct several hundred young men and women through an ideologically divided, wide-open city? The solution, as one Western observer described it, belied the event itself: beyond scheduled appearances, the East Europeans "were practically not there."[43]

For defenders of Zhdanov's Iron Curtain, travel to West Berlin ranked as one of the worst trespasses possible in 1951. And by all accounts, non-communist foreign delegates held the same opinion.[44] Although the Soviet sector remained a far cry from the utopia that ex-residents Marx, Liebknecht, Luxemburg, and Lenin had envisioned, festival visitors believed what their hosts told them. First, that the grim panoramas were the cards capitalism had dealt them. Second, that whereas the eastern half of the city was "the refuge from the Fascists," as one festival chant asserted, the west side was their refuge—a beachhead for fascism's decade-old war on communism.[45] A Latin American anti-communist admitted that the warnings published in the festival's daily quadrilingual newspaper were so effective that "even he was a little worried about what the Americans would do to him if he crossed." Non-Europeans, furthermore, had added reason to oblige East German requests. The twenty-person Chilean group had paid its fare to Berlin, but not a single peso of the trip home, nor for the month of East European sight-seeing in between.[46] Nelson Mandela's comrade Ahmad Kathrada appears to have traveled from South Africa to Berlin free of charge, all at WFDY's expense.[47]

In attempts to explain why so few non-German festival delegates paid "free" Berlin a visit, Western officials blamed exhausting daily regimens, arguing that back-to-back performances, "friendship meetings," meals, and rehearsals provided even "those specialized in 'making themselves scarce' no escape from the plan."[48] But this was an imagined explanation. Kathrada's account of "social gatherings where people met and talked, sang, danced, ate, drank, kissed, embraced and pledged everlasting friendship" suggests neither imposition nor exhaustion. Similarly, no one prohibited London's Peter Waterman from breaking off from his planned activities, boarding a west-bound el-train to Zoo Station, and then riding back again.[49] Delegates from nonsocialist states were as free as Berliners to go where they pleased.

Foreign delegates, as Waterman's excursion suggests, were not always as obedient as the GDR would have liked. As Perry Anderson points out, Stalinist internationalism was a paradox "without equivalent before or since," according to which human progress hinged on "rejecting any loyalty to [one's] own country and displaying a limitless loyalty to another."[50] Among communists, Anderson's contradiction could be felt, but never said. For nonparty members, however, honesty came easily. When Britain's ideologically diverse, 1,200-head delegation arrived in their grade-school dormitory, its leaders caused a stir by demanding that Stalin's portrait be removed from all the walls.[51] On a tour through Cecilienhof Palace, the site of the 1945 Potsdam Conference, a Trinidadian delegate nudged his interpreter and grinned: enough about where the great Generalissimo Stalin once sat, slept, and ate; ask the guide "which toilet Stalin used."[52] Finally, at one of many whistle-stop celebrations held to welcome festival-bound "peace trains" as they passed through the bloc, a poorly slept Italian communist spotted a café inside the train station and went inside. Minutes later, as plainclothes Czechoslovak police dragged him back onto the platform, he allegedly made a racket, shouting that all he wanted was "to kill the horrible taste of the cider he'd drunk at the previous station."

A half hour later, when Tortora came across the trespasser smoking a cigarette out the train window, it appeared that his PCI (Italian Communist Party) superiors had talked some sense into him. "It is imperative that each individual recognize the needs and wishes of the state and its ordained representatives," Tortora recalls him saying.[53] Aware of where he stood, the trespasser pledged to speak and act accordingly.

Tortora, as his feat of persuasion in Padua's public gardens showed, was himself not averse to manipulative language. It may therefore be that he rephrased the Italian's statements to satisfy his American readers' (or better yet, publishers') McCarthy-era expectations. But even so, and even if the conversation on the train never happened, the tension it illustrates was integral to the festival experience. By virtue of its heterogeneity and decentralized power structure, this communist spectacle not only let impostors in but also, as we will see below, permitted them to question what they saw.

QUESTIONING THE CURTAIN

If the festival's internationalist spirit germinated en route to Berlin, it blossomed inside Walter Ulbricht Stadium on August 5, 150 meters from the British sector. In spite of the rockets that popped overhead, showering 80,000 spectators with invitations to West Berlin, and notwithstanding a US helicopter that circled the stadium for much of the afternoon, the proceedings were peaceful. Unlike the somber, militant face worn at most National Socialist and Communist spectacles, dedicated to collective sacrifice and fallen martyrs, the mood in Ulbricht Stadium was euphoric and nonaggressive. Drew Middleton of the *New York Times,* fresh from the Moscow desk and therefore no stranger to mass demonstrations, found "the fanatic enthusiasm that the young people exhibited . . . terrifying."[54] Whereas most communist rallies carried strong national undertones, added the US embassy, this one's multicultural program "affirmed rather than diminished" its internationalist message.[55] Even Bonn, home to one of the most anti-communist governments in the world, conceded victory to the GDR. By assembling the "crème de la crème of communism," and by doing so within shouting distance of the Iron Curtain, festival organizers had made sure "enthusiasm reigned."[56]

But to attribute the ceremony's élan solely to its multiethnic program and leftist consensus is to underestimate the festival organizers' achievement. The ceremony articulated two political principles, each of which resonated deeply among postwar youth. First, it exemplified a participatory style of democracy characterized by doing the collective good collectively, "eliminat[ing] the distinction between the rulers and the ruled."[57] Unlike representative democracy in the West, which to many socialists and all communists divorced "the people" from drafting and enacting policy, average citizens in the East could help draft policy by joining the party and help enact it by living, working, and celebrating *with* the society.[58] In this sense, the opening ceremony was exemplary. On the stadium field, German gymnasts crouched to spell PEACE МИР FRIEDEN on all fours, while sixty-six others, standing along the sidelines, pirouetted and doubled over to form BEREIT ZUR ARBEIT UND VERTEIDIGUNG DES FRIEDENS (Ready to work and defend the peace). Here, democratic participation was staged. But a short while later, it reappeared, this time haphazard and carefree. One archived photograph of the ceremony shows delegates of all descriptions milling around on the field, carrying a jumble of flags and portraits in no particular order, spectators interspersed among delegates on the grass.[59] The contrast between this friendly disorder and the gymnasts' crisp formations is striking. And judging by East German novelist Harry Thürk's fictionalized account—based, it appears, on personal experience—the contrast was true to the festival's ethos. Soon after the protagonists of Thürk's debut novel take their seats at the festival's opening ceremony, one exclaims ruefully, "To think we can't get down there . . . !" Then the Vietnamese appear on the track, and a roar wells up from the crowd. One of the young trio makes "a giant leap over three rows of [emptied] seats" and joins the crowd on the track to meet the freedom fighters.[60] In democracy as Thürk imagined it, the boundary between participant and spectator need not exist.

Notwithstanding ovations for guerrillas from Vietnam and North Korea, the opening ceremony's second defining principle was peace. Dressed in a white suit to match his white hair, GDR president Wilhelm Pieck told the crowd: "The supreme purpose of the World Festival lies squarely in the fact that it provides the most vivid and by far the most radiant evidence for that simple yet oh so capacious truth: in peace lies the peoples' happiness!"[61] Hyperbole notwithstanding, Pieck's message was compelling. Western journalists howled at Pieck's salute to Stalin as the "the great *Führer*"; they mocked the likeness between FDJ blueshirts and

Hitler Youth brownshirts; and citing last June's North Korean invasion, they inveighed against the doublespeak of festival "peace."[62] Even so, the assumption that Konrad Adenauer planned to march east just as Syngman Rhee had (allegedly) marched north lent Pieck's appeal to peace a special weight, especially for young West Germans with "potent fears" of renewed mobilization.[63] The fact that Ulbricht Stadium was built from war debris; that the blocks around it contained more walls than buildings; and, finally, that West Berlin insisted on delivering its leaflets via rocket—it all added urgency to Pieck's syllogism: unity is to peace as peace is to happiness.[64]

For some participants, admittedly, the festival's location had the opposite effect, cheapening rather than affirming the demand for peace. Among Third World delegates, this opinion was rare. To Indians or Egyptians, the villain of recent history was colonialism, not fascism.[65] For orthodox communists, meanwhile, East Germany's exemplary performance proved Marxism-Leninism right: National Socialism inhered in late capitalism, not in German culture. Romanian delegates, according to an émigré who did his best to befriend them, noted that unlike the rest of Eastern Europe, "in Eastern Germany Communism had *really* conquered the youth."[66] Soviet officials were equally impressed. East Germans were not only well taught in "the spirit" of communism; their urban beautification campaign and construction projects had "rendered Berlin unrecognizable"—a tidy wasteland in place of a mess. Regarding peace, the FDJ's commemoration of (and disassociation from) Nazi crimes at the Red Army memorial, amplified by German invalids' pledge that "German youth will never [again] raise weapons against the Soviet lands," was especially poignant. Poignant enough that a Polish youth leader spoke for many East European delegates when he replied to Honecker's solemn vow of nonaggression, "We believe in the FDJ."[67]

Provocative questions and discussions, not surprisingly, stemmed more often from ideologically diverse delegations than from state-sponsored ones. Britain's Tom Madden, like the United States' Halsted Holman, was a medical student who held a leading position at Prague's IUS. Madden procured festival cards for five "young apprentices" and remembers watching them depart for Berlin with "great enthusiasm," only to see them return "angry and disappointed. Although impressed by the cultural events and kind hospitality, they were profoundly disaffected by what they learned of the suppression of East German workers."[68] Another group of Britons came across an open door marked "choirmaster" inside East Berlin's House of Children and decided to enter. Curious to see what songs German communists sang, they leafed through books on the choirmaster's desk until one boy stopped short. In his hands was a National Socialist songbook opened to the Hitler Youth's *Horst-Wessel-Lied* anthem. They rushed down the hall, determined to find the House director. When they did, their question, "Do the teachings of this song belong to the 'House of Children' program?," no doubt galled him. Duly obedient to the festival's inverse etiquette, the director nonetheless apologized and assured that it was a misunderstanding; the FDJ had no truck with Nazi martyrs. The Stasi assigned an "informer" to keep an eye on the choirmaster, an otherwise trusted, dues-paying party member. True to festival tradition, it left the British upstarts alone.[69]

Inasmuch as the festival reinforced negative stereotypes of the fanatical German, it also worked against them. Standing near one of many open-air stages one afternoon, a twenty-three-year-old French student asked twenty-two-year-old GDR playwright Heiner Müller a provocative question. He handed Müller a stack of faded photos, each of a graphic crime committed by German soldiers against French civilians, and said "he'd come to Berlin to see what had become of the Germans—whether what occurred yesterday could happen again tomorrow." Despite his rhetorical skills, Müller failed to convince the Frenchman that this Germany was different enough to preclude barbarity. Two days later, overlooking a massive 1.5 million-person FDJ Peace Parade on Unter den Linden boulevard, the French delegate was spotted tearing photographs to shreds on the tribune. As he did so, an FDJ troop marched past with a portrait of Raymonde Dien—the "latter-day Joan of Arc" who had lain across the train tracks near Tours in February 1950, blocking a shipment of tanks to Indochina.[70] Young Germans celebrating a young Frenchwoman, it appeared, had accomplished what Müller's words could not.

At the third festival, the question of the Iron Curtain was latent rather than explicit. Fifteen-year-old London communist Peter Waterman recalls how impressed he was by East Germans' openness to the world. But he also remembers that the "uniformity" of life there "did not sit well with us"—especially not with Jews like himself, who made up a sizable minority of both the British and US delegations.[71] Waterman recalls sitting in an East Berlin doctor's office soon after his arrival, wondering, "How could I possibly tell the (ex-Nazi? ex-SS?) doctor who gently and efficiently treated my . . . ankle that it was a Jewish one?" On the street, Berlin's helmeted firemen bore an unsettling resemblance to Wehrmacht soldiers. FDJ regimentation clashed with what young Britons considered normal, much less progressive. And yet at the end of his fortnight in socialism, Peter Waterman held the blueshirts in high esteem. What they lacked in humor and eccentricity, the Free German Youth made up for in "democratic, communist, anti-fascist" integrity.[72]

RECASTING THE CURTAIN

It was the object of the 1951 World Youth Festival to impart Waterman's impression on a much wider audience than Berlin could accommodate. By demonstrating a *new* Germany, East Berlin hoped to counteract the West's diplomatic boycott on the GDR as a legitimate, sovereign state. If done right, deputy Minister of State Security (Stasi) Erich Mielke predicted, the festival would "boost the GDR government's prestige around the world."[73] Foreign delegates hence slept in beds with three sheets, dined on "massive portions of succulent veal, roast beef or roast pork," and rode public transport for free. "Judging from the amount of free literature, transport and even accommodation . . . pressed on all—whether they wanted any or not," noted one British delegate, "money appears to have been no object."[74] The event's prohibitive cost forced FDJ participants to sleep in musty cellars and sweltering attics and sometimes to go days without food. But foreign guests felt no such pinch. It was a clever strategy, acknowledged John McCloy, Washington's top civilian officer in Germany. "Early emphasis in the demonstration on the theme of international friendship made a deep impression, even on anti-Communist participants," so much so that "[h]ad this theme been kept in the foreground throughout the whole demonstration, the Communist gains would have been much greater."[75]

McCloy's critique is apt. The third festival appears to have undermined anti-communist prejudice best when its spirit of international amity was strong, and worst when political bias got in the way. As Perry Anderson reminds us, noncommunists were not the only ones to take exception. Stalinist internationalism's fealty to the USSR caused trouble on two counts at the festival in August 1951. The first was Soviet predominance in athletic and artistic competitions, in which Soviet musicians, sculptors, and painters won 30 of 38 gold medals. Of the team sporting events that they entered, Soviet teams won the gold every time. And in individual events, Soviet athletes took home 259 of 558 total medals.[76] Not surprisingly, not all spectators were willing to attribute these results to Soviet superiority. Moscow Dynamo's 2-0 victory over the GDR's all-star football club provoked a chorus of boos and whistles from the hometown crowd. The game's most valuable player, Berlin spectators were convinced, was the Russian referee.[77]

The second check on festival internationalism was the "national gala performances" held by each delegation to showcase its cultural canon. Galas from the West were generally slapdash medleys of poor quality. Third World delegations were often too small. And with the exception of the Soviets, who staged a superbly produced, largely apolitical show, zealotry impinged on the creativity and quality of many Second World programs.[78] There was "nothing at all subtle," for example, in the Chinese delegation's tawdry, four-hour opera about an evil landlord's disenfranchisement by the new regime.[79] A North Korean play about a mother and child caught under American bombs was even cruder. After throwing two grenades to avenge her infant's death, the mother is at the mercy of three US soldiers, their guns drawn and mouths "chew[ing] gum violently." Suddenly a band of partisans leaps onto the stage, armed with spears, ready to battle the Americans back. At this point, the drama onstage gave way to one in the crowd. The 1,500 spectators were on their feet, chanting "Kim il Sung!" until the curtain fell.[80]

If festival planners set out to soften socialism's public image through "peace and friendship," why did they permit such provocative shows on stage? The simple answer is timing: With the "anti-imperialist" Korean War in full swing, Korean and Chinese communists could hardly be expected to champion pacifism. But embedded in this statement is a more precise and, to my mind, more convincing explanation. The 1951 festival's federalized planning apparatus permitted militancy, and as a result distracted attention from McCloy's "theme of international friendship." Archival findings suggest that the International Preparatory Committee (IPC) knew less about oncoming delegations than today's International Olympic Committee knows about oncoming teams. Pre-festival correspondence might confirm that a delegation existed and offer a sense of its size, but artistic composition, like delegate selection and self-policing, was left to each country's communist-led National Preparatory Committee. A late-July progress report to Komsomol's First Secretary and future Minister of Culture Nikolai Mikhailov thus predicted thirty national orchestras in Berlin, fifty national galas, and "mass theatrical performances" by 300-odd Italians. But there it stopped; the report said nothing about the message the repertoire would convey. The Italians were to sing and dance in honor of the fiftieth anniversary of Giuseppe Verdi's death, and the Chinese were to put on an opera called "The Girl with Seven Hairs."[81] That there was "nothing at all subtle" about the latter was either unknown or inconsequential to the Komsomol or the IPC, or both. To Mikhilov and the festival's sponsors, the semblance of "world culture" evidently mattered more than the content.

It is reasonable to assume that in 1951, Mikhailov and the IPC defined its target audience as Western "fellow travelers." To assure West Europeans that the true threat to peace lay in US encroachment on European politics, not in peace-minded Communist Parties; this was the message, and the festival was the vessel. But the planning apparatus outlined above was poorly suited to the message. For non-Soviet communist delegation leaders, the object of gala shows and even football matches was to please Moscow, not to impress Social Democrats. Whether the latter liked "The Girl with Seven Hairs" was of no consequence to the Chinese. What really mattered was what Mikhailov wrote home to Moscow.

Judging by Mikahilov's reports to Stalin's supposed successor, Georgii Malenkov, the Komsomol chief liked what he saw. Not only in Berlin, but in places like Saalfelden, Austria, "youth again saw who are their friends and who are their enemies." They saw that "a choreographic collective is not a tank division" and that "meetings between young friends of peace . . . are not meeting[s] of the High Command [*nachal'nikov voennykh shtabov*]." The third festival had thus served its purpose. Not only was the East open, the Red Army was nowhere to be seen. By mollifying the East and discrediting the West, the event had pushed the Iron Curtain from East to West, off of Zhdanov's desk and onto Chuchill's.[82]

Stationing eleven thousand armed police along the Lower Saxony border had resulted in three deaths.[83] News of the shootings inspired a "can-you-top-this session in telling atrocity stories," reported Goodman.[84] "When East Berlin got word that one young [would-be] participant had died in a bold attempt to cross the Elbe," added West German ex-communist Willy Haas, "the battle for the hearts of the youth" appeared finished—"won by the Communists."[85]

The most conspicuous of the converts were the 280 Britons in Innsbruck, few if any of whom foresaw or forgave their hold-up at the "western" curtain. The heroes' welcome that they received in East Berlin—after going south into Italy on train tickets paid for by Austrian trade unions, then doubling back to Berlin via Austria's Soviet Occupied Zone—carried special meaning. The celebrity treatment given to Raymonde Dien was now theirs. The cheap holiday had become a political rite of passage.[86] The son of one British "conservative counsillor" went so far as to call for a suit against His Majesty's government for failing to defend freedom against American fiat.[87] For the British public, the scandal confirmed old contempt for American vulgarity. For western communists like Haas, to enter East Germany was "to tread on the political promised land" of the foreseeable future.[88] And for publicists across the Soviet bloc, the news from East Berlin was even sweeter. True to their hopes, the third festival had frightened Western imperialism out of its liberal rhetoric, proving civil liberties contingent and the threat of brutality omnipresent. Had the West responded more liberally to the festival, attendance might have been higher, but the press would have been quieter. As an East German press statement announced in italics on August 7, the "maneuvers by the enemies of peace" had shown the world "*who the authors of the iron curtain between the peoples really are.*"[89]

CLOSING THE CURTAIN

The GDR and USSR had succeeded on two counts out of three at the World Youth Festival of 1951. Their West German and US nemeses reacted brutally, killing three West Germans, battering a British woman with a train, and cutting an eight-stitch gash across a London School of Economics student's forehead. Foreign guests, in turn, had acted with integrity, venturing rarely into West Berlin and entertaining few doubts about which side was right when they did. Unfortunately for Erich Honecker, the third leap of faith—trust in his Free German Youth (FDJ)—had landed gracelessly. In the mania of mass-event preparation, Honecker had pegged his FDJ quotas too high. Emboldened by FDJ vigilance at East Berlin's massive Germany Rally the year before, he had expected the blueshirts to behave like interwar communists, sacrificing individually for the good of the society. As a result, 1.4 million young East Germans came to the capital expecting to see the world. On account of unsavory food and unventilated attics, as many as two-thirds discovered West Berlin instead.[90] For Honecker, the betrayal was all but catastrophic. Had it not been for SED General Secretary Walter Ulbricht's intervention, he likely would have wound up like Georgii Malenkov: ordered to march down the party ladder he had worked so hard to climb up.[91]

For the GDR and the World Youth Festival, however, the exodus to West Berlin was not as bad as it first appeared. For one, the perceived "traitors" were not always enamored of what they saw. According to *Der Spiegel,* young Easterners made a habit of saying, "Admittedly, you've got it better. What matters, though, is that while you're going down, we're building up."[92] Even more important was the trespassers' presence. To anyone who did not know better, including foreign delegates, it was every (East German) Saxon's and Thuringian's "right to leave any country, including his own, and to return" as he pleased. The GDR did lose 3,000 blueshirts to West Berlin over the course of the festival, and would have lost many more had Western authorities been more accommodating.[93] Still, a 0.2 percent defection rate was no great loss. His career hanging by a thread, Honecker had sent a mob into West Berlin to provoke "fascist" violence and had emerged victorious. Photographs of East German girls in hospital beds echoed the grim shots of GIs leading Britons at bayonet-point through Saalfelden. By opening the curtain at the "divided centre of the divided centre" without police to hem East Berlin in, festival planners had put the event on the world's front page, where it had always meant to be.

Until recently, the "Iron Curtain" was anchored so deep in Cold War historiography that it required no qualification, much less a definition. Despite the ebb and flow of scholarly fashions, and despite the bounty found in East European archives since the 1990s, the curtain remained where Winston Churchill had set it. That the Soviet bloc co-opted the metaphor and that the anchor swung from one side of Europe to the other in 1951 went unnoticed. In her recent account of a chestnut-lined road between two postwar German towns, Edith Sheffer presents a local study of this chapter's global theme. Originally named for the burnt logs used to build it, the "Burned Bridge" between socialist Thuringia and capitalist Bavaria acquired its proverbial meaning in the late 1940s. After a series of state-sponsored mass crossings, the GDR imposed "sharp measures" against trespassers on one side, while Bavaria's Interior Ministry hired more police to defend the other.[94] Borders were best in safe hands, the adversaries agreed. Bridges between East and West Germany were therefore better burned than crossed.

The reimposition of border control along the Soviet bloc's western edge a few days after the third festival's end followed a similar logic. In Bohemia, checkpoints and armed police reemerged from the woods. At German border crossings, the three cigarettes, ping-pong tables, and a "refreshing drink" that had welcomed West German delegates to socialism were put back in their boxes.[95] After a few weeks of chaos, the Iron Curtain returned to normal.

For young Germans who had spent the festival watching "national galas" in socialist theaters, chatting with foreigners on East Berlin sidewalks, or laughing at Laurel and Hardy in West Berlin cinemas, the return to provincial life was difficult. Four days after her arrival in Delitzsch, a small town in Saxony, seventeen-year-old Marianne Heidecke wrote in her diary,

> Everything is terribly quiet. One day follows the next, without somehow something unordinary happening. The only thing that keeps one on one's toes is work. And the only amusement is the radio. I darn stockings and other necessary garments to [the radio]; the day passes very quickly to it. The wash wants to be washed, and you don't even notice how quickly it's evening—and despite all this, it's still boring.[96]

For Marianne, the boredom had two escapes: the radio (most likely West Berlin's Radio in the American Sector, or RIAS), and memories. "I always find myself thinking back on Berlin," she wrote on September 12, where "nobody meddles in his neighbor's business. If only I could get back there really soon and see nothing more of Delitzsch."[97] Two years later, newly enrolled at East Berlin's Humboldt University, Marianne got her wish. And eight years after enrolling, she watched workers construct the wall—a project overseen by former FDJ chairman Erich Honecker. In August 1961, precisely ten years after Marianne Heidecke and the Iron Curtain spent two weeks in the West, the border became impassable. Whatever ambiguity the line once had held was lost. Marianne and the Iron Curtain belonged to the East.

NOTES

1. For the metaphor's origins, see Ignace Feuerlicht, "A New Look at the Iron Curtain," *American Speech* 30, no. 3 (October 1955): 186–89. For the speech itself, Win-

ston Churchill, *The Sinews of Peace: Post-war Speeches* (New York: Houghton-Mifflin, 1949), 100.

2. See "Stalin's Reply to Churchill" (transl. from *Pravda*), *New York Times,* March 14, 1946, 4.

3. Quoted in Vladimir Pechatnov, "The Big Three after World War II," Cold War International History Project [CWIHP] Working Paper no. 13 (Washington, DC: Woodrow Wilson Center, 1995), 23.

4. Milovan Djilas, *Conversations with Stalin,* trans. M. Petrovich (New York: Harcourt-Brace, 1962), 114. In 1974 Molotov affirmed Djilas's statement. See Albert Resis, ed., *Molotov Remembers: Inside Kremlin Politics: Conversations with Felix Chuev* (Chicago: Ivan Dee, 1993), 59.

5. On CIA vote-rigging in postwar Italy, see CIA officer Mark Wyatt's compelling account at http://www.gwu.edu/~nsarchiv/coldwar/interviews/episode-3/wyatt3.html (accessed April 2013).

6. For the original text: *Pravda*, September 21, 1946; for an English translation: Andrei Zhdanov, *Central Committee Resolutions and Zhdanov's Speech on the Journals* Zvezda *and* Leningrad, trans. Felicity Ashbee and Irina Tidmarsh (Royal Oak, MI: Strathcona, 1978), 71.

7. Legal historian Johannes Morsink attributes communist UN delegates' abstention on the global "Bill of Rights" not to the matter of travel, but to its silence regarding nazism and fascism. See Morsink, *The Universal Declaration of Human Rights: Origins, Drafting, and Intent* (Philadelphia: University of Pennsylvania Press, 1999), 24.

8. Joseph Wechsberg, "Letter from Bucharest," *New Yorker,* September 12, 1953, 67.

9. J.K. "Frontier or Front?" *East Europe and Soviet Russia*, September 13, 1951, 12.

10. Walter L. Hixson, *Parting the Iron Curtain* (New York: St. Martin's, 1997), 151.

11. The *New York Times* included further coverage of athletics at the Prague festival. Since these articles make no reference to the festival itself, only to athletics, I exclude them from my tally. For the number of US delegates in 1949, see "Rift of U.S. Group in Budapest Noted," *New York Times,* September 3, 1949, 3.

12. The foreign delegate total for 1949, according to official festival documentation, was 10,400. See Pia Koivunen, "The 1957 Moscow Youth Festival: Propagating a New, Peaceful Image of the Soviet Union" in *Soviet State and Society under Nikita Khrushchev*, ed. Melanie Ilic and Jeremy Smith (London: Routledge, 2009), 49.

13. Bertolt Brecht, *Journals,* trans. Hugh Rorrison, ed. John Willett (London: Methuen, 1993), 401.

14. Timothy Garton Ash, *In Europe's Name* (New York: Random House, 1993), 15.

15. Russian State Archive of Socio-Political History, Komsomol division (RGASPI-M), fond 4, opis' 4, delo 3, list 17; d. 15, l. 3.

16. Though no statistical records of gender at the festival exist, US participant Vincent Tortora's memoir notes that males were "far in the majority amongst the delegates" on the train to East Berlin. See Tortora, *Communist Close-Up: A Roving Reporter behind the Iron Curtain* (New York: Exposition Press, 1953), 27–28, 32, 60.

17. Huge thanks to Stepan Ruckl for this quotation and translation. See Národní Archiv České Republiky, Prague (NAČR), ČSM kr. 1602–13, folder: Průběh I Světového Festivalu.

18. The Iron Curtain did not actually pass between Czechoslovakia and Austria's Soviet Occupied Zone in 1951; both belonged to the Soviet "sphere of influence." Nevertheless, a border checkpoint no doubt stood there. Tortora, *Communist Close-Up*, 27.

19. Interview with Peter Waterman, The Hague, March 28, 2009. The fact that the *Batory* evacuated Britons from the same pier eleven years earlier to escape the German army only heightened the excitement.

20. Speech by US delegate Joyce Silver, printed in *Tägliche Rundschau,* August 12,

1951. Howard Fast "was extolled by the propaganda machine [of the Soviet bloc] as the greatest living American writer" in the early 1950s, recalls Bulgarian writer Georgi Markov. See Markov, *The Truth That Killed,* transl. L. Brisby (London: Weidenfeld & Nicholson, 1983), 195.

21. These reports derive from Komsomol world press summaries. RGASPI-M, f. 4, op. 4, d. 3, ll. 128–38.

22. Acheson to Frankfurt (telegram), May 23, 1951, in National Archives and Records Administration, Washington, DC (NARA), 59/250/40/23/1, box 4374.

23. British National Archives, Kew (BNA), Foreign Office (FO) 371/93658/CD 2041/23.

24. Charles Ringmore to Acheson, August 30, 1951, NARA, 59/250/40/23/1, box 4375, 1–10.

25. Photographs of the LSE student and the gash above his eye appeared in the *Daily Worker.* Report by Colin Sweet, written in Innsbruck, August 7, 1951, BNA FO 371/93667/CD 2041/168, 1.

26. Letter to the Editor from D. Simpson of Oldham, *Manchester Guardian,* August 17, 1951.

27. *The Economist,* August 25, 1951; letter to British consul (Innsbruck), August 28, 1951, BNA, FO 371/93667/CD 2041/176; NCCL letter to Morrison, August 15, 1951, FO 371/93661/CD/2041/67; FO 371/93668/CD/2041/188.

28. John L. Gaddis, *The Strategies of Containment* (New York: Oxford, 2005), 123.

29. Gifford to Morrison, October 8, 1951, BNA, FO 371/93669/CD 2041/108, 3; Vienna to Secretary of State (telegram), August 7, 1951, NARA, 59/250/40/23/1, box 4374.

30. A Foreign Office press release stated: "The Western Authorities, while ready as always since 1948 to abolish the [interzonal pass] requirement for all passengers, were not prepared to make an exception only in the case of persons in whom the Soviet Authorities were politically interested." BNA, FO 371/93664/CD 2041/108, 2; ibid., CD 2041/114.

31. One example is British communist Monty Johnstone, a son of the aristocracy who grew up in Sir Walter Scott's manor and attended the elite Rugby School before joining Oxford's class of 1952. See Johnstone's obituary by Eric Hobsbawm in *The Guardian,* August 23, 2007.

32. Bericht, July 27, 1951, Federal Archive for State Security Records, Berlin (BStU), MfS-AS 341/67, 208.

33. Tortora, *Communist Close-Up,* 23–24.

34. Despatch No. 532 from Santiago to Dept. of State (DOS), October 30, 1951, NARA, 59/250/40/23/1, box 4375.

35. Tortora, *Communist Close-Up,* 15–19.

36. The term is quite popular in contemporary social science. See Henry Farrell, *The Political Economy of Trust: Institutions, Interests and Inter-Firm Cooperation in Italy and Germany* (New York: Cambridge University Press, 2009).

37. In Budapest in 1949, the US delegation expelled one member, a Virginian named Regina Bartley, "for allegedly spreading rumors that a Hungarian girl's fingernails and hair had been pulled out by the Hungarian police." Though Bartley tearfully denied the charges, she was sent home. See "Rift of US Group in Budapest Noted," *New York Times,* September 3, 1949, 3.

38. On surveillance of delegates, see Willy Haas, *Der Abschied vom Paradies, das keines war* (Böllingen: Tykve, 1988), 139. Günter Rodegast, a teenaged interpreter assigned to several Trinidadians, used to file a report on the daily activities each night before going to sleep. Rodegast, unpublished memoir, 17 (in author's possession).

39. Hannah Arendt, *The Origins of Totalitarianism* (New York: Houghton-Mifflin, 1994 [1951]), 323, 325.

40. Self-policing, one might argue, was a hallmark of Soviet communism. See Sheila

Fitzpatrick, "Signals from Below: Soviet Letters of Denunciation of the 1930s," *Journal of Modern History* 68, no. 4 (December 1996): 831–66. The reach of national autonomy in postwar Eastern Europe remains a point of debate between historians. Regarding security, however, the debate narrows considerably. For the bloc-wide "show trials" of 1949–52, for example, Stalin's Kremlin provided not only an impetus, but also a precedent. In the realm of propaganda, by contrast, Soviet influence was less overt. The World Youth Festival, for instance, had no Soviet model to follow. On the Stalinization of Eastern Europe, see Vladimir Tismaneanu, ed., *Stalinism Revisited: The Establishment of Communist Regimes in East-Central Europe* (Budapest: Central European University Press, 2010).

41. Memo from Hauptabteilungsarbeiter Betriebsschutz to Kameraden des Betriebsschutzes, July 14, 1951, Bundesarchiv Berlin-Lichterfelde (BArch-B), DO/1/27547, folder: Jugendtreffen, 6.

42. To appreciate why Goodman's compatriots suspected him, consider the postcard he sent the *Harvard Crimson* from East Berlin a few days before being expelled: "Well, here we are at the big youth festival and jiminy crickets, is it something. Holy cow, you should see it. Gee whiz, yesterday there was a big peace demonstration and a million Free German youth marched, and then released doves—the birds of peace. You could even say this whole magnificent demonstration is for the birds . . . ." See "Youth Festival 'Crashed,'" *New York Times,* August 16, 1951, 3; "College Senior Invades Red Festival at Berlin," *Harvard Crimson,* September 20, 1951.

43. Although various Western sources agree that Soviet bloc delegates were a rare sight at the festival, a Bonn press office report notes that Soviet delegates not only "go for walks in civilian clothes," but that empty pockets obliged them to "loiter on streets, squares and train stations." See "Berlin Youth Festival: Émigré view thereon," Paris to DOS, August 30, 1951, NARA, 59/250/40/23/1, box 4374, 7–9; Presse- und Informationsamt der Bundesrepublik, "Information aus der Sowjetzone . . . ," August 8, 1951, Bundesarchiv Koblenz (BArch-K), B/106/16026, Folder: Weltjugendfestspiele Berlin 1951, 3.

44. "Soviet Zone Speaks Out," September 7, 1951, NARA 466/250/68/15/3, box 136, 3.

45. For the full chant, see Tortora, *Communist Close-Up*, 66–67.

46. Communist Parties subsidized the travel of delegations from particular countries (i.e., the French party subsidized delegates from France's colonial territories). Considering the prohibitive cost, the fact that the Finns alone outnumbered all Third World delegates in 1951—a mere 4.4 percent of 26,000 foreign delegates—is not surprising. For the cited text: Despatch No. 532 from Santiago to DOS, 3–4. For festival demographics: RGASPI-M, f. 4, op. 4, d. 64b. For the Finnish delegation, see Pia Koivunen, "Bridging the East and West—Informal Interactions at the World Youth Festivals in the 1940s–60s," paper presented at the 2010 Aleksanteri Conference (Helsinki), 2n4.

47. Considering that Kathrada traveled to Europe not only for the festival's sake, but to begin a two-year stint at WFDY headquarters in Budapest, and considering the meager finances of South Africa's anti-colonial movement, it is highly unlikely that he paid his way.

48. Haas, *Abschied,* 139.

49. Ahmed Kathrada, *Memoirs* (Cape Town: Zebra, 2004), 91; interview with Waterman, The Hague, March 28, 2009.

50. Perry Anderson, "Internationalism: in Breviary," *New Left Review* 14 (March–April 2002): 15.

51. Interview with Waterman, The Hague, March 28, 2009.

52. Rodegast, unpublished memoir, 17.

53. Tortora, *Communist Close-Up*, 35–37.

54. Drew Middleton, "Berlin Youth Rally Whipped into Frenzy against the U.S.," *New York Times,* August 6, 1951, 1.

55. Berlin to DOS (telegram), August 6, 1951, NARA, 466/250/68/15/3, box 136.

56. "Information aus der Sowjetzone: 'Weltfestspiele' [. . .] Erster Sonderbericht," Presse- und Informationsamt, August 8, 1951, BArch-K, B/106/16026, folder: Weltjugendfestspiele Berlin 1951, band I, 2.

57. Arendt, *Origins of Totalitarianism,* 325.

58. The best articulation of the ideological distinction remains Isaiah Berlin's 1958 Oxford speech, "Two Concepts of Liberty," in *Four Essays on Liberty* (Oxford: Oxford University Press, 1969).

59. BArch-K, bild M 0202/300 N.

60. Harry Thürk, *In allen Sprachen: Eine Reportage von den III. Weltfestspielen der Jugend und Studenten* (East Berlin: Verlag Neues Leben, 1953), 25, 31.

61. "Im Frieden liegt das Glück der Völker," *Tägliche Rundschau,* August 6, 1951, 3.

62. See the August 11, 1951, article from Ljubljana's *Slovenski Porocevalec* in NARA, 59/250/40/23/1, box 4374.

63. Helga Müller, "Jugendpflegerische Arbeit in den Heimen," Landesarchiv Berlin (LAB), B Rep. 013, nr. 12, folder: Weltjugendfestspiele.

64. Peter Waterman, unpublished memoir (in author's possession).

65. Kathrada, *Memoir,* 91. For Third World attendance, see n. 46.

66. Italics mine. "Berlin Youth Festival: Émigré view thereon," 8.

67. RGASPI-M, f. 4, op. 4, ll. 34; f. 4, op. 4, d. 15, ll. 42, 134–35, 138; "Unsere Freundschaft ist unbesiegbar," *Junge Welt,* August 10, 1951, 1. Fourteen months earlier, the FDJ judged "the greatest words" spoken at May 1950's *Deutschlandtreffen* (Germany Rally), the unofficial dress rehearsal for the 1951 festival, to be those of WFDY president (and future Eurocommunist) Enrico Berlinguer, who assured his German audience, "We have trust in you." *Dokumente zur Geschichte der FDJ* (Berlin: Neues Leben, 1960), 2:90. The decision to hold the third festival in Berlin struck many East Europeans as outrageous. A Slovenian newspaper went so far as to liken the festival to the NSDAP's 1939 Parteitag for Peace—an event that would have opened on September 2, 1939, had Hitler not invaded Poland the day before. The aforementioned Romanian émigré informed the US State Department that Socialist Unity Party (SED) members conveyed an abiding pro-Nazi bias, characterized by "tak[ing] a sort of malicious joy in the danger in which the Allies are today and which compensates them partly for the bitterness they feel for having lost the war." Seeing as neither Slovenians nor Romanian émigrés adhered to Stalinist internationalism, it follows that they spoke more critically and candidly than Polish or Czechoslovak delegates. See Despatch from Belgrade to DOS, August 20, 1951, NARA, 59/250/40/23/1, box 4374.

68. Tom Madden, unpublished memoir, 54 (in author's possession).

69. BStU, MfS-AS, nr. 1/52, bd. 4a, 8.

70. Heiner Müller, "Anekdote," *Aufbau* (September 1951): 810. On Raymonde Dien: "France: Martyrdom Denied," *Time,* June 12, 1950, http://www.time.com/time/magazine/article/0,9171,812654,00.html (accessed April 2013).

71. Interview with Waterman, The Hague, March 28, 2009. Komsomol First Secretary Nikolai Mikhailov's summary report to Georgii Malenkov states that the "overwhelming majority" of Americans at the 1951 festival were "blacks and Jews." RGASPI-M, f. 4, op. 4, d. 15, l. 2.

72. Waterman, unpublished memoir; interview with Waterman.

73. On the boycott, see William G. Gray, *Germany's Cold War* (Chapel Hill: University of North Carolina Press, 2003), 13–29. For Mielke: Dienstanweisung von Erich Mielke an MfS Landesverwaltung Brandenburgs, BStU, Mfs-BdL/Dok. 000014, 3.

74. Tortora, *Communist Close-Up,* 68–69; copy of the British National Union of Students' (NUS) report on the 1951 festival in the Komsomol archive(!), RGASPI-M, f. 4, op. 4, d. 12, ll. 198–203.

75. McCloy (Berlin) to DOS (telegram), August 19, 1951, NARA 466/250/68/15/3, box 138, folder: August 1951.

76. Soviet composers won the first-, second-, and third-best song, the winning number titled, "March of the Soviet Youth." RGASPI-M, f. 4, op. 4, d. 15, ll. 6–8, 11, 48.

77. A Hungarian marathon runner received wild cheers from East Germans at the end of the race after three Soviet runners "bumped" and "boxed" him out of first place. See *New York Times,* August 16, 1951, 39; Rodegast, unpublished memoir, 17.

78. With the exception of a white marble statue of Stalin and a map of the USSR hanging over the stage, the Soviet gala program was all art: three hours of classical Russian music and ballet interspersed with Karelian, Tajik, and Ukrainian folk dance. For the closing act, performers and audience rose to sing Lev Oshanin's "World Youth Song," the last line of which reads: "Our song flies over the borders—friendship is victorious!" In light of recent work on Stalinist nationality policy, one might argue that the blend of classical and folk works was prototypically Stalinist. Even so, and even if oxymoronic, the multicultural program conveyed a distinctly internationalist national identity. Soviet supremacy was that of a system, the program suggested, not of a nation. See Thürk, *In allen Sprachen*, 54–59; NARA, 59/250/40/23/1, box 4374, 6; Francine Hirsch, *Empire of Nations* (Ithaca: Cornell University Press, 2005).

79. Visit to Chinese Communist National Program, August 13, 1951, NARA, 59/250/59/30/4, box 6345.

80. Tortora, *Communist Close-Up*, 75–76; see also Haas, *Abschied,* 151–52.

81. Report from K. Orlov of the Antifascist Committee of Soviet Youth (AKSM) to Mikhailov, July 26, 1951, RGASPI-M, f. 4, op. 4, d. 12, ll. 135–38.

82. Only the first report in this series is signed from Mikhailov to Malenkov, dated August 24, 1951. The quotation comes from the fourth, unsigned report in the series. RGASPI-M, f. 4, op. 4, d. 15, l. 38.

83. "Polizei verhindert illegalen Grenzübertritt der FDJ," *Neue Zeitung,* July 30, 1951; Michael Lemke, "Die 'Gegenspiele': Weltjugendfestival und FDJ-Deutschlandtreffen in der Systemkonkurrenz," in *Die DDR in Europa,* ed. H. Timmermann (Münster: Lit, 2005), 471.

84. George Goodman, "I Crashed Stalin's Party," *Collier's Weekly,* November 10, 1951, 47.

85. Haas, *Abschied,* 127.

86. Ringmore to Acheson, 5.

87. *Daily Worker* (London), August 15, 1951.

88. Haas, *Abschied,* 134.

89. *Dokumente zur Geschichte der FDJ,* 2:241.

90. See Lemke, "Die 'Gegenspiele.'"

91. W. Berlin to DOS (telegram), August 16, 1951, NARA, 466/250/68/15/3, box 138, folder: August 1951; Heinz Lippmann, *Honecker: Porträt eines Nachfolgers* (Cologne: Verlag Wissenschaft und Politik, 1971), 136.

92. "Ostfestspiele: Es muß etwas passieren," *Der Spiegel,* August 15, 1951, 5.

93. Lemke, "Die 'Gegenspiele,'" 490.

94. Edith Sheffer, *Burned Bridge: How East and West Germans Made the Iron Curtain* (Oxford: Oxford University Press, 2011), chs. 1, 4.

95. Ibid., ch. 4.

96. Marianne Heidecke (nee Kirschke) diary, August 27, 1951, entry (in author's possession).

97. Ibid., September 12, 1951, entry.

4

SOCIALIST ENCOUNTERS

Albania and the Transnational Eastern Bloc in the 1950s

ELIDOR MËHILLI

In the summer of 1961, a group of East Germans found themselves in something of an ordeal. They were stationed in Kurbnesh, an isolated locale in the mountainous area of Mirditë, in northern Albania. A small village situated close to copper reserves, Kurbnesh was undergoing a stormy transformation into an industrial town. When authorities decided to build a copper enrichment factory there, they brought in specialists from East Germany to supply their advanced industrial experience.[1] In their reports to Berlin, however, the visitors voiced frustration. The Albanian hosts, they complained, seemed uninterested in the advice they had to offer. Local engineers appeared ill trained, the managers mischievous, and the intelligentsia indifferent to the factory. They detected an excessive "self-consciousness" and a "distinct arrogance in technical and economic issues" for which they blamed constant Party of Labor (PLA) propaganda. Decisions had often been taken counter to German suggestions; the visitors' advice was heeded only when these decisions had led to disaster.[2]

The Albanian hosts drew an entirely different picture of the conflict. They singled out delays in machine shipments from East Germany and blamed the visitors for not working hard enough. The copper enrichment factory was originally supposed to start operating on April 1, 1960,

Versions of this chapter were presented at the Woodrow Wilson Center for International Scholars in Washington, DC, and at the Modern Europe Workshop at Princeton University. I gratefully acknowledge the thoughtful comments of the participants. The chapter has greatly benefited from the suggestions and criticisms of Stephen Kotkin, Marc Frey, and the editors of this volume.

but construction of segments was still lagging behind.[3] Reading the reports from both sides, it would seem that the East German transfer of technology to Albania was an utter failure. True, a factory did eventually emerge, but socialist cooperation seems to have been anything but "fraternal." Still, the point is not whether the East German experts exaggerated local conditions, or whether the hosts blamed the visitors for their own planning failures. After all, by mid-1961, political relations between Tirana and Moscow had deteriorated, so these records may reflect straining relations with Berlin as well. The tensions between the East Germans and the Albanians also had a lot to do with the unintended consequences of transnational socialist exchange. The point, therefore, is to ask how such encounters came about in the first place.

It was not a handful of foreigners, either. By 1960, some 114 Soviet and Eastern bloc specialists were employed in design and construction projects alone (urban planning bureaus, factories, nationalized brickworks, agricultural enterprises).[4] To contextualize that number, it should be noted that by 1960 there were 105 Albanian architects, urban planners, civil engineers, geometers, and drafters *in the whole country.*[5] One year later, foreigners working in mines and at geological sites alone numbered 155 (most of them from the Soviet Union).[6] Similar contingents were dispatched to other industrial branches, planning agencies, and schools. In addition to Soviet officers, advisers, and engineers, a small army of men and women, including East Germans, Czechoslovaks, Poles, Hungarians, and Bulgarians, descended on Albania to help build socialism. They were brought in to execute industrial designs, supervise assembly, and teach locals how to operate imported machines. They constituted, in short, the transnational agents of the Eastern bloc.

Among the excellent accounts of the establishment of communist regimes in Eastern Europe, classics by Hugh Seton-Watson, Zbigniew Brzezinski, and François Fejtö emphasized Soviet strategy to extend Moscow's sphere of influence.[7] Following the "archival revolution" of the 1990s, important new works reassessed the postwar period by utilizing a range of declassified materials.[8] These studies point to the Soviet Union as a total model of socioeconomic development, involving nationalized means of production, central planning, and pervasive party rule. Indeed, Soviet influence was manifested not only in postwar Eastern Europe but also in North Korea and China.[9] This chapter, however, introduces the Eastern bloc as another important level of analysis. Official propaganda may have exaggerated its cohesion, but the bloc was not less real than any of its constitutive parts. It was more than a geopolitical concept or military alliance; it also came about through formal and informal interactions, coercive and voluntary transfers and circulations enabled by communist parties and centralized economies. Much has been written about post–World War II development politics and modernization campaigns in the Third World, but the transnational history of the so-called Second World has been largely overlooked.[10] In an influential article on Eurasia as an arena of "influences and interactions," Stephen Kotkin observed that the Soviet Union "created standardized national infrastructure for the republics but also transnational infrastructure, as well as transnational political habits, transnational economic relations, and transnational ways of behaving, still visible in many of the successor national republics."[11] Studying this "globalization within an autarky" requires sensitivity to Soviet controls, but also to transnational currents of exchange and internalized practices within the Eastern bloc.[12] In addition to replicating dynamics of center-periphery, the Eastern bloc provided career opportunities, privileges, and access to well-connected agents.

Postwar Albania offers compelling examples of the contradictory features of this state-directed traffic of peoples, ideas, and practices. Though peripheral, the Balkan country became an important experimental arena in the efforts to cure backwardness through socialist planning. Emerging from Italian and Nazi occupation, Albania initially flirted with the idea of joining the Yugoslav federation under Tito but then found itself an eager Soviet satellite after 1948. Domestic planning became utterly dependent on foreign aid. (In less than six years the Soviets built some eighteen industrial projects, including textile mills, a cement factory, and a sugar-processing plant.) Until the 1960s, when Albanian party chief Enver Hoxha denounced Nikita Khrushchev's handling of Sino-Soviet disagreements, these Soviet and Eastern bloc specialists sought to integrate the isolated country into the socialist commonwealth. Of course, these integration efforts were profoundly shaped by political and economic developments in Western Europe. But the Albanian example shows that there were also comparisons to be made *within* the Eastern bloc. Expanding transnational contacts made these comparisons inevitable—between East and West, but also between Moscow, Berlin, Prague, and Tirana. Guided by the logic of central planning, socialist development aid put so-called proletarian solidarity to the test: encounters between foreigners and locals in 1950s Albania brought to surface feelings of superiority and inferiority, bred misunderstandings, and created unexpected conflicts.

EXCHANGE IN AND OUT OF THE BLOC

Eastern bloc bureaucrats insisted that cooperation among socialist states was uniquely molded by a sense of proletarian solidarity and internationalism. Relations among the people's democracies, the official line went, were "relations of a new type" based on socialist solidarity and disinterested cooperation.[13] Not so under capitalism, allegedly, where international relations were said to be shaped by the rule of dominant and aggressive powers over small and frequently helpless states. And yet socialist exchange was inevitably informed by expanding international transfers and communication in the postwar period.[14] Take, for example, the establishment of the Council for Mutual Economic Assistance (Comecon), the first organization of socialist states. Originally composed of Bulgaria, Czechoslovakia, Hungary, Poland, Romania, and the Soviet Union, it added Albania to its ranks within a month of its inception in January 1949 and East Germany in 1950. China, North Korea, Vietnam, Cuba, and Yugoslavia took part in various meetings as observers, with Mongolia, Vietnam, and Cuba gaining membership in the 1960s and 1970s.[15] From the outset, the Comecon was envisioned as a response to the Marshall Plan. Specifically, its most direct Western counterpart was the Organization for European Economic Cooperation (OEEC), founded in 1948 and responsible for administering reconstruction aid in postwar Western Europe. The OEEC was also instrumental in setting up the European Free Trade Area and eventually the European Common Market. As one author has observed, this Cold War arrangement effectively divided the continent along lines of wealth conforming "to the postwar pattern of trade blocs—'horizontal integrations' at broadly the same level of development." It departed from the dominant prewar system in which wealthy centers dealt with underdeveloped peripheries (though this feature did not altogether disappear).[16]

In the background of nascent socialist exchange were also such developments as the creation of UN technical assistance programs, championed by US president Harry S. Truman, which utilized government donations to send experts to underdeveloped countries. A precursor to the United Nations Economic and Social Council (ECOSOC), these aid programs signaled an enduring approach in the West that considered technology transfer to be the crucial ingredient in "curing" underdevelopment. Another similar body was the European Productivity Agency (EPA), an outcome of the Marshall Plan, which was established in 1953 within the OEEC and was also funded in large part by Washington. Finally, international scientific cooperation also expanded remarkably throughout the 1950s in areas like the geophysical sciences. In urban planning and architecture, too, the Union Internationale des Architectes, founded in Lausanne, Switzerland, in 1948 grew into an international body seeking, often unsuccessfully, to cross Cold War fault lines by holding its fifth congress in Moscow in 1958.

Just as it increasingly shaped Soviet policies, this in-built comparative drive with the capitalist West also became internalized within the bloc, where it had important repercussions for the socialist integration project as a whole. Made evident by increasing competition in areas like science, technology, and consumption, this competitive urge nurtured a sense of cohesion around the bloc and offered a rationale for technical assistance to such underdeveloped member states as Albania. "Even among capitalist countries there is cooperation in the realm of science and technology," admitted Albert Cohen within the GDR Planning Commission on the occasion of the signing of an exchange agreement with Poland in 1950, "but capitalists view such scientific realms as frivolous, so it happens only infrequently." Cohen argued that capitalist countries were driven by reckless self-interest and that they would use any weapon available to them—espionage, threats, blackmail—to obtain technical supremacy. Political and economic strength, he reasoned, trumped any genuine cooperation in science and technology. As an example he took the fuel used by the US bombers that demolished German cities, which, he explained, had been produced according to IG Farben patents—the ominous result of the convergence of imperialist interests with technical expertise. By contrast, people's democracies based technical transfer on "a stable and profound friendship."[17]

Despite Comecon's existence, socialist exchange between 1947 and 1955 was mostly limited to bilateral agreements.[18] There were a number of reasons for this. During Stalin's lifetime, the Comecon was scarcely envisioned as a supranational body (indeed, "sovereignty" had been made the guiding maxim to counter the "imperialism" of US authorities in Western Europe).[19] The organization merely served to reinforce existing and independently running central plans and sustain the transfer of the Soviet economic management model to the newly acquired bloc. In this context, Comecon's early activities were limited to the coordination of a handful of research projects, and it largely remained "an institution for pursuing (or at the very least presenting) national interests" to Moscow.[20] Each member state enacted its own economic plans and established its own research institutions. Imported Soviet models, to be sure, resulted in considerable uniformity (party structures, planning mechanisms) in Eastern Europe in the early 1950s, but this had more to do with applied Sovietism than a coordinated effort of integration.[21]

Khrushchev's call to compete with capitalism implied a more central role for science and technology in socialist planning, and it also ushered in a period of increased exchange across the bloc. In December 1954 the Soviet leader famously railed against Stalin-era urban planning and architecture at the All-Union Convention of Construction Workers.[22] He criticized architects and Moscow's skyscrapers and took the construction industry to task for having long invoked the tenets of socialist realism to justify extravagant budgets and financial folly. He warned against superfluities in construction while advocating simplicity in design and an expansion of industrial building methods. This turn had important repercussions across the Eastern bloc. It signaled the rising stakes in a competition waged with the capitalist West not only in armaments but also in consumption and design. At the American National Exhibition in Moscow in 1959, Soviet visitors would witness not the might of the US military but the intoxicating power of consumer goods, modern household appliances, and lavishly appointed model homes. The ensuing Kitchen Debate between Khrushchev and Nixon was the culmination of this longstanding competition in design standards. American propaganda in material culture, Greg Castillo has observed, "encouraged the Soviet bloc to measure its progress through direct comparisons with Western per-capita private consumption, the Achilles heel of economies based on state-owned heavy industries."[23]

Efforts to integrate socialist economies intensified in the late 1950s. The May 1958 meeting of socialist representatives in Moscow was intended to reinvigorate the Comecon and outline a new international socialist division of labor. At the meeting, the Albanian delegation argued that its requests for substantial aid were reasonable given the fact that even in the 1970s the standard of living in Albania would still be much lower than elsewhere in the Eastern bloc. During the proceedings, the East Germans also requested substantial assistance to increase *their* standard of living, arguing that West Germany posed a threatening example of consumerism and well-being. In supporting the East German request, Khrushchev observed that both East Germany and Albania bordered on the capitalist world and thus deserved substantial assistance. The GDR, the Soviet leader said, ought to become a socialist showpiece to counter West Germany, while Albania was to become an example for the Arab world.[24] Improbable as it may seem in retrospect, this parallel between Albania and the GDR aptly reflects the external constraints (Western borders) impacting the socialist world.

Khrushchev's attempts to spearhead further integration, however, faced serious obstacles. Even with a charter adopted in 1959 and an Executive Committee established in 1962, the effort to centralize the Comecon did not fundamentally alter its character.[25] Soviet measures designed to establish a common planning structure and economic enterprises across the bloc, in turn, later met with intense Romanian objections. Significantly, constraints to socialist integration were built into the economic infrastructure of member states. Planning centered around physical production targets, a feature that also shaped international trade within the Eastern bloc. Central plans, moreover, required constant tweaks, which further complicated cooperation among member states. "The disparity between members is not," wrote Michael Kaser, "as wide as it is within OECD, EEC, or EFTA; nor, at root, is it the crucial obstacle to integration. The difficulty seems rather to lie in the *forms* of central planning to be harmonized."[26] Socialist economies had notorious difficulties with multilateral trade. "As in relations between centrally managed enterprises within each country," observed one economic historian, "money was not allowed any such active role as expressing purchasing power capable of acquiring any product at a posted price."[27] The result was that multilateral trade acquired barter-type dynamics. Due to the demands of central planning, moreover, disparities in pricing among the bloc countries, the shielding of domestic prices, and the prevailing focus on imports, trade arrangements started—as a rule—with a list of products to be adjusted to balance payments. This setup might have worked for bilateral relations, but it was ill suited for multilateral agreements. Relations among socialist countries, in short, were shaped by the limits and arrangements of central plans, even as, crucially, relations with capitalist countries demanded the adoption of other terms. Comecon's paradox, one author wrote, was that "under Stalin the USSR had the power, but not the will, to impose any degree of economic unity short of outright annexation; while under Khrushchev it had the will but not the power."[28] In light of the challenges at hand, it was surprising that *any* exchange could take place at all.

Trade was only one facet of socialist exchange. The latter also involved the circulation of specialists, industrial blueprints, and technological innovations, and in this area socialist exchange achieved considerable results. Formal agreements provided for the transfer of building plans, patents, and technical descriptions as well as formulas, models, and samples. The documents outlining these terms of exchange themselves exuded uniformity, since they were often copies of bilateral agreements between individual countries and the Soviet Union. There was also the uniformly translated bureaucratic-speak: The ubiquitous label "technical-scientific cooperation" began to permeate the planning bureaucracies of the bloc (*nauchno-tekhnicheskoe sotrudnichestvo* in Russian; *technisch-wissentschaftliche Zusammenarbeit* in German; *bashkëpunimi tekniko-shkencor* in Albanian.) Within the overlapping webs of socialist international relations, it was not always possible to fully differentiate technical exchange from other government agreements providing for capital assistance, training programs, or even cultural diplomacy or similar provisions attained through party channels. But the adoption of this bureaucratic term pointed to a clear effort to differentiate and standardize such practice among socialist states. Here, too, uniformity was an indication of pervasive copying at all administrative levels, of the prevailing ethos of planning, and of an all-out drive to make exchange a routine state matter.

In order to differentiate socialist exchange, bureaucrats decided to create even more bureaucracy. Scientific and technical exchange was supposed to occur systematically, according to bilateral negotiations taking place annually. During these meetings, provisions would be passed on payments and costs, which were mostly (but not always) carried by the recipient country. Intergovernmental bodies were set up to effectuate these agreements. Formalities were also standardized throughout: meetings alternated between the capitals of the countries involved, the language of business was Russian, and each side was supposed to prepare technical requests well in advance.[29] The crucial assumption behind this form of technical transfer was that negotiators directly relied on centrally approved plans. Each side was supposed to predict—at least in theory—short-term

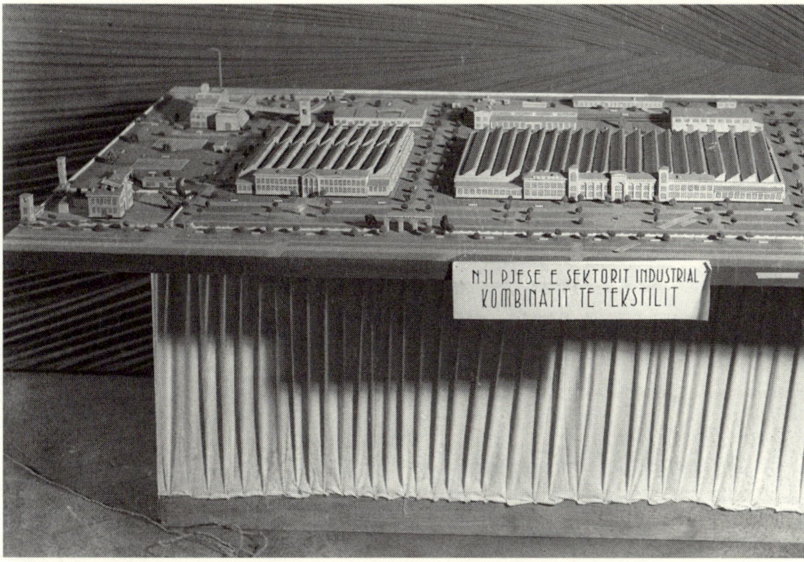

Figure 4.1. Architectural model of the Soviet-designed Stalin Textile Works, outside of Tirana, Albania, February 1951. Courtesy Agjencia Telegrafike Shqiptare.

Figure 4.2. Industrial equipment arriving in Albania from the Soviet Union, 1951. Courtesy Agjencia Telegrafike Shqiptare.

needs and allocations in virtually all sectors of the economy. But it was also necessary—again, in theory—to determine the relative strengths of each Eastern bloc partner. Technical transfer assumed a certain level of information, or the ability to obtain it, in addition to a robust centralized system.[30]

Official Soviet sources heavily emphasized the centrality of Soviet technical aid to the people's democracies. They reported, for example, that most of the Eastern bloc countries (except the GDR and Czechoslovakia) were primarily recipients of Soviet technical expertise. According to one estimate, the Soviet Union sent some 31,778 technical documents between 1948 and 1961 to Eastern bloc countries as well as Mongolia, North Korea, North Vietnam, and China. It received, in return, some 8,877.[31] The biggest recipient of Soviet technical documents in this period appears to have been China, and the largest contributor Czechoslovakia. These numbers, of course, need to be contextualized. For example, they reflect official Soviet calculations of formalized exchange, but not the extensive industrial machines and resources that the Soviet Union picked up across Eurasia and shipped back home. Referring to a kind of "imperial scavenging," Austin Jersild has highlighted this Soviet campaign to adopt Eastern bloc technical knowledge and innovations. Driven by a sense of competition with the capitalist West, Soviet technical and managerial elites scoured the bloc to appropriate everything they deemed beneficial to their science and technology. This "scavenging" mentality, Jersild observes, pushed them toward the west (Prague) more so than the east (Beijing), with the Chinese increasingly seen in the 1950s as unable to offer much of value to the Soviet technical revolution.[32]

As conceived, techno-scientific exchange among socialist countries produced its own institutions (in and out of the Comecon) and employed its own agents. It thus offers a productive angle not merely into the politics of modernization and building socialism in individual countries but also the role of a broad range of actors, including party apparatchiks, planning bureaucrats, and managerial elites, all the way down to local bosses and ordinary workers. As "a socialist division of labor" became the new Soviet mantra, so technical transfer within the Eastern bloc gained urgency. But beyond Soviet calculations, Eastern bloc countries also increasingly engaged in exchange among themselves. Czechoslovakia and Bulgaria, for example, became involved in less developed Comecon members like Albania. And although fewer technical documents and patents made it there

Figure 4.3. Adolf Krusemark and Erna Siegmund of VEB Gubener Wolle prepare a shipment of fabric to Albania, December 2, 1954. Using wool from the Soviet Union, China, and Mongolia, the East German factory manufactured fabric for the rest of the Eastern bloc. Photo by Krueger. Courtesy Bundesarchiv, bild 183-27466-0002.

relative to other Eastern bloc countries, the impact could have arguably been as significant, if not greater, given the party-state's heavy investment in industrialization and Albania's relative underdevelopment.

THE TRICK OF COMPARISON

The Eastern bloc specialists who took up jobs in 1950s Albania spoke of proletarian solidarity and disinterested development aid. Not all of them were experienced; some, in fact, were recent university graduates. A trip to Albania was largely an experiment. In fact, it sometimes proved difficult to find specialists who were willing to move to Albania for long periods of time, as only few were allowed to take their families with them. Even when such individuals were identified, there was the additional hurdle of having to ensure their political loyalty, as a high-level official at the Polish Foreign Ministry admitted.[33] Nevertheless, some volunteered for the jobs, driven, it would seem, by enthusiasm and the professional challenge of building socialism under challenging circumstances. To be sure, there were special salaries and privileges to be had, but these did not necessarily contradict a genuine sense of passion in imparting advanced "socialist experience" to a backward country. A group of Polish civil engineers and planners, for example, volunteered to plan the entire transportation system in the capital Tirana.[34] Though exaggerated, the widely propagated solidarity among the people's democracies was not spurious. Domestic interests and calculations certainly drove socialist exchange, but unprecedented professional opportunities, political considerations, and actions animated by prevailing beliefs about the communist world were important too.

Socialist solidarity, however, did not guarantee that this inflow of technical assistance would be free of problems. Albania did not even have enough trained negotiators, translators, and technical personnel to attend international meetings, let alone implement Eastern bloc decisions and blueprints.[35] The place that Eastern bloc personnel occupied in the country's enterprises, moreover, could be ambiguous. They were far better qualified than most of their native colleagues, but, unlike the ubiquitous Soviet advisers, they were often unable to shape outcomes or influence planning. East Europeans were at the same time part of the chain of command and as outsiders, merely relegated to an "advisory" position. Their technical skills were in demand, but their authority was difficult to pin down. Nor was it any easier to establish with certainty whether Albanian workers were subordinate to them. Of course, foreign specialists could make use of their contacts at their respective embassies in Tirana—they frequently did, especially when misunderstandings arose. Problems could also be "solved" through party channels or by going straight to the enterprise director or even the minister. But the issues were also deeper: exchanges of personnel in technology created a vague space of authority within Albanian planning and building agencies. Official rhetoric drew a sharp distinction between the legacy of "colonialist" Italian engineers who arrived in the 1930s and early 1940s, or the "scheming" Yugoslav personnel of the late 1940s and the Soviet and Eastern bloc staffs in the 1950s. And yet, relations between foreigners and locals remained fraught with tension.

Nothing exemplified this tension better than questions of pay and privileges.[36] According to some guidelines, Soviet specialists were supposed to receive the same wages that their Albanian counterparts obtained for the same task.[37] In reality, Albanians officials initially paid the Soviet specialists much more than locals and afforded them privileges, prompting the Soviet ambassador to criticize Hoxha in 1952.[38] For many positions, moreover, there were hardly any local counterparts to serve as comparison.

Guidelines were also not clear on non-Soviet personnel. Would they earn the same wages? Well into the 1950s the issue was also complicated by the presence of various other foreigners. Italian specialists and a range of Yugoslavs, as well as a smaller assortment of foreign-born individuals who had moved to Albania in the interwar period, had taken up jobs in construction and were often intentional targets of government policies. It was necessary to formally distinguish between these and the personnel from the "fraternal countries," but it remained unclear how to do so. When the older law regulating wages of foreign personnel was abrogated in 1950, it was decided to pay foreigners who "had been in the country for a while" as if they were Albanians, thus differentiating these from newly arrived Soviet and Eastern bloc personnel.[39] Pay, in other words, was supposed to separate politically useless, or even suspect, foreigners on the one hand and politically significant agents of socialist countries on the other.

This might have worked had it not proven difficult for the authorities themselves to distinguish between foreigners. Back in 1948, for example, they had struggled with a certain Ivan Chekvenik from Trieste, who might have been considered either Italian or Yugoslav.[40] A couple of years later, a construction enterprise faced a similar dilemma when trying to ascribe a nationality to a certain Mikhail Rudmenkin. Records showed that he had come to Albania from Yugoslavia, but since he was a White Russian and had recently obtained Soviet citizenship, it was unclear how he ought "to be treated."[41] Needless to say, for Rudmenkin it made a whole lot of difference if authorities decided to treat him as a Yugoslav or as a Soviet citizen. In the aftermath of the Stalin-Tito split, a number of Russians had moved from Yugoslavia to Albania where they often took jobs in construction. Like Rudmenkin's, their background was at best unclear and possibly suspect.[42] Authorities found it easier to underpay an Italian engineer or a former Yugoslav resident carrying a suspicious past than the personnel of Eastern bloc fraternal states. In the end, classification and pay were as much an outcome of arbitrary decisions as much as a matter of formal guidelines.[43]

The question of foreigners in 1950s Albania was a complicated one. Seemingly technical discussions about pay rates and working conditions actually concealed deeper concerns about political loyalty and the country's geographical isolation from the Eastern bloc. An Interior Ministry report to the Politburo in 1953 identified certain resident foreigners as potential state enemies. Chief among them were recent Yugoslav immigrants, who numbered a little less than 500 (but over 40 had been arrested as alleged spies). Of the other 21,775 foreigners living in Albania, the report noted, it was necessary "to carry out a selection among them and expel undesirables (Lebanese, French, Turks, Jews) as well as repatriate the nationals of friendly countries."[44] A closer look at the report reveals that Mikhail Aristov, an engineer in the same group as Rudmenkin, had been charged as a *bielloguardist* saboteur in construction.[45] The tiny Jewish population in Vlorë, the report claimed, was "connected to American espionage efforts," with a chief of the secret police adding that a Bulgarian ship had made it possible for some of the Jews to even send letters to Israel. There was also the Greek minority in the south that needed to be forcefully told, as Hoxha put it, that "beyond our border is hell and on this side it is heaven."[46] Though authorities seem to have not manifested any political suspicion toward Eastern bloc specialists, they were nevertheless aware that not all of them were party members either.

When it came to decisions to pay foreign specialists, the expectation of sustaining standard norms with Eastern bloc partners could be self-defeating. As rationing was being phased out in 1956, for example, the Czechoslovak embassy in Tirana suggested that resident Czechoslovak specialists receive a bonus to make up for the fact that they would need to purchase food at market prices. It turned out that the Czechoslovak request was supported by a clause in a mutual agreement signed with the Albanian side, which allowed for salary raises in case of domestic measures affecting the standard or living. Yet no similar provision existed with the Soviet Union and the other people's democracies. What was to be done? The Albanian side at first refused, concerned that other countries would follow suit and demand higher salaries for their own specialists—a negative manifestation, as it were, of the tendency of the Eastern bloc to imitate itself.[47] But when Albanian authorities later tried to remove the clause, the Czechoslovak side also refused, arguing that this would upset their specialists.[48] Similarly, when Hungarian premier András Hegedüs asked the freshly arrived Albanian ambassador in Budapest for higher wages for Hungarian specialists in September 1956—a month before the Hungarian Revolution would throw both men into panic—it became clear that Eastern bloc diplomats and officials closely followed agreements and terms among other people's democracies.[49]

Equality among socialist states implied that there ought to be a uniform treatment of the socialist advisers as well. But it was written nowhere that, say, Bulgarians and Czechoslovaks employed in local construction sites were supposed to earn the same wages and receive the same monthly bonus. Here, too, the problem was that bilateral agreements between states and Comecon-related arrangements were often in tension, which was heightened by a prevailing expectation of uniformity. The Albanian position was to try to have it both ways. As early as 1949, trade officials closely observed how much Soviet advisers and technical staff were paid in Bulgaria—information that they used to bargain lower costs in negotiations.[50] Internal secret reports translated from Czech into Russian also provided the Albanians with basic data about cooperation between Czechoslovakia and the USSR as well as the rest of the bloc.[51] Whenever it was beneficial, Albanian authorities used examples of arrangements with the Soviet Union, which were generally favorable to Tirana, to seek similar concessions from the bloc. More often than not, Eastern bloc planning bureaucrats, grudgingly perhaps, made the concessions. But when Albanians were asked to increase contributions, they stalled. To details that Czechoslovak and Polish specialists had complained about tough living conditions, Shehu responded by asserting that even the government's ministers "do not live as comfortably as the Czech specialists here."[52] Being the least developed member of the Comecon seemed to provide room for party and planning authorities to maneuver.[53]

The appearance of uniformity, then, rested on the novel possibilities for comparison that the Eastern bloc brought about. In matters of wages and payments, the achievement of uniformity seemed against all odds. Take, for example, the financial rules regulating the wages of Soviet specialists dispatched to Albania. They were supposed to vary according to professional rank, level of education, and range of experience as well as the nature of the contract signed. That is to say, those Soviet specialists sent according to special government arrangements received wages according to preapproved schedules, which often also included provisions for local travel and vacations.[54] Others' wages, however, were regulated by separate contracts. As it turned out, some Soviet specialists received their allowances in Albanian currency and some in rubles. When they returned to the Soviet Union, the former had effectively earned significantly more due to exchange rates. Some unspoken law of uniformity had been broken, apparently, and the Soviet ambassador promptly requested a revision of technical exchange guidelines.[55]

Looking at payroll records, it becomes clear that there was a hierarchy comprising government advisers and managers, going all the way

Figure 4.4. Albanian Politburo member Gogo Nushi inspects light bulbs at the East German factory VEB Berliner Glühlampenwerk, July 14, 1958. Photo by Rudolf Hesse. Courtesy Bundesarchiv, bild 183-57000-0527.

down to mid-ranking officials, employees, and technical aides. The latter, nevertheless, earned substantial wages compared with the local Albanian workforce.[56] Soviet academics sent to organize schools were also among the highest earners. In the early 1950s Soviet and Eastern bloc specialists earned an average of 10,000 to 12,000 lekë (chief engineers earned more), or twice as much as Albanian specialists. Soviet advisers to branch ministries earned a remarkable 18,000 lekë.[57] Toward the end of the decade, too, records show that the construction branch ministry employed sixteen foreign specialists who were all paid significantly more than any Albanian employee, except the minister, the deputy ministers, and several chiefs of national construction enterprises.[58] As it turned out, officials frequently followed a case-by-case approach when dealing with wages, opting to stretch budgets as far as possible and relying on political maneuvering—the recital of the tenets of socialist solidarity among fraternal countries—when it was financially expedient to do so.

Socialist exchange provided a field for endless comparisons: wages, numbers, percentages, and costs. The Comecon was its formal embodiment, but there were also important informal arrangements at play. This did not mean that Albania always abided by examples drawn from the Eastern bloc, but it did mean that this comparative dimension became increasingly unavoidable. Every Eastern bloc country was constantly engaged in comparisons. Delegations of workers dispatched for study trips compared the working conditions back at home with what they saw in the various people's democracies they visited. Eastern bloc specialists compared achievements in their own countries with the bleak conditions they found in Albanian construction sites or factories. Because comparisons were powerful, it was not possible to control how one employed them. Managers and workers could employ comparisons with other Eastern bloc countries to justify shortcomings or to expose the errors of a colleague. One presumably stood a better chance with authorities if one's reasoning was supported by examples drawn from the people's democracies. Beyond the official propaganda, the press, and the radio, in other words, the bloc was also recreated through contacts and encounters across factories and construction sites.

UNPREDICTABLE ENCOUNTERS

The transfer of socialist experience implied, above all, a movement of peoples. Like the Soviet staff accompanying tractors and industrial machines shipped to Albania during the first Five-Year Plan, Eastern bloc specialists came to the country and locals were sent abroad for training. Numerous encounters took place at all levels of society—in remote villages, in rising industrial towns, in enterprises, mines, construction sites, branch ministries, and in the army. The adoption of discrete socialist practices implied an ongoing process of translation, a negotiation between perceived foreign examples and local circumstances. Throughout this process, the possibility of misunderstanding loomed large.

Faulty translations were often blamed for these misunderstandings. But in matters of industrial design and technology, mere misunderstandings could conceivably produce machine breakdowns, a shortfall in production, and substantial financial loss. These, in turn, could be deemed intentional acts, signs of political subversion. By 1956, for example, there were several reports drawing attention to the cost of translation errors.[59] Translation was a common problem across the Eastern bloc, but it was more widely felt in a country where even cadres capable of using the Russian language were in short supply by the mid-1950s and where they were shuffled around incessantly. Frequently, Albania failed to send trainees or study groups simply because there was a shortage of individuals who spoke the required languages. It became necessary to establish special language courses, but bureaucrats in Tirana complained that they merely delayed planning targets. Even as recent graduates of Soviet and Eastern bloc universities took up positions back home, the problem of translation hardly waned. Technical documents arrived in the hundreds. Given tight budgets and saving campaigns, spending resources on translations often seemed unfeasible. As with Soviet films, which were translated by students enrolled in Soviet universities, technical documents were often informally translated by Soviet advisers or local managers who happened to read Russian. Some of the latter were eager to obtain the assignments as a way of supplementing their wages. But the arrangement also meant that translations could take months, even years.

Although the image of harmony pervaded official propaganda of socialist relations, disagreements among visitors and the local workforce were not uncommon. Conflict often arose because of living conditions, even though foreigners—as a rule—received far better treatment than locals. But some foreigners enjoyed better living conditions than other foreigners. A Soviet doctor brought in to care for the party leadership, for example, also had access to the "leaders' store" (*dyqani i udhëheqjes*), a special retail unit in the capital catering to Politburo and Central Committee chiefs.[60] High-level government advisers enjoyed the same privilege. Housing was another major point of conflict. Soviet and Eastern bloc specialists slept in various hotels because there were no apartments. In one instance, Soviet specialists housed in Hotel Dajti in Tirana were moved out to make room for delegates visiting the capital for a congress.[61] But when the congress had ended, the specialists had not been allowed back into their rooms, which were subsequently occupied by other Eastern bloc specialists. In yet another example, Bulgarian urban planners were housed in an apartment reserved for a Soviet agriculture adviser, who was left without shelter, prompting officials to warn that the incident was "an embarrassment not only for our enterprise but for our state itself."[62] Like wages, housing allocation was supposed to follow professional status. Chief engineers and other high-ranking officials were supposed to be allocated two rooms, with lower-ranking engineers, academics, geologists, and specialists of a similar rank eligible for a single room and a smaller quantity of furniture. Last on the list were ordinary technical workers who were supposed to get shared rooms and were eligible for only basic supplies.[63] In reality, there was less of everything, and it was often allocated arbitrarily.

Take, for example, the reports of the East German mining specialists in Kurbnesh, who wrote in detail to Berlin about their daily impediments. They had been housed more than a kilometer away from the worksite in newly built one-story buildings composed of two rooms, a hallway, a kitchen, and a bath. While there was adequate power, water was available only when the supply pipe from a nearby spring did not freeze or dry up. The group of men had been provided with two women who cooked and cleaned for them, with an additional man entrusted with the task of supplying firewood and foodstuffs. (Due to "chronic laziness," one of them pointed out, this man had proven "practically useless.") Indeed, by local standards, the East German group appears to have been living well, when bearing in mind that ordinary miners and factory construction workers were ravaged by disease and did not even have a cafeteria. Still, the visitors deemed the provision of foodstuffs "distinctly bad." Except bread, sugar, and tea, all other goods had to be brought in by car from Tirana. On rare occasions, there was meat, fruit, and vegetables in the local market. But for the most part, the East Germans observed, "only when German food was delivered was it possible to somewhat adequately feed oneself." Medical services were similarly modest: a young doctor had been stationed in Kurbnesh at some point, but teeth in need of repair required a trip to the polyclinic in Tirana. Regular mail from Kurbnesh to Tirana took three or four days whereas a letter to Germany took fourteen (packaged goods mailed from Germany took two to four months to arrive). In terms of entertainment, old Soviet films were screened in a nearby barrack three or four times a week. Trips to other cities required special permission (*autorizim*), which could only be obtained in a town two hours away. That was reason enough, the East Germans concluded, for the team to refuse any extension to their work contract.[64]

Socialist encounters, then, exposed feelings of superiority and inferiority and dynamics of power replicated within "fraternal states." A Polish group was chastised by the Interior Ministry in 1955 for taking pictures of such "non-socialist" scenes across the countryside as destitute children and gypsies but also "beggars, badly dressed peasants along with their animals, old dirt roads, ruined houses." Such images, the note asserted, "do not correspond to the reality of our country."[65] In their daily work, too, Soviet and Eastern bloc specialists discovered problematic practices at construction sites and enterprises, problems that might have otherwise have gone unreported. A Czechoslovak by the name of Antonin Stupka worked in an Albanian automobile plant from February 1957 to June 1959 (though it was three weeks after he began that he was finally provided with a translator). The working conditions, he reported, were poor and the workers generally unskilled. (It is worth noting here that a large number of the transportation units throughout Albania at that point, like the various Škoda vehicles, were Eastern bloc products.) "Workers generally work as they please," he observed, "without any effective guidance or any controls in place. One can hardly speak of discipline under these conditions."[66] Stupka attempted to enact changes in the plant, but he was forced to intervene directly with the minister to get anything done. In any case, the plan was not fulfilled during his tenure at the plant. Local managers blamed the scarce resources available; the Czechoslovak, however, blamed existing labor practices and poor organization.

Yet another group of East Germans registered similar complaints. One team, sent to Albania to help standardize the production of children's wooden toys, found that the local "industry" consisted merely of two plants, seven smaller shops, and numerous craftsmen who worked with little central supervision. The East Germans also visited a shop specializing in wood products, headed by a Soviet technician. It lacked heating, they observed, and the walls were exposed brick erected on a concrete floor and supporting a shoddy ceiling made of clay bricks and cardboard. Some sectors seemed like temporary structures—indeed, the whole building seemed like a series of poorly executed expansions. The equipment was invariably old. Rooms were filled with dust and covered in chipping.[67] One East German specialist, a certain Linke from VEB Sachsendruck, visited Albanian printing presses in October 1960. He encountered the same shabby equipment and low-skilled workers operating them. But he also made note of poor organization and management problems, and he left detailed reports on how to improve production as well as lists of tasks.[68]

Foreign specialists were both technically useful and politically significant. But they were also a daunting presence, since they served as a constant reminder of the glaring limitations of Albanian industries. By merely doing their work, they were constantly exposing faults. One Czechoslovak specialist, for example, was brought to work in a plant producing pipes used in housing units. The problem was that much of the plant's output came out defective. As the visitor soon discovered, the annual production plan was more than twice as high as the maximum possible output given the plant's capacities. To make up for the shortfall, the plant's workers would significantly cut the heating time for each unit. In addition, they would also fill ovens beyond capacity to increase production quantities. Even if the ambitious plan was ultimately fulfilled, the result was increasing numbers of leaking pipes in newly erected housing units. In another example, a group of East German housing specialists came to experiment with local building materials and the design of low-cost dwellings in the late 1950s. Beyond the usual problems with transportation, the visitors were surprised by the utter lack of a qualified workforce. Eventually, it dawned upon them that the locals had assumed that the East Germans would be building all of the housing units by themselves.[69]

Local managers were not pleased with the foreigners' criticisms and complaints, especially when they exposed deeply entrenched problems. Foreign specialists were also eager to boast about their achievements under such drastic and harsh conditions in Albania. Their reports lingered at length on the immense obstacles they had faced and heroically overcome. While prone to exaggerations and hyperbole, their written reports nevertheless provide clues to the tensions that socialist exchange created at the ground level. At the center of these encounters was the unquestionable enthusiasm about the *potential* of socialist exchange and the deeply entrenched belief that socialist experience could indeed be imparted from a developed country like East Germany or Czechoslovakia to a backward country like Albania. Relations had to be built *as if* the transfer of socialist experience was the only logical outcome. This posture was constantly tested out on the ground, where conflicts inevitably arose due to living and working conditions, misunderstandings, questions of uncertain authority, and foot dragging.[70]

As political relations between Albania and the rest of the Eastern bloc turned sour in the early 1960s, foreign specialists were faulted for missing planning targets and failed operations. This was the other side of socialist exchange. When the Kurbnesh copper enrichment plant failed to go into operation in April 1960, for example, Albanian authorities launched an investigation into the causes of the delay. The minister of mines accused the East German specialists of not working hard enough. "I must note," he wrote to party boss Enver Hoxha, "that the comrades in Kurbnesh also told me that some of the German specialists are not very good." In conclusion, the minister suggested putting pressure on the German ambassador in Tirana to get the East German specialists to comply with local planning targets.[71] Once again, party officials were forced to intervene. Friendly relations seemed to have turned decidedly unfriendly.[72]

Socialist transnational contacts were shaped by the ideological tenets of international socialism just as much as by seemingly objective criteria and comparative advantages. But the paradox of these encounters ran deeper. The factors that helped foster socialist cooperation seem to have been exactly the same ones limiting further integration in the Eastern bloc. Nationalized industries, for example, greatly facilitated exchange among socialist states insofar as they enabled more efficient controls and transfers of personnel "from above." Licenses and patents, similarly, could be freely distributed among centrally planned economies. But centrally planned economies also had a tendency to overemphasize vertical hierarchies to the detriment of horizontal ties between enterprises and agencies. As with trade, techno-scientific cooperation was driven by output considerations, often turning the process into little more than an artifice of the central plan. It was not that *actual* exchange did not occur; rather, it was notoriously difficult to reliably assess its efficiency, or even its overall impact. In short, socialist exchange was both enabled and constrained by radical centralization, output-focused economies, the parallel structure of the party-state, and the formal and informal channels maintained between socialist states. This accounts, in large part, for its contradictory nature: vastly ambitious but inherently self-limiting; planned but also informally arranged; increasingly pervasive but difficult to measure. Its "socialist logic" was manifested both in formal interactions, which were ideologically framed, and the handling of the unintended consequences of those interactions, as illustrated in the factories and construction sites of 1950s Albania. Conceived, in part, as an answer to the Marshall Plan, socialist cooperation entailed the circulation of personnel, patents, and designs, but also ideas, expectations, and terms of comparison. The novelty was that it came to embody all of these imperatives.

NOTES

1. List of foreign specialists working in the enterprises of the Ministry of Mining and Geology, April 25, 1961, Arkivi Qendror Shtetëror (Central State Archives of the Republic of Albania, Tirana, hereafter AQSH), fondi (f.) 537, viti (v.) 1961, dosja (dos.) 156, fleta (fl.) 5; Ministry of Mines and Geology, Section on Foreigners to the Ministry of Interior, December 7, 1960, AQSH, f. 537, v. 1960, dos. 348, fl. 6. Other East Germans (twenty, by mid-1960) had worked in Kurbnesh at one point or another. For examples, see lists contained in a memorandum from the Ministry of Mining and Geology, Foreigners' Sector, October 26, 1961, AQSH, f. 537, v. 1961, dos. 158, fl. 1–13.

2. DDR-TWZ-Gruppe Kurbnesh, "Zusatz zum Abschlussbericht der TWZ-Gruppe (Nur für die deutsche Seite bestimmt!)," September 23, 1961, Bundesarchiv (Archive of the Federal Republic of Germany, Berlin, hereafter BArch), DE1/25483, 55–71.

3. Memorandum on the beginning of operations at the copper enrichment plant in Kurbnesh (Secret), August 11, 1960, AQSH, f. 537, v. 1960, dos. 219, fl. 3–7.

4. List of foreign specialists working on the design and construction of public works in Albania, n.d., AQSH, f. 499, v. 1960, dos. 604, fl. 1.

5. Ministry of Construction statistics on workforce, AQSH, f. 499, v. 1960, dos. 430, fl. 6.

6. List of foreign specialists working in the enterprises of the Ministry of Mining and Geology, April 25, 1961, AQSH, f. 537, v. 1961, dos. 156, fl. 5.

7. Hugh Seton-Watson, *The East European Revolution* (London: Methuen, 1950); Zbigniew Brzezinski, *The Soviet Bloc: Unity and Conflict* (Cambridge, MA: Harvard University Press, 1960); François Fejtö, *A History of the People's Democracies: Eastern Europe since Stalin* (New York: Praeger, 1971).

8. An important early volume was Norman Naimark and Leonid Gibianskii, eds., *The Establishment of Communist Regimes in Eastern Europe, 1944–1949* (Boulder, CO: Westview, 1997). See also Norman Naimark, *The Russians in Germany: A History of the Soviet Zone of Occupation, 1945–1949* (Cambridge, MA: Harvard University Press, 1995); E. A. Rees, "The Sovietization of Eastern Europe," in *The Sovietization of Eastern Europe,* ed. Balázs Apor, Péter Apor, and E. A. Rees (Washington, DC: New Academia Publishing, 2008), 1–28; and the most recent contribution to the subject matter, Vladimir Tismaneanu, ed., *Stalinism Revisited: The Establishment of Communist Regimes in East-Central Europe* (Budapest and New York: Central University Press, 2009). For a useful summary of Russian historiographical approaches to these issues, see Norman M. Naimark, "Post-Soviet Russian Historiography on the Emergence of the Soviet Bloc," *Kritika* 5, no. 3 (Summer 2004): 561–80.

9. Stephen Kotkin and Charles Armstrong, "A Socialist Regional Order in Northeast Asia after World War II," in *Korea at the Center: Dynamics of Regionalism in Northeast Asia,* ed. Charles K. Armstrong et al. (New York: M. E. Sharpe, 2006), 110–25; Thomas P. Bernstein and Hua-yu Li, eds., *China Learns from the Soviet Union, 1949–Present* (Lanham, MD: Lexington Books, 2010).

10. Overviews include David C. Engerman and Corinna R. Unger, "Introduction: Towards a Global History of Modernization," *Diplomatic History* 33, no. 3 (June 2009): 375–85; Frederick Cooper, "Writing the History of Development," in *Modernizing Missions: Approaches to "Developing" the Non-Western World after 1945,* special issue of *Journal of Modern European History* 8, no. 1 (January 2010): 5–23; and Marc Frey and Sönke Kunkel, "Writing the History of Development: A Review of the Recent Literature," *Contemporary European History* 20, no. 2 (May 2011): 215–32. Some historians of science and technology have been more attuned to the mechanics of transmission within the socialist world. See, for example, Paul Josephson, *Would Trotsky Wear a Bluetooth?: Technological Utopianism under Socialism, 1917–1989* (Baltimore: Johns Hopkins University Press, 2010).

11. Stephen Kotkin, "Mongol Commonwealth? Exchange and Governance across the Post-Mongol Space," *Kritika* 8, no. 3 (Summer 2007): 487–531, quotation on 525.

12. In advocating for a transnational approach to Soviet history, Michael David-Fox has pointed to the European approaches of *Histoire croisée* and *Transfergeschichte.* See Michael David-Fox, "Multiple Modernities vs. Neo-Traditionalism: On Recent Debates in Russian and Soviet History," *Jahrbücher für Geschichte Osteuropas* 54, no. 4 (2006): 535–55.

13. Referring to state-led techno-scientific exchange among socialist countries, one official pamphlet put it this way: "World History knows of no such examples when scientific and technological achievements worth hundreds of millions of rubles were handed over gratis to other countries to help them accelerate their progress." Council for Mutual Economic Assistance, *A Survey of 20 Years of the Council for Mutual Economic Assistance* (Moscow: CMEA Secretariat, 1969), 64.

14. For an overview of Soviet and Eastern bloc exchanges and planning assistance to the developing world, in the context of more broadly transnational currents, see Stephen V. Ward, "Transnational Planners in a Postcolonial World," in *Crossing Borders: International Exchange and Planning Practices,* ed. Patsy Healey and Robert Upton (London and New York: Routledge, 2010), 47–72.

15. On the Comecon, see Michael Kaser, *Comecon: Integration Problems of the Planned Economies,* 2nd ed. (London: Oxford University Press, 1967); Andrzej Korbonski, "Comecon," *International Conciliation* 549 (September 1964): 3–62; Kazimierz Grzybowski, *The Socialist Commonwealth of Nations: Organization and Institutions* (New Haven and London: Yale University Press, 1964), 64–171; Henry W. Schaefer, *Comecon and the Politics of Integration* (New York: Praeger, 1972); Adam Zwass, *The Council for Mutual Economic Assistance: The Thorny Path from Political to Economic Integration* (Armonk, NY: Sharpe, 1989), esp. 3–52.

16. Kaser, *Comecon,* 10.

17. "Technisch-wissenschaftliche Zusammenarbeit, das ist Freundschaft," November 1950, BArch, DE1/10676.

18. Techno-scientific cooperation agreements between Eastern bloc countries were first signed in 1947, though informal arrangements had been reached before then. For example, Albania requested Czechoslovak specialists as early as in 1945. When asking (via Belgrade) for Czechoslovak specialists in a range of areas from agriculture and water management to fishing and mining, as well as a special envoy for matters of information and propaganda, the Albanian side spoke of "a moral assistance to our Democratic Government." See Ministry of Economics, Department of Trade, to the Council of Ministers, November 26, 1945, AQSH, f. 490, v. 1945, dos. 124, fl. 1.

19. For a brief assessment of the argument that Comecon's activity during the period 1949–53 was almost wholly inconsequential, see Włodzimierz Brus, "1950 to 1953: The Peak of Stalinism," in *The Economic History of Eastern Europe 1919–1975,* ed. M. C. Kaser (Oxford: Clarendon Press, 1986), 3:4, esp. note 1.

20. Brus, "1957 to 1965: In Search of Balanced Development," in Kaser, *Economic History of Eastern Europe,* 3:73.

21. There were some efforts to intensify socialist exchange via the Comecon in 1953. The Albanian ambassador in Moscow, who received Comecon instructions that year, reported that technical exchange was "a new form of cooperation among our countries"—one that did not and could not exist under capitalism. Moscow to Tirana, October 31, 1953 (Top Secret), Arkivi i Ministrisë së Punëve të Jashtme (Archive of the Ministry of Foreign Affairs of the Republic of Albania, Tirana, hereafter AMPJ), v. 1953, dos. 51, fl. 81.

22. Albrecht Martiny, *Bauen und Wohnen in der Sowjetunion nach dem Zweiten Weltkrieg: Bauarbeiterschaft, Architektur und Wohnverhältnisse im sozialen Wandel* (Berlin: Berlin Verlag, 1983).

23. Greg Castillo, *Cold War on the Home Front: The Soft Power of Midcentury Design* (Minneapolis: University of Minnesota Press, 2010), xi.

24. Transcript of meeting of the Party of Labor of Albania (PLA) Politburo, May 28, 1958, AQSH, f. 14/ap (PLA Central Committee), Organe Udhëheqëse (Leading Organs), v. 1958, dos. 13, fl. 39. See also Russian Embassy in Tirana to the Soviet Ministry of Foreign Affairs, forwarded to Mikhail Suslov, "O polozhenii s ispol'zovaniem kreditov, predostavliaemykh Albanii Sovetskim Soiuzom i stranami narodnov demokratii" (Secret), September 24, 1956, Rossiskii Gosudarstvennyi Arkhiv Noveishei Istorii (Russian State Archive of Contemporary History, Moscow), f. 5, op. 28, d. 391, l. 194.

25. On the endurance of bilateralism in Soviet–Eastern bloc trade, see Charles Gati, *The Bloc That Failed: Soviet-East European Relations in Transition* (Bloomington: Indiana University Press, 1990), 124–35.

26. Kaser, *Comecon,* 5, emphasis added. The Organization for Economic Cooperation and Development (OECD) succeeded the OEEC in 1961. The European Free Trade Association (EFTA) was established in 1960. Kaser observed that problems of socialist integration were increasingly linked to questions of domestic economic reform in the various member countries, but most importantly the Soviet Union: "The absence of criteria whereby the Soviet economy can measure its own goals and its own performance has for fifteen years been the crucial issue on which Comecon integration has foundered" (26).

27. Brus, "1957 to 1965," 116.

28. P. J. D Wiles, *Communist International Economics* (New York: Praeger, 1969), 311.

29. See, for example, "Die zweiseitige wirtschaftliche und technisch-wissenschaftliche Zusammenarbeit," n.d., BArch, DE1/25483, 853–58.

30. For an overview of socialist techno-scientific exchange written by a Comecon official, see T. Azarov, "Problems in Coordinating the Scientific and Technical Research of Comecon Countries," *Eastern European Economics* 2, no. 4 (Summer 1964), 11–16. Other overviews include O. A. Chukanov, ed., *Nauchno-tekhnicheskoe sotrudnichestvo stran SEV: Spravochnik* (Moscow: Ekonomika, 1986); US Bureau of the Census, *Integration of Science and Technology in CEMA,* Foreign Economic Report No. 21 (Washington, DC: US Government Printing Office, 1983), 3–7; Kaser, *Comecon,* 56–57; Aleksandr Numovich Bykov, *Nauchno-tekhnicheskiie sviiazi stran sotsializma* (Moscow: Mysl,' 1970); and Bykov, *Soviet Experience in Transfer of Technology to Industrially Less Developed Countries* (New York: UN Institute for Training and Research, 1973).

31. Bykov, *Nauchno-tekhnicheskiie sviiazi,* 68–69.

32. Austin Jersild, "The Soviet State as Imperial Scavenger: 'Catch Up and Surpass' in the Transnational Socialist Bloc, 1950–1960," *American Historical Review* 116, no. 1 (February 2011): 109–32. "Scavenging," nevertheless, does not explain unreciprocated development aid in the Eastern bloc.

33. Albanian diplomatic mission in Warsaw to the Ministry of Foreign Affairs, April 14, 1950, AMPJ, v. 1950, dos. 88, fl. 6 (verso).

34. "Varshava, 5.12.1959," letter typed in Russian, AQSH, f. 490, v. 1959, dos. 1199, fl. 53.

35. Albanian planning chief Spiro Koleka admitted as much in 1958. See memorandum on the conference of representatives of the communist and workers' parties of member states of Comecon (Top Secret), May 27, 1958, AQSH, f. 14/ap, ou, v. 1958, dos. 13.

36. Already in 1949, the Soviet government took up the issue of standardizing the salaries of Soviet specialists dispatched to Korea and Albania, but also Romania, Hungary, Czechoslovakia, and Bulgaria. See Andrei Gromyko's letter to Stalin dated October 6, 1949, printed in V. Volokitina et al., eds., *Sovetskii faktor v Vostochnoi Evrope, 1944–1953: Dokumenty,* (Moscow: ROSSPEN, 2002), 2:182–84.

37. "Relacion mbi çështjen e këshilltarëve dhe specialistëve të vendeve miq që ndod-

hen në vendin t'onë (me përjashtim të ushtarakëve)," memorandum on advisers and specialists from friendly countries present in Albania with the exception of military personnel, December 24, 1956, AQSH, f. 490, v. 1956, dos. 1079, fl. 62.

38. "Zapis' besedy," memorandum of conversation between K. D. Levychkin (Soviet ambassador) and Hoxha dated August 9, 1952, printed in Volokitina et al., *Sovetskii faktor,* 2:678–80.

39. Office of the Prime Minister, Section on Organizational Structures and Categorizations, August 25, 1951, AQSH, f. 490, v. 1951, dos. 160, fl. 2.

40. Ministry of Construction correspondence, AQSH, f. 499, v. 1948, dos. 117, fl. 1.

41. Ministry of Construction correspondence, AQSH, f. 499, v. 1951, dos. 160, fl. 46.

42. In the aftermath of the Stalin-Tito split, some seventy-three "Russian immigrants" arrived in Albania from Yugoslavia, most of them holding Soviet citizenship. PLA leaders were immensely suspicious of this group, and in 1951 Hoxha urged Stalin to repatriate them. Hoxha to Stalin, March 6, 1951, AQSH, f. 14/ap, ou, v. 1951, dos. 4, fl. 1. The particular group referred to here, attached to the design enterprise, had started work in Albania at some point between December 1949 and January 1950. See Ministry of Public Works, Personnel Branch, to Office of Prime Minister, March 4, 1950, with attached list of employees, AQSH, f. 499, v. 1950, dos. 104, fl. 5–6.

43. Ministry of Foreign Affairs memorandum on foreign specialists and their wages, AMPJ, v. 1956, dos. 26/1, fl. 61/1.

44. Report of Mehmet Shehu on party and state enemies to the PLA Politburo, January 20, 1953, AQSH, f. 14/ap, ou, v. 1953, dos. 8, fl. 14–15.

45. Ibid., fl. 18.

46. Ibid., fl. 107.

47. Embassy of Czechoslovakia in Tirana to Shinasi Dragoti, January 9, 1956, AQSH, f. 490, v. 1956, dos. 1079, fl. 1–3.

48. Note from the Embassy of Czechoslovakia in Tirana to Ministry of Foreign Affairs, July 19, 1956, AMPJ, v. 1956, dos. 74, fl. 7.

49. Embassy of Albania in Budapest, "Relacion," memorandum on the ambassador's meetings during August and September 1956, AMPJ, v. 1956, dos. 14/6, fl. 20–22.

50. Correspondence on trade terms with Bulgaria, AQSH, f. 490, v. 1949, dos. 437, fl. 65–66 (verso).

51. "Informatsiia o nauchno-tekhnicheskom sotrudnichestve v 1955 godu" (Secret), n.d., AQSH, f. 490, v. 1955, dos. 1163, fl. 151–69. In addition to containing statistics, these Czechoslovak reports provided the Albanian side with a blueprint on how to organize technical transfer. See, for example, "Raport mbi punën e B. T. Shkencor," memorandum on technical-scientific cooperation, March 1, 1956, AQSH, f. 490, v. 1956, dos. 1060, fl. 18. The Albanians were not the only ones engaging in these kinds of comparisons. GDR planning bureaucrats, who, like the Soviets, fully subsidized the transfer of technology to Albania, consulted with Poland and Czechoslovakia to figure out what kind of aid they were providing. See "Aufstellung über die finanziellen Zuwendungen an die Volksrepublik Albanien" (Streng vertraulich), July 28, 1959, BArch, Stiftung Archiv der Parteien und Massenorganisationen der DDR (hereafter SAPMO), DY30/IV2/20/98; "Finanzierung der technisch-wissenschaftlichen Zusammenarbeit," n.d. (dated 1956 by hand), BArch, DE1/1963.

52. "Proçes-Verbal," transcript of meeting of the Council of Ministers, February 6, 1957, AQSH, f. 490, v. 1957, dos. 1168, fl. 30. The Czechoslovaks were, in fact, the highest paid specialists of all, including Soviet ones.

53. Memorandum on foreign specialists, AMPJ, v. 1956, dos. 26/1, fl. 61.

54. Office of the Prime Minister, Organograms and Categorization Sector, to all ministries, August 25, 1951, AQSH, f. 490, v. 1951, dos. 160, fl. 2.

55. Memorandum to premier Mehmet Shehu (Top Secret), June 2, 1955, AMPJ, v. 1955, dos. 79, fl. 53.

56. "Vendim," Council of Ministers decision no. 442 on the specification of wages of Soviet specialists and technical staff, July 5, 1952, AQSH, f. 490, v. 1952, dos. 464, fl. 1.

57. Government circular on foreign specialists, AQSH, f. 499, v. 1951, dos. 160, fl. 9.

58. Ministry of Construction schedules of wages of foreign engineers during the period September 16–30, 1958, AQSH, f. 499, v. 1958, dos. 956/2, fl. 2, 160.

59. Ministry of Foreign Affairs memorandum on problems in the sector of technical-scientific cooperation, n.d., AMPJ, v. 1956, dos. 26/1, fl. 10.

60. Section on Technical Cooperation to the Ministry of Trade on the status of the Soviet doctor Nikolai Ivanovich Tulipov, June 18, 1952, AQSH, f. 490, v. 1952, dos. 464, fl. 6–7.

61. Soviet specialists living in the hotel included professors, deputy directors at various enterprises, and advisers in state agencies and at the Soviet-designed Stalin Textile Works in the outskirts of Tirana. "Mbi lëvizjet e teknikëve dhe specialistëve të huaj në Dajti, me rastin e festës 29 Nëntor," memorandum from Hotel Dajti on the relocation of Soviet specialists, December 29, 1952, AQSH, f. 14/ap, ou, v. 1952, dos. 66/2, fl. 71–72.

62. Information for the minister of construction Josif Pashko and deputy premier Koço Theodhosi on foreign technical personnel, April 6, 1956, AQSH, f. 499, v. 1956, dos. 190, fl. 6.

63. Schedules of furniture provisions and supplies to the foreign technical personnel divided in categories, n.d., AQSH, f. 499, v. 1956, dos. 194, fl. 1–3.

64. DDR-TWZ-Gruppe Kurbnesh, "Zusatz zum Abschlussbericht," BArch, DE1/25483, 55–71.

65. Ministry of Interior to premier Mehmet Shehu (Top Secret), September 22, 1955, AQSH, f. 490, v. 1955, dos. 743, fl. 1.

66. Final memorandum of Antonin Stupka between January 1957 and June 1959, June 18, 1959, AQSH, f. 490, v. 1959, dos. 1188, fl. 6.

67. Siegfried Wiedemann, VEB Seiffener Spielwaren, "Studienbericht," October 22, 1958, BArch, DE1/26906.

68. Filed reports from Linke, October 29, 1960, December 1, 1960, and January 10, 1961, BArch, DE1/26906.

69. Memorandum to the deputy premier Koço Theodhosi, August 6, 1959, AQSH, f. 490, v. 1959, dos. 1195, fl. 1.

70. Eastern bloc disagreements were not limited to Albania. By the late 1950s and early 1960s, GDR planning officials noted several instances of disagreements with the Bulgarians and Romanians on technical aid terms. See the correspondence of the GDR-Romanian mixed commission, June 12, 1958, BArch, DE1/25478; and "Weiterführung der zweiseitigen Zusammenarbeit mit der Volksrepublik Bulgarien," October 19, 1960, BArch, DE1/25484, 874.

71. Ministry of Mines and Geology to Enver Hoxha and Mehmet Shehu (Secret), April 7, 1960, AQSH, f. 537, v. 1960, dos. 219, fl. 1–2.

72. Meanwhile, in Berlin, East German planning officials complained that Albania lacked the necessary cadres to fully absorb socialist experience, which had led Germans specialists to spend far more time with Albanian problems without obtaining satisfactory results. See "Zusammenarbeit der DDR-VRA," October 12, 1960, BArch, DE1/21355. From then on, GDR officials reasoned that exchange terms with the country would have to follow the same rules as with any other country. See Staatliche Plankommission, "Beschluss," n.d., BArch, DE1/25484, 927.

5

THE SOVIET-SOUTH ENCOUNTER

Tensions in the Friendship with Afro-Asian Partners, 1945–1965

CONSTANTIN KATSAKIORIS

Devastated, divided, and reduced, post–World War II Europe could hardly envisage the near future with much optimism or self-assurance. In the East, Stalin was redesigning the boundaries and establishing Soviet control over half of the continent. In the South, the colonial possessions, those territories of vital importance both for the wartime effort and for the postwar recovery, symbols of pride and strength, were in revolt against the weakened or humiliated metropoles.[1] National independence movements were gaining momentum, many of them professing a radical agenda. Mao's victory in China, the establishment of communism in North Korea, the communist insurgency in British Malaya, and Ho Chi Minh's liberation movement in French Indochina were more than inauspicious presages. The list of potential communist leaders and countries was long. After Eastern Europe and China, would communism spread over the Southern Hemisphere? Would the paths of the East and the South cross, and what would be the outcome of their encounter?

From the early years of the Cold War the expansion of communism in the colonial and newly independent world became a distressful concern that haunted many Western observers, politicians, journalists, and scholars. Global developments and the rise of Soviet power were giving this concern firm ground. After the Asian independence movements, Africa's decolonization occurred during a period in which the Soviet Union was professing its economic development and scientific superiority and was all the more assertive in global affairs. In the West, prominent political scientists were mobilized in order to map out and forecast Soviet policies and to explain the appeal of communism for Third World nationalists. For all their attentive analysis and reservations about the prospects of the Soviet-South alliance, they emphatically pointed out that Moscow was advancing a well-orchestrated political offensive and that among its most vulnerable targets were intellectuals, middle-class nationalists, and youth.[2]

Contemporary scholarship on Soviet-South relations still draws from the work of Cold War political scientists. However, capitalizing on the opening of many archives, as well as on the distance that separates them from the period of the superpowers' rivalry, historians of the post–Cold War era have contributed to a significant readjustment of earlier mainstream interpretations. This readjustment mainly consists of the rejection of the ideas of Soviet tutelage and grand strategy, as well as in the acknowledgment and significant revaluation of the agency of Third World partners and allies in the tug-of-war of the Soviet-South relationship.[3] At the same time new research, which brought into focus concrete cases of cooperation and exchange, has revealed the tensions and ambiguities of this relationship, as well as the deceptions engaged in by both sides beyond the façade of their public statements.[4]

This essay revisits those years when the Africans and Arabs, in revolt against colonialism, encountered the Soviet superpower, and concentrates on the tensions and frustrations that resulted from their postwar contacts. The aim here is to deny neither the strength of the Soviet soft power nor its appeal to the Third World. It is rather to point out that the nationalist "friends" of the communist superpower often adopted a very critical stance regarding both the international policies and the friendship offensive of the USSR. Their stance took shape in the face of the ambiguities and the volte-face of Soviet policies and was clearly expressed in the course of their tumultuous encounters with Soviet cultural officials and writers. Besides political and ideological frictions, disillusionment loomed large when news about hostile attitudes and violent incidents against darker students in the Soviet Union overshadowed what was conceived of as a cornerstone of the Soviet-South friendship: the training of students at Soviet educational institutes. Students themselves were the first to reconsider their assumptions.

On the Soviet side too, beyond the official rhetoric of internationalism, disinterested solidarity, and people's friendship, the encounter with the Southerners generated serious reservations, deceptions, and reactions.

Cultural officials expressed their frustration and sometimes adopted dismissive attitudes vis-à-vis their African and Arab counterparts. Many Soviet citizens also reacted to the presence of the students of color who came to study in the USSR. If, despite their frustration, officials and scholars had to maintain their mission to convince the Southerners of the superiority of the Soviet Union, students and citizens were more eager to react and did not seem to subscribe either to the objectives or to the rhetoric of the Kremlin. Some of them overtly expressed their disappointment with their own country's regime to the Southern guests, while others took umbrage at what they considered to be the visitors' freer and more privileged life. Their reactions evidenced that they were angry at their government's generosity to the Third World guests. And their exasperation was not only fomenting tensions but also undermining the Soviet Union's assumptions of superiority over the backward Southerners that it sought to educate, modernize, and liberate from Western exploitation.

This exploration of the discrepancies between the official discourses and various unofficial attitudes aims at shedding some new light on the views and the mutual appraisals of both sides.[5] In the first and second parts of this essay I examine the establishment and the early development of relations with African and Arab activists and intellectuals. The third part will be devoted to the tensions that emerged in the early sixties, when students started arriving at the Soviet Union.

MOSCOW AND THE ANTI-COLONIAL MOVEMENTS: FROM DISDAIN TO RAPPROCHEMENT

In the aftermath of World War II the independence of African and Arab countries was not an issue of primary importance for Soviet international policy. The Pyrrhic triumph over the Third Reich had left the Soviet Union ruined and exhausted. The task of domestic reconstruction was urgent and colossal, while the consolidation of Soviet power from the Balkans to central Europe constituted Stalin's strategic imperative. Ambitions for expansion in the Middle East and the Mediterranean existed, yet, in the face of a firm Anglo-American stance, Moscow did not persist in its demands for a Soviet mandate and naval bases in the former Italian colony of Libya, and pulled the Soviet army out of northern Iran.[6]

Although unsuccessful, such attempts to seize opportunities for quick geopolitical advances were compatible with Stalin's views on the conduct of foreign policy. However, any Soviet commitment in the noncommunist Afro-Asian countries was overtly incompatible with the Soviet leader's ideological convictions and world perceptions. His repulsion for Afro-Asian nationalism had been cemented in 1927 when Chiang Kai-shek, until then supported by the Soviet Union, turned his arms against his Chinese communist allies. After the war, tactful suggestions for a more flexible stance toward independent India had no impact on Soviet policy. In 1952 at the Nineteenth Party Congress Stalin vigorously denounced the bourgeoisie as the chief enemy of any liberation movement.[7] Stalin remained extremely suspicious of the bourgeois nationalist proclivities of even such an accredited communist leader as Ho Chi Minh.[8]

In that ideological and political climate Moscow's official position regarding decolonization in the global South was clear: any support for the so-called bourgeois nationalist movements was meaningless, because countries liberated from colonialism yet ruled by native bourgeois governments were not truly independent, but remained integral parts of the Western capitalist system. True independence could be assured only through the rule of a workers' party implementing an anti-capitalist program and serving the interests of the working class. The leading figure among the few Soviet Africanists, Ivan Potekhin, praised the "anti-imperialist union of workers and peasants" in British East Africa, while expressing his distrust for the "national bourgeoisie and intelligentsia."[9] In the same official line, the young Orientalist Evgenii Primakov underscored that the growth of the working class in the Arab world, and particularly in Saudi Arabia and Egypt, was opening revolutionary prospects for the future.[10] But where the working class was small, the conditions for support were not fulfilled and Soviet detachment was justified.

The Soviets' reluctance to involve themselves in the colonial question constituted a serious impediment to the efforts of European communists to rally the Arab and African sympathizers to their cause. This was particularly the point of view of French communists in Algeria who were addressing letters to Soviet organizations asking them for a more active cultural policy. French trade unionists were decrying the living conditions of the Algerian working class and condemning the discriminations imposed by the metropole. In support of their demands for justice and equality of rights they argued that "Algeria is a French department and not a colony."[11] The leading French members of the Algerian Association of Friends of the

Soviet Union were pressing the Soviets to invite Arab sympathizers and give them the chance to visit the Soviet "Muslim republics, so that with their return they will be able to speak in front of Muslims and tell them their impressions of the Soviet Union."[12] Addressing the French demands, the All-Union Society for Cultural Relations with Foreign Countries (VOKS) received in 1950 a delegation from Maghreb composed almost exclusively by Arab members, among which was the Algerian communist writer Kateb Yacine.[13] Upon their return to Maghreb two Algerian trade unionists wrote a letter to the VOKS expressing their admiration for the achievements of Soviet industry and promising to do "their best possible in order to propagate everywhere" what they saw in the USSR.[14] Kateb Yacine himself published in the Algerian press his poem "The Red Star" and an account of his impressions from the USSR and particularly from Uzbekistan, stressing that Soviet rule had eliminated both "racism and religious persecutions."[15]

Pressure from the French comrades was thus crucial in the establishment of contacts between the Soviets and the Arabs. Behind their insistence lay the idea that Arab travelers to the Soviet Union would be convinced by the Soviet example and support the line of the French Communist Party (PCF) that the French Union should be transformed according to the model of the Soviet Union. The need to mobilize Arab communists and sympathizers against those nationalists who demanded immediate independence was an argument that the French invoked in their discussions with the Soviets and that the latter seemed to share.[16] An important premise of this political line was that neither Arabs nor Africans were mature enough for independence. The idea of transforming the French Union according to the model of the Soviet Union implied that since the Russians had the upper hand inside the USSR, the French should preserve their dominant role inside the French Union. From that position they would lead the Arab and African peoples of the socialist French Union down the path of progress as the Soviets had done, thanks to Bolshevik rule, for the Asian and Caucasian nations of the Soviet empire.[17] For all the adherence of Arabs and Africans to the idea of equality of rights inside the French Union, it soon became clear that such a political perspective was alienating the biggest part of the politically active population, especially in the Maghreb.[18]

French friends of the Soviet Union also played a significant role in the extension of the network of the World Peace Council. This Soviet-led international organization, campaigning for disarmament and against a third world war, had gained the support of African American personalities such as Paul Robeson and W. E. B. Du Bois. Another prominent member of the council was Ceza Nabaraoui, the cosmopolitan Egyptian feminist who also became the representative of Afro-Asian women in another Soviet-led organization, the International Democratic Federation of Women.[19] But besides those famous participants, the president of the council, the French physician Frédéric Joliot-Curie, and the secretary-general, Jean Lafitte, made constant efforts to integrate representatives from Arab and African peace committees of the French Union into the council's activities. As a result, the Congress of the Peoples for Peace, which took place in December 1952 in Vienna under the auspices of the council, brought together anti-colonial activists from all over the French Empire.

The Vienna congress gave the Southern activists an important tribune to denounce imperialism and to formulate their political claims. However, at the same time, it revealed a serious divergence of views between, on the one side, Soviets and Europeans and, on the other, the representatives of the colonial South. Two African delegates, Latyr Camara and Jacques N'Gom, expressed their repugnance for American imperialism and racial discrimination in the United States, but they also did not miss the opportunity to denounce the French imperial yoke and to call for self-determination and independence of the colonial countries.[20] The Arab representatives were even more adamant in their political views. A delegate from Algeria denounced the French inclusion against the will of Algerians, and added that peace was conceivable only when people live free following "their customs, their traditions, their own national life." Quoting both Roosevelt and Stalin, another delegate called for the immediate national independence and sovereignty of Algeria. Delegates from Morocco and Tunisia also demanded the end of the protectorate and the proclamation of national independence. References to the Gospels and the Koran were used in support of these anti-colonialist claims.[21]

The interventions of the African and Arab delegates were clearly against the wishes of the organizers. The Southerners had seized the opportunity of the peace congress to put forward their claims for national independence, or, in other words, for peace through decolonization. For the Soviets and for their French comrades, however, world peace did not mean decolonization but common struggle against capitalism and American imperialism. The independence of the African and Arab countries was not a prerequisite for peace. Commenting on the participants of the peace movement, a Soviet report demarcated the European and Asian organizations from those in "Africa, Near and Middle East," acknowledging that for the latter "the struggle for national independence has a primary significance, but this is not sufficiently articulated with the struggle for peace," adding that this political line was not compatible with the "directives of the World Peace Council and the peoples' aspirations."[22]

Obviously the Soviets did not know the "peoples' aspirations" better than the Africans and Arabs themselves. Seeing the South through the lens of Stalin's doctrine, Soviet officials faced the demands of their guests with indifference and mistrust. Arabs' and Africans' national and religious rhetoric irritated the Soviets, and this became evident not only in the peace congress, but also in the course of their encounters in the Soviet Union. In fact, from the beginning of the 1950s delegations of trade unionists from the colonial countries started arriving in the USSR, either following their training at the School of the International Federation of Trade Unions in Budapest or at the invitation of Soviet organizations. Many trade unionists were suspicious of the Soviet Union and provoked the embarrassment of their hosts with their demands to visit churches and mosques in order to interview the priests and muftis and to examine the important question, for them, of religious freedom in the USSR.[23] Apart from their religious sensibilities, their Soviet hosts took a dim view of their lack of class consciousness and nationalist world view. Two Ghanaian trade unionists, who visited the Soviet Union in 1954 after their training in Budapest, were depicted as members of the "petit bourgeois Convention People's Party," as the nationalist party of Kwame Nkrumah was still catalogued. One of them, the secretary-general of the trade union of sailors and longshoremen, was criticized by the Soviet guide because "he was very hastily associating the struggle of workers in the Gold Coast with national liberation," expressed petit bourgeois opinions, and behaved like a tourist.[24] A delegation of African trade unionists, which visited the USSR in 1957 for the anniversary of the October Revolution, also left their hosts with mixed impressions. A Soviet official commented that one of them "considers himself a communist, but has not read Lenin," a second one "goes far beyond the narrow ideas of nationalism" but was still using a racial rhetoric and depicting his fellows as "whites with black skin," while for a third trade unionist "the narrowness of his nationalistic world view does not allow him to consider the achievements of the Soviet government from an international point of view." At the end of his report the Soviet official argued that the sojourn had a positive impact on the foreign guests, but that still "the discussions which took place among delegates demonstrated that not all of what they saw and learned is clear to them, yet obviously, they made efforts to understand it, even if sometimes it was very difficult for them."[25]

Such comments and conclusions were characteristic of the Soviet attitude vis-à-vis colonial activists and their claims. Being incompatible with the priorities of Soviet international policy, their national aspirations were considered immature and nonprogressive. Progressive, for the Soviets, meant subscribing to their state's international policy and downplaying national aspirations. Contrary ideas or remarks were considered as a failure to understand the Soviets' sophisticated arguments. This failure to appreciate the rightness of Soviet assumptions became an easy and typical conclusion that the Soviets generally attributed to the impact of Western colonialism and propaganda and to the subsequent petit bourgeois mentality of many Southerners.

On the African and Arab side, however, there was clearly little misunderstanding. For the majority of activists the priorities were self-determination and independence, and as far as the Soviets were ignoring or downgrading their claims, their attitude provoked disenchantment. Disenchantment with the Soviets and European communists was a reason for, and at the same time a strong message in, the very influential book *Pan-Africanism or Communism,* published by the onetime Comintern cadre from Trinidad, George Padmore, in 1955. Padmore was decrying the "political and cultural totalitarianism of the East" and the efforts of the Soviets, through the British and French communist parties, to infiltrate African trade unionism and to subordinate anti-colonial nationalism to the interests of Moscow's foreign policy.[26] Padmore's message to all African nationalists was clear: they should have no illusions about Soviet and European intentions and they had to oppose the communists' maneuvers.

The disenchantment of Arab anti-colonialist activists was especially a consequence of the ambiguous stance that the Soviets and their French comrades maintained vis-à-vis the Algerian question and of Moscow's tacit acquiescence to favor political solutions inside the framework of the French Union. The decisive blow to the influence of communists came after the decision of the French Communist Party, in March 1956, to vote for the accordance of special powers to the French government to settle the Algerian question—in other words, to stamp out the revolution. That decision provoked the disillusionment of Arab sympathizers and the resignation from the Algerian Communist Party of such members as the writers Kateb Yacine and Malek Haddad. In 1962 the latter, during a trip to the Soviet Union, reminded his Soviet hosts that "the attitude of French communists towards the fighting Algeria did not attest even a single Leninist principle of proletarian internationalism," that the Algerian Communist Party "was discredited in the eyes of people," and that "in Algeria they will remember for a long time the communists with bitter words."[27] Nevertheless, behind the blame assigned to the French communists, the Soviets had also been stigmatized as responsible for the stance against independence.

Significant tensions had been thus accumulated in the relations between Soviets and Southerners during the first postwar decade, notably because of conflicting views on the anti-colonial movements in Africa and elsewhere. The Soviet critique of nationalism and of bourgeois-led self-rule, as well as the entente with European communists, had alienated the Southerners and marked Soviet-South encounters with frustration and distrust. Yet, after 1953, in the face of growing national assertiveness, the Algerian revolution, and the impact of the Bandung Conference, Stalin's international policy came under attack. The new Soviet leadership repositioned the Soviet Union in global affairs and inaugurated a decisive turn toward addressing the demands of the Third World.

Capturing the Afro-Asian nationalisms became a major objective for Nikita Khrushchev, who seemed convinced that the time of the colonial world's awakening had come and that the Soviet Union had to stand on the right side of history. The Suez crisis gave him the chance to engage in Afro-Asian politics, through the Middle East, and to build bridges with new desirable partners. Moreover, by backing Nasser, who was an anti-communist, Moscow sent the clear message that the Soviet Union was ready to put aside its previous ideologically justified reluctance and to pursue an alliance with nationalist regimes against the West, on the basis primarily of anti-imperialism and secondarily of anti-capitalism. The formerly dismissed Afro-Asian bourgeois nationalists thus became the targets of a Soviet friendship offensive. This shift in Soviet global policy was imprinted on the new hierarchy of international allies for peace and against imperialism that the communist parties of the socialist countries proclaimed in Moscow in November 1957. Behind the "invincible camp of the socialist countries, guided by the Soviet Union" stood "the Asian and African nationalist governments, which maintain an anti-imperialist stance and constitute, together with the socialist countries, a vast zone of peace." Beyond them were enlisted the international working class, the massive peace movements, and finally, in this unorthodox yet very revealing hierarchy, the neutral European and Latin American countries as well as the popular masses of the imperialist countries.[28]

This shift in the mid-1950s was certainly of enormous importance. However, building friendships and alliances with African and Asian countries was not at all an easy task. As already noted, the decision of the PCF in March 1956 to back the French government against the Algerian revolutionaries dramatically damaged the influence of communists in the Maghreb. In this same period the report of Nikita Khrushchev at the Twentieth Congress of the Communist Party of the Soviet Union (CPSU) and the revelation of Stalinist crimes had a profound impact not only in the West but also in the South. One of the most resounding reactions to these revelations was undoubtedly the *Letter to Maurice Thorez,* through which the Antillean intellectual Aimé Césaire made public his resignation from the PCF, denounced Stalinism and the Soviet system, and expressed his sympathy for the anti-Soviet and independent socialist movements in Eastern Europe. In his letter Césaire did not miss the opportunity to decry the attitude of the PCF toward Algeria and the exploitation of the colonial question both by the USSR and by the Stalinist PCF for their own political interests.[29]

Public interventions such as the ones of Aimé Césaire and George Padmore were formulated precisely at the moment that the Soviet Union was about to change its domestic course with de-Stalinization as well as the course of its international policy with support for the Afro-Asian movement and decolonization. In that sense such voices not only gave vent to accumulated frustration for the attitude of communists, but also marked the moment of the Soviet turn to the South and constituted a counterbalance to the communism of such figures as W. E. B. Du Bois. In fact they sealed a significant political and psychological rupture between Afro-Asians nationalists and Soviet and Western communists, while presaging that Southern intellectuals would not be easy targets for the new Soviet policy. Aimé Césaire's intervention, in particular, demonstrated that Southerners were careful observers not only of the communists' African policy, but also of the domestic situation in the USSR and Soviet tutelage over the majority of European communist countries and parties.

The degree to which Soviet conduct abroad mattered for Southerners was also confirmed a couple of months later by the reactions of the two existing Soviet-Southern friendship associations following the Soviet invasion in Budapest. Founded in 1956 not by Europeans but on the initiative of native sympathizers, the first in independent Tunisia and the second in French Madagascar, both associations had expressed their strong commitment to friendship and engaged in direct contacts with and sent delegates to the USSR.[30] Yet, for all their positive feelings toward the USSR, the bloody crash of the Hungarian revolt provoked embarrassment among their members or even condemnatory reactions. In a letter that he addressed to the VOKS, the president of the Madagascar-USSR association told the Soviets that the events in Hungary and the subsequent denunciation of the Soviet invasion by numerous progressive French intellectuals had divided the members of the association and spread "anxiety and sadness" among them.[31] More adamant and condemnatory was the reaction of the vice president of the Cultural Association Tunisia-USSR. In his letter to the VOKS he accused the USSR of unjustifiable military intervention which flouted the principles of the Bandung Conference, deplored the fact that the Warsaw Pact was turned against the people, and exhorted the Soviets "to let Hungarians continue their revolution, without slandering them as counter revolutionaries."[32]

The public interventions of Padmore and Césaire, as well as the lesser-known reactions of the friendship associations, were evidence that the Soviet policy regarding the decolonization of Africa, Soviet imperialism in Europe, and authoritarianism inside the country did not pass unremarked, and that these criticisms were not due to Western propaganda. Despite the positive impact that Soviet involvement in the Suez crisis definitely had on colonial and newly independent countries, all these issues lay heavy on the establishment of Soviet-South ties, and this partly explains why African and Arab governments, even the so-called radical ones, did not roll out a red carpet for their Soviet friends. The building of friendships with the noncommunist Southern countries therefore required perseverance and commitment, which the Soviet Union now seemed ready to undertake.

OPENING A NEW PAGE OF SOVIET-SOUTH FRIENDSHIP

The year 1956 constituted a turning point for Soviet international policy. In February, at the Twentieth Party Congress, Nikita Khrushchev proclaimed his faith in peaceful coexistence between the communist and the developed capitalist countries. Yet in October and November, at the same time as the revolution in Hungary, the Suez crisis was putting to the test the very idea of peaceful coexistence. Suez did not resurrect the Stalinist doctrine of the inevitability of war, but it did accelerate Soviet involvement in the Third World. For if peaceful coexistence was aimed at increasing contacts with the West, it also meant the competition of the two systems for influence and hegemony over the South.

The years following Suez were thus marked by the intensification of efforts to establish ties with the Afro-Asian countries and by a spectacular development of cultural exchanges. In the new foreground of the Afro-Asian world the Soviet Union engaged in the peaceful battle for the hearts and the minds of millions of people now considered natural allies. The milestone of the Khrushchevian thaw, the Moscow Youth Festival of 1957, gave the opportunity for an unprecedented encounter between Soviet people and Afro-Asian youth. During the festival the members of the African students' delegation enthusiastically supported Soviet-African friendship, and one of them affirmed being "impressed by the internationalist spirit of Soviet people."[33] Two Soviet friendship associations, the first one with Arab countries and the second with African peoples, were founded in 1958 and 1959 respectively in order to undertake the development and coordination of cultural exchanges.[34] One year later Khrushchev inaugurated in Moscow the People's Friendship University for the training of students from Asian, African, and Latin American countries, which shortly afterward was renamed Patrice Lumumba University in the memory of the Congolese nationalist hero and symbol of the anti-colonial struggle.

The new policy of friendship with the South was founded on important political premises for both the international and the bilateral potential of the relationship between the USSR and the emerging postcolonial countries. At the same time it was motivated by a powerful ideology, which envisaged noncapitalist development and a successful socialist course for the Afro-Asian world, as well as a leading position for

Moscow in the Soviet-South partnership. The turn to the South was also symptomatic of the fact that, while after the Khrushchev report and the Hungarian Revolution the Soviets found themselves in a very awkward position vis-à-vis the European left, they were eager and still very comfortable giving lessons to their non-European potential and desirable allies. The Soviets considered themselves to be the teachers and the Southerners to be disciples, and the lessons were based on the Soviet historical experience, which theorists and policy makers adapted to what they considered to be the political priorities and the developmental needs of the underdeveloped countries. They were the representatives of a developed society, which had solved problems similar to those that postcolonial countries were facing after their political independence. A prominent role in this policy was played by Soviet Asian and Caucasian officials who incarnated the progress of their formerly backward republics and the integration of their peoples into the socialist union. Khrushchev himself was inviting the representatives of the postcolonial countries which were in search of their path to development to "take a look at the prospering republics of Soviet Central Asia and at the other regions . . . which, after October, bypassed the painful capitalist path."[35] The Soviet Union lay thus as their model. It was an empire of tangible, time-tested, and rational solutions, ideal for transmission to underdeveloped postcolonial countries. The Soviets were obviously convinced that they already possessed the visible proof to show their prospective partners and allies and that they had the wisdom and the method to allow them to rapidly achieve similar progress. The sense of superiority over the backward Southern countries conditioned the conduct of Soviet cultural policy and lay behind the optimism of Khrushchev's grand overture to the South.

At the same time, while there was a tacit assumption of superiority, internationalist solidarity and disinterested aid to non-Western peoples became recurrent references in Soviet discourse and fundamental arguments justifying Soviet involvement. Nikita Khrushchev was praising the "internationalist duty [of the CPSU] to help peoples which are on the way to gain and to consolidate their national independence" and elevating "the alliance with peoples that cast off the colonial yoke, as one of the cornerstones of its international policy."[36] On the one hand, throwing aside their previous indifference and disdain, their vigorous support for nationalist anti-colonial movements and postcolonial countries gave the Soviets a much-needed (after 1956) possibility to claim moral superiority over the imperialist West. On the other hand, consistency with this claim required engagements and commitment that were constantly probed in the course of the burgeoning Soviet-South relationships.

Relying on their assumptions, the Soviets intensified their efforts for cooperation with the Afro-Asian movement, which after Bandung had emerged as a major independent political platform beyond the two blocs. Capitalizing on the support accorded to Nasser during the Suez crisis, they became initiators of the Cairo conference that, in December 1957, gave birth to the Afro-Asian People's Solidarity Organization (AAPSO). The organization adopted the stance of an anti-colonial international. It developed as a network of national solidarity committees in most Afro-Asian countries, but quickly became an ideological battlefield between its members and, most notably, the Soviets and the Chinese.[37]

Aiming at a hegemonic role, in September 1958 the Soviet Solidarity Committee organized the first Afro-Asian writers' conference in Tashkent. With participants such as W. E. B. Du Bois, Nazim Hikmet, Mario de Andrade, Sembène Ousmane, and many others, the conference was destined to mark the ideological rapprochement between Soviets and Afro-Asian intellectuals and to inaugurate their anti-imperialist entente. In reality, however, it also revealed the serious reservations of the Southerners and their disagreements with the Soviet policy. The boycott of the conference on behalf of Arab committees and the acute intervention of the Algerian delegate, who called on the Soviets to back the revolutionaries (FLN) and to recognize their Provisional Government of the Algerian Republic (GPRA), were reminders of the Arab discontent concerning the Soviet stance in Algeria and of their strong reservations regarding the credibility of Moscow's friendship offensive.[38]

Not less reserved was the attitude of the Société Africaine de Culture (SAC).[39] Its secretary-general, Alioune Diop, quit the conference at the preparatory sessions in protest against the organizers' refusal to let the SAC select a group of African delegates. The incident evidenced that the SAC was extremely suspicious of Moscow's intentions and in no case wanted to participate in a conference ideologically dominated by the Soviets. The host organizations were particularly annoyed with Diop, whom they depicted as a "bourgeois nationalist Negro" who "tried to undermine" their conference. Illustrative in this regard was the reaction of Ivan Potekhin, the president of the Soviet Association for Friendship with African Peoples and director of the Soviet Institute of Africa. Guardian of orthodox Marxism-Leninism, he was a fervent opponent of African cultural and racial nationalism and particularly of the theory of négritude that two prominent members of the SAC, Aimé Césaire and Léopold Sédar Senghor, had formulated. Being skeptical of the prospects of entente with Africans and dismissive of their ideologies, he warned his Soviet colleagues that "the heads of African intellectuals are filled with an immense quantity of prejudices" and advised them to study those prejudices "in order to find the way to approach those minds and hearts."[40]

In many respects the Tashkent conference constituted a crash-landing for Soviet cultural policy. The outcome of the conference fell short of the initial optimistic expectations, while the responses to it demonstrated that a big gap existed between the expectations of each side. In the face of the African and Arab reactions Soviet cultural officials had recourse to the usual explanations, such as the petit bourgeois mentality of colonial intellectuals. But in reality such arguments put into question the feasibility of Khrushchev's new Third World policy, which had anticipated finding common ground with the noncommunists. At the same time they also had recourse to an Orientalist rhetoric in order to explain the "prejudices" of the Southerners and the pitfalls in the first grand attempts at Soviet-South friendship. Characteristic in this regard was the stance of Mirzo Tursunzade, the Tajikistani poet and president of the Soviet Afro-Asian Solidarity Committee, the man in the Afro-Asian forums who embodied the progress and integration in the USSR of the formerly backward peoples of the Russian Empire. On his return from Guinea, where he headed the Soviet delegation at the second Afro-Asian Solidarity Conference, Tursun Zade reported on that primitive African country "full of natural gifts, pineapples, bananas, coconuts, but with illiterate people . . . simply big kids." Asking the rhetorical question, "now that they are free from the yoke of colonialism. What are they doing?" he answered that "they are getting out in the streets, singing and dancing." At the same time he made an appeal to his Soviet colleagues "to take care of those pure peoples, to give them correct education and enlightenment, so that their country takes a right path."[41]

The paternalistic Orientalist discourse, the references to "big kids" and to "pure peoples" who needed "correct education and enlightenment" illustrated the superiority that Soviet cultural officials felt when they encountered Southerners and especially the Africans. At the same time this discourse, which had striking similarities with the Western Orientalist one, also conveyed feelings of embarrassment in the context of the new Soviet cultural policy. The nervous cultural officials had to demonstrate perseverance in the face of the immature Southerners, despite the unconcealed ideological compromise that they had made by embracing "bourgeois nationalism" and despite the cold reception of the Soviet friendship offensive by many Afro-Asians. In fact, if paternalism and the consequent language of "affection" constituted one facet of the Soviet reaction, another was disaffection. Many Soviet officials felt estranged by the African and Arab reactions and Southerners' refusal to subscribe to Soviet views. Convinced of the rightness of their assumptions, they could hardly tolerate the unorthodox anti-imperialist diatribes from representatives of backward societies with a dubious class background and an even more dubious political vision. Moreover, their disaffection was easily transformed into anger against the Southerners' disobedience, all the more so because they felt that the Soviet Union was sacrificing its precious resources and offering substantial aid, while the Southerners remained thankless and abused Soviet friendship, support, and hospitality. Such considerations were in fact having a significant impact on the Soviets' regard for the Southerners. There was thus nothing extraordinary in the fact that the paternalist Mirzo Tursun-zade was expressing his ire for the African students in the USSR, some of whom had received their scholarships from his committee. The cause was that many students complained about their living conditions and adhered to the ideology of pan-Africanism instead of adopting Soviet views. "Those students are eating the bread and the salt of our Soviet people and we cannot stay neutral," Tursun-zade stated during a meeting of the solidarity committee, implying that those benefiting from Soviet aid had to subscribe to Soviet views.[42]

These kind of expectations or requirements were fomenting clashes with the "opinionated" Southerners, such as the one that Algerian activist Mohammed Harbi recalls in his political memoirs. A delegate of the FLN at the congress of the World Peace Movement in New Delhi in 1961, Harbi confronted the eminent Soviet writer Ilya Ehrenburg. Angry at the Algerians' refusal to back the Soviet positions, Ehrenburg told the Algerian delegation that "the Soviet Union is pulling the bread out of her mouth in order to give it to you." Ehrenburg's allusion clearly implied that the Soviet Union was already making great sacrifices in order to support the Algerians and other Third World peoples and that the latter had to be grateful for that aid and side with the USSR. The incident ended, thanks to the intervention of the Turkish poet Nazim Hikmet. Still, it signified the mutual disenchantment and conflicting considerations that often led to tensions during Soviet-South encounters.[43]

The frustration of Soviets over the ungrateful attitude of the Southerners was colliding on the other side with the frustration of the Southerners with the Soviets' half-hearted support for their cause. This had been particularly evident in the case of Soviet-Algerian relations. Even after the agreements for Algerian independence and official Soviet recognition had been reached, the legacy of mistrust could hardly disappear. Behind the façade of very warm relations, the Algerians were keeping their distance from their Soviet partners, contesting their advice and maintaining a critical view of both international and domestic Soviet policies. This became clear to a delegation of Soviet writers that visited the country in 1965. Their mission was to advise Algerians on the development of literature in their multinational state and to promote the idea of socialist realism, but they were given a cold reception by Algerian officials. Hocine Zahouane, a senior member of the Political Bureau and head of the Department of National Orientation of the FLN government under Ahmed Ben Bella, for instance, delighted the Soviet guests by repeating Ben Bella's well-known statement that "if the Soviet Union did not exist, we would have to invent one." Yet, disputing both the USSR's hegemony and its cultural policies, Zahouane criticized the interference of the party in cultural life, praised the Algerian example of "artistic freedom" and the coexistence of "many schools of art"—including eminently Western "abstractionism"—and finished by asserting to his Soviet guests that in Algeria "no such conflicts like the 'Pasternak case' could occur." The reference to the disillusioned Nobel prize winner insinuated that Algerians too were quite disillusioned with the Soviet paradigm. They also seemed to have enough pride and self-confidence to envisage their own more liberal cultural model, which they considered better than the Soviet one. Similarly disillusioned, the delegation returned to Moscow having realized the limits of the Soviet aura in Algeria.[44]

Such encounters revealed that postcolonial partners often had a very cautious and critical regard for the motherland of socialism and that they were well aware of the cause of Soviet writers who were defying the regime's orthodoxy. Evoking those writers or trying to establish friendships with them, instead of favoring relations with the cultural officials, was a way not only to express sympathy for their cause, but also to demonstrate alienation and independence from the Soviet model. In this respect the response of Léopold Sédar Senghor to the invitations of Soviet cultural officials was particularly meaningful. The poet and president of Senegal was a close friend of Alioune Diop, who had protested the participation of the SAC in the Tashkent conference of 1958. The following year Senghor received the invitation of Ivan Potekhin to visit the Soviet Union, a trip that he never made.[45] In a letter that he addressed to Potekhin, Senghor did not hide his disaffection from the sharp critic of the theory of négritude, which he described as a form of "African socialism" that incorporated "all the elements of the traditional Negro-African civilization."[46] When in July 1961 he received in Dakar a delegation of Soviet writers, he insisted that in the future one form of socialism would prevail, "either the one of Senghor or the one of Potekhin."[47]

However, besides his overt ideological polemic with Potekhin, Senghor had a more incisive way to demonstrate his disenchantment with the Soviet Union. This was to invite to Dakar, on the occasion of the first Festival of Negro Arts, Evgenii Evtushenko, the poet whose critique of Stalinism as well as of the falsification of history in the USSR had made of him a symbol of dissent and a fighter for freedom and truth in the noncommunist press. In his letter of invitation in March 1963 Senghor wrote Evtushenko that he had read most of his poems and "almost everything that was written" about him "in the French press." He meaningfully expressed his "great admiration for the man and the poet" and his conviction that Nikita Khrushchev's new policy "would allow the peoples of the Soviet Union to express their real message to humanity." In Evtushenko's poetry Senghor found the message of "tenderness for the salvation of humanity," which for the poet of négritude was clearly an insinuation against the brutality of the previous Soviet regime. "What brings Slavic peoples and Black peoples closer is, along with their capacity to suffer, the maintenance of tenderness in their hearts," Senghor concluded, drawing an explicit parallel between the psychic force and the sufferings of both peoples in their historical march. In overt conflict with the Soviet narrative, Senghor's words would probably have embarrassed or irritated most Soviet cultural officials.[48]

Not by chance, Evtushenko was invited to Dakar together with Andrei Voznesenskii, another poet of the Thaw generation who had been targeted by the authorities and particularly by Khrushchev for his alleged admiration of the West as well as for his nonconventional poetic and personal style. As Senghor put it in another letter, at the festival the poets should "not represent the Soviet government" but "Russian literature" and "the most sparkling sources of Slavdom."[49] Beside Senghor's attachment to an essentialist perception of cultural identity, which the two poets were supposed to incarnate, lay his criticism of the communist modernity that was strangling the culture of Slavic peoples just as Western colonialism had done in Africa. In Senghor's eyes the Soviet path to modernity that Moscow was displaying as a paradigm for the postcolonial countries constituted a dangerous threat to African peoples' culture.

Evtushenko accepted Senghor's invitation with enthusiasm and attended the festival in April 1966, accompanied not by Voznesenskii but by Evgenii Dolmatovskii. This was Evtushenko's second trip to Dakar. Honorary guest of President Senghor, with whom he held a private and friendly discussion, he participated in an evening of Soviet-African friendship. During the event, and notably in the presence of the Soviet ambassador, Evtushenko defended his country's ideology and international policies. Yet in their report submitted after the trip he and Dolmatovskii underscored the progressive and anti-colonialist character of the festival and tactfully criticized the dismissive stance of Soviet cultural officials with regard to the ideology of négritude, a stance that was alienating many Africans.[50] On the margins of the official exchanges Africa became for Evtushenko a source of poetic inspiration, a land of mysterious beauty, exotic and strange, yet akin to his own mysterious country. As one scholar suggests, Evtushenko's verses lauding African freedom and the empathy of the Russian taiga for the African savannah were hardly empty of political meaning. Written in 1962 among expectations and struggle for a freer post-Stalinist Soviet country, they hid the message of liberalization within an exaltation of African liberation. His ideologically ambiguous tribute to African freedom bore no resemblance to the typical representations of Third World peoples' struggle in Soviet public discourse.[51]

In any case, the cultural encounters between Soviets, Africans, and Arabs were diverging significantly from the strict framework that the rulers in Moscow had envisaged. Seen through the eyes of many Southerners, the Soviet Union was neither a staunch ally nor the ideal model for their own countries' postcolonial paths. On the Soviet side of the interaction, too, the reactions vis-à-vis these prospective allies varied from distrust and frustration to empathy or admiration. But if significant tensions and contradictions came up in the course of encounters between activists, intellectuals, and cultural officials, it was also the reception of Southern students in the USSR that seriously put to the test the assumptions of both sides and the "romance" of the Soviet-South friendship.

AFRICAN AND ARAB YOUTH IN THE SOVIET UNION

From the late 1950s onwards the training of students in the USSR became a keystone in the Soviet partnership with Third World countries. For the latter it constituted a great opportunity to educate the young specialists that they terribly needed for their state-building and economic development. For the USSR it was a serious investment with several objectives. Apart from demonstrating internationalist solidarity and gaining the gratitude of the Southerners, the Soviets also hoped that, through this formative experience, the students would became true friends of the USSR and assimilate the scientific paradigm of Marxism-Leninism. As both good friends and "progressive" specialists, the Soviet-educated youth would constitute a bridge for the transfer of Soviet ideas as well as a pillar for the implementation of "progressive" socialist reforms, which would detach the South from the tutelage of the capitalist West and pave the way for its alliance with the communist East. Under such considerations and in response to the growing demand from foreign governments, the CPSU steadily increased the number of scholarships granted to Third World students. In 1965 there were 2,623 Arabs, 2,794 Africans, and 2,111 Latin Americans enrolled in Soviet universities and technological institutes. In 1975 their numbers had almost doubled, and a decade later there were approximately 20,000 Arabs, 18,000 Africans, 17,000 Latin Americans, and 27,000 Asian students in the USSR. Foreign guests in such numbers and from such alien, remote, and diverse countries had never before been received by the peoples of the Soviet Union.[52]

In contrast to political and cultural visitors, who were accompanied by guides and had a rigid and tight schedule, students spent around five years in the Soviet Union. They spoke Russian, entered into relations with Soviet citizens—many of them married Soviet women—and, by Soviet standards, enjoyed a free everyday life. In the course of their long stays they became familiar with Soviet reality and with the mood of the Soviet people. Indeed, their experiences in the USSR constituted a major chapter in the Soviet-South relationship. On the one hand, both students and the governments of their countries expressed very positive views of the quality of education and gratitude for the generous scholarships offered to them by the Soviet authorities. On the other hand, the experiences of students often made them reconsider their assumptions and realize that the Soviet state and society differed significantly from the images presented in propaganda.

In many cases such realizations were the outcome of friendly exchanges that the foreign students had with their Soviet colleagues. Living side by side, the visitors often heard their classmates' grievances about the situation in their own country. Reports of the Komsomol, the Soviet youth organization, pointed out several such cases, including one involving a Soviet student "who was living together with an Iraqi student and was ceaselessly telling him defamatory lies about the Soviet reality."[53] Another report referred to the case of a Lithuanian student, the roommate of Cuban colleagues in a residence of Leningrad State University, "who was expressing to the Cubans his disappointment with the domestic situation of the country and was criticizing the Soviet reality" until he was finally denounced to the rector by his Cuban roommates.[54] A report on the life of foreign students at the Medical Institute of Tbilisi underscored the fact that Georgian students had discussions with their foreign colleagues on the subject of "the Russian imperialism in Georgia."[55] In another case, illustrative of anti-Soviet mood, citizens of western Ukraine "were distributing leaflets of nationalist content to the foreign students of L'vov."[56] Without doubt, these kinds of experiences constituted significant lessons about the discontent of citizens as well as the tense relations between peoples of different nationalities. As such, they dissipated many of the students' illusions about the democracy, internationalism, and popular support of the regime that Soviet propaganda was presenting to them as a model.

At the same time, besides these revelatory exchanges, foreign students often experienced dismissive or violent attitudes on the part of Soviet students and citizens. From the beginning of the training programs incidents of verbal and physical violence both inside and outside the campuses were in fact very frequent. Such altercations played a definitive role in the disillusionment of the students and additionally of the comrades and progressive friends of the USSR in African and Arab countries. Even if the authorities made efforts either to prevent the "undesirable incidents" or to keep them secret, the clashes were recurrent, the students protested vigorously, and the news and rumors circulated. A delegation of leading

Nigerian trade unionists, which visited the USSR in 1961, met Nigerians students in Tbilisi and heard their serious complaints. Upon their return to Moscow the trade unionists told their Soviet counterparts that the students "were terrorized by the attitude of the local youth and were afraid to get out in the street." They affirmed that this was not proof of "internationalist spirit" and requested the students' transfer to another city.[57] An Algerian student, a member of the Algerian Community Party and brother of a communist poet, did not hide his disenchantment after his experiences in Moscow. While in a restaurant with his Russian girlfriend he was insulted because of his African look, and after he responded the couple was led to the police station, where the police treated his girlfriend in a humiliating manner. Following the event, the student addressed his protest to the Union of Soviet Writers and affirmed that he was going to report his grievances both to the party in Algeria and to the students' organization.[58]

In every respect the frequent incidents of violence dissipated the students' illusions and seriously harmed Soviet-South relations. In 1962 a student from Basutoland, a fellow of the Soviet Afro-Asian Solidarity Committee, was found dead in Kiev. The tragic event provoked indignation and terror in the city's African community and serious concerns inside the pro-Soviet Basutoland Congress Party, which sent a delegate to meet the students in the Soviet Union and calm them down.[59] In December 1963 a Ghanaian student was found dead on the outskirts of Moscow under mysterious circumstances. His death gave vent to the African students' exasperation with racism and violence in the USSR. Their massive demonstration in Red Square caught the Soviet authorities by surprise and was reported with astonishment in the world media.[60] Two years latter another Ghanaian student was found dead in Baku. Once again students protested, in addition to boycotting their courses and squatting in the railway station with the intention of leaving Baku. Terrorized and disillusioned, a group of Kenyan students left the Soviet Union in a move that constituted yet another blow to the image of the USSR in Africa.[61]

These tragic events and the recurrent incidents of physical and verbal violence were evidence that racism persisted in the Soviet socialist society. In the majority of cases the victims were black Africans, who constituted the most visible targets, and this was indicative of the racial facet of Soviet xenophobia. Nevertheless, blacks were not the sole victims. Other Third World students had been attacked several times or insulted both by Soviet students or citizens, and they had protested to the authorities. Latin American students at the Peoples' Friendship University denounced the fact that in the transport facilities they often heard citizens calling them "spongers" who "came to hang at our necks."[62] Students from several Third World countries had been beaten by hooligans, who also stole their clothes and watches.[63] A report of the Komsomol admitted that "the cases of beating and insult" against Iraqi students in Kharkov and other cities of Ukraine were "so frequent" that "their association sent an official protest to the rector asking for protection."[64] Successive reports from the 1960s underscored the numerous "undesirable incidents" against darker-skinned students pointing both to the tense relations with their Soviet colleagues and to the hostility of the population. The fact that so many darker-skinned men from so many alien countries and cultures suddenly appeared in Soviet campuses and cities certainly played an enormous role in the outburst of xenophobic reactions.[65] Nevertheless, numerous conflicts also indicated that the motives behind the Soviet reactions were not solely racial or cultural.

Tensions between Soviet and Southern students emerged from the very beginning, and a significant cause was the scarcity of places in both the residences and in the universities. In the face of growing domestic and foreign demand the authorities were obliged to give priority to the foreigners over Soviets. In several cases Soviet students were ordered to quit their rooms, some of them returning to live with their families, while some families living in the residences were also forced to move.[66] At the coveted prestigious medical and technological institutes of Moscow, Kiev, and Leningrad, toward which the Soviet government was directing the bulk of foreign students, the shortage of housing was much more acute. With thousands of Soviet students on waiting lists for placement in the residences, those schools in fact refrained from enrolling Soviet candidates from provincial towns who also needed accommodation.[67] Such problems were certainly chronic and could by no means be attributed only to the arrival of Third World students. Nevertheless the Komsomol did not miss the opportunity to decry the better accommodations and "exceptional conditions" reserved by the authorities for Third World students.[68] Soviet students also complained that the foreigners were taking their places in the institutes, the residences, and the libraries.[69]

One more strong reason for Soviet students' resentment toward their Third World colleagues was the large scholarships that the latter were receiving from the Soviet government or Soviet organizations.[70] In contrast to the Soviet students, who had a stipend of 30 to 35 rubles per month, Third World undergraduates were receiving 90 rubles and PhD candidates 100. For certain periods some national groups were even receiving a surplus from their own governments, while many individual students also had the financial support of their families.[71] The result was that the Southern students generally enjoyed a life without vital material constraints and spent more on consumer goods and entertainment. However, this situation, and especially the generosity of the Soviet government, was denounced by Soviet students, professors, and officials and led to numerous conflicts with the Southerners.[72] Along with the automatic access to better schools and residences, the larger scholarships and the better standards of living provoked the envy of Soviets who never subscribed to the "positive discrimination" that their government had established in favor of the Southern guests.

Additionally, in the eyes of the Soviets, foreign students had other important privileges. They traveled abroad, returning to their warm countries in the summer and sometimes in the winter, or visited Western Europe. Students from former French colonies often traveled to France to spend holidays with relatives and friends, as did Somalis to Italy, and Nigerians and Ghanaians to England "to buy every kind of garment," as one report meaningfully pointed out.[73] Upon their return to the Soviet Union many of them not only were dressed in the latest fashions, but also were bringing back clothing and other Western goods to sell to Soviet colleagues and citizens in order to make some extra money.

All these "privileges" of the Southern students had a very negative impact on Soviet popular opinion. The foreign students from noncommunist countries had a freer and supposedly easier life than the Soviets. They were, or were alleged to be, wealthier than Soviet citizens because—as certain Soviets seemed to believe—many of them were the offspring of rich families and members of the bourgeois milieu.[74] "It is well known that in many Asian and African countries secondary education is a privilege of the wealthy classes. This explains the fact that people of no use or simply enemies often come to our country," a Komsomol report argued.[75] The opinions of many Soviets regarding the Southern students was thus particularly negative; yet much more negative was their opinion of the Soviet government, which was spending the country's precious resources for undesirable friends and dubious allies. At a time when the Soviet people aspired to better standards of living and to a bigger share in the country's resources, the government's funding for the Third World appeared to them extravagant. The darker-skinned students in the USSR who embodied the absurd, costly, and illegitimate policy of Soviet-South friendship thus became the targets of Soviet ire, but the racism and the violent incidents against them did not evidence only racial prejudices. They were also the outcome of the Soviet people's negative opinion of their own government, which was reinforced by their encounters with Third World students—an opinion that the Soviet regime had striven to avoid yet, due to its international and domestic policies, had unintentionally intensified.

CONCLUSION

The unexpected reactions against the Third World students and the incidents of verbal and physical violence caught the Soviet authorities by surprise. Much greater was their surprise when African students demonstrated in Moscow and in other cities to protest against racism. Embarrassment and dissatisfaction had been equally pervasive among cultural officials after the Tashkent conference and other encounters, despite their enthusiastic declarations to the contrary. The fact was that behind Khrushchev's friendship rhetoric and Ben Bella's statements of tribute to the USSR lay an undercurrent of tensions that loomed large at the middle and especially at the lower levels of the Soviet-South interaction. Those tensions, as noted, reflected the skepticism of cultural officials who did not seem to share Khrushchev's optimistic assumptions regarding the Soviet-South friendship. The early Soviet frustrations heralded the public dismissal of bourgeois nationalism and the adoption of a more realistic approach toward postcolonial countries after Khrushchev's eviction.[76]

Among the Africans and Arabs, both officials and students held Soviet technology and sciences in high esteem, which was confirmed through the training of Southern youth in Soviet schools.[77] They also needed Soviet support and cooperation to counterbalance Western influence, gain or consolidate independence, and advance their goals of sovereignty and development. Realism and, to a large degree, ideology constituted strong motives behind the quest for partnership with Moscow. Yet, as it quickly became clear, most Africans and Arabs also had strong reservations about accepting Moscow's superiority in political and ideological affairs. From the aftermath of the war to the 1960s, Soviet ideology and policy regarding their countries in many respects failed to meet Third World nationalists' expectations and disappointed them. Beyond the public stance of George Padmore and Aimé Césaire against Moscow's policy, disagreements and frustration were constantly expressed during conferences and cultural meetings or in private exchanges with the friendship associations. Awe of the Soviet superpower did not prevent sharp critiques of both its international and domestic policies. Suspicion of Moscow and the self-confidence of the nationalist movements were also important reasons behind their cautious and independent stance. The experiences of foreign students in the early sixties and the disillusionment of many of them, which did not pass unremarked in their countries of origin, became indeed an inextricable part of the Soviet-South relationship.

On the Soviet side, an attentive regard to the attitudes of cultural officials and those of students and citizens vis-à-vis the Africans and Arabs reveals that beyond the evident discrepancies, there existed also common Soviet perceptions. Soviet officials, students, and citizens seemed to share the opinion that Soviet citizens were making enormous sacrifices, taking bread from their mouths in order to offer it to those Southerners "eating the bread and the salt of Soviet people." Such allusions echoed the popular depictions of the Southerners as "spongers" living at the expense of Soviet people. Nevertheless, for cultural officials the crucial issue was whether the Soviet policy of friendship with the postcolonial countries, in the way that it was conducted, would bear the expected fruits. Despite their anger at the Southerners and their serious doubts about whether these people could or should be considered as friends and allies, Soviet officials never questioned their country's involvement in the alien and remote South, out of which they were in fact making their living and gaining their status. But for Soviet students and citizens the issue was not expressed in the same terms. The policy of the Soviet-South friendship seemed to them to bring concrete losses instead of gains. Their reactions against foreign students demonstrated that they rejected both their government's choices and the internationalist duty required of them by the CPSU.

At the same time, the hostile attitudes of Soviet citizens not only demonstrated the limits of Soviet internationalism but also revealed signs of the contestation of the other major assumption of the same policy, Soviet superiority. Once again, if superiority vis-à-vis the backward Southerners was taken for granted by cultural officials, many Soviet citizens did not seem to subscribe to their government's propaganda. The depictions of the Southerners as wealthier, freer, and more privileged were evidence that many Soviets did not consider themselves as members of a superior society or of a model country. At the very least they were not at all concerned about the transfer of the Soviet model in the Third World.

Toward the end of the 1970s a small group of audacious Soviet scholars started overtly questioning the noncapitalist path of development and refrained from praising the Soviet model for Third World countries.[78] It is worth mentioning that popular opinion had anticipated their findings. Deriding the superiority of Soviet socialism and its transplantation to the Third World, one popular joke asked: "When will socialism be constructed in Cuba?" And the meaningful answer was given: "When Cuba starts importing sugar."[79]

NOTES

1. For the regard of the European countries toward their overseas possessions after 1945, see Tony Judt, *Postwar: A History of Europe since 1945* (New York: Penguin Press, 2005), 7–8, 278–88.

2. Walter Laqueur, *Communism and Nationalism in the Middle East* (New York: Praeger, 1956), 14, 272–75; Alexandre Bennigsen, "Le front national dans la nouvelle politique soviétique au Moyen Orient," *Politique étrangère* 21, no. 5 (1956): 614–24; Roger E. Kanet, "African Youth: The Target of Soviet African Policy," *Russian Review* 27, no. 2 (1968): 161–75.

3. Two reviews of the new trends and perspectives of the field: David C. Engerman, "The Second World's Third World," *Kritika: Explorations in Russian and Eurasian History* 12, no. 1 (Winter 2011): 183–211; and Tobias Rupprecht, "Die Sowjetunion und die Welt im Kalten Krieg: Neue Forschungsperspektiven auf eine vermeintlich hermetisch abgeschottete Gesellschaft," *Jahrbücher für Geschichte Osteuropas* 58, no. 3 (2010): 381–99. Some reference studies: Ilya V. Gaiduk, *Confronting Vietnam: Soviet Policy toward the Indochina Conflict* (Stanford: Stanford University Press, 2003); Ragna Boden, *Die Grenzen der Weltmacht: Sowjetische Indonesienpolitik von Stalin bis Brežnev* (Stuttgart: Franz Steiner, 2006); Sergei V. Mazov, *Politika SSSR v zapadnoi Afrike, 1956–1964. Neizvestnye stranitsy istorii kholodnoi voiny* (Moscow: Nauka, 2008); Lorenz M. Lüthi, *The Sino-Soviet Split: Cold War in the Communist World* (Princeton: Princeton University Press, 2008).

4. Thomas Bernstein and Hua-Yu Li, *China Learns from the Soviet Union, 1949–Present* (Lanham, MD: Lexington Books, 2010); Julie Hessler, "Death of an African Student in Moscow. Race, Politics, and the Cold War," *Cahiers du Monde russe* 47, nos. 1–2 (2006): 33–64; Maxim Matusevich, *No Easy Row for a Russian Hoe: Ideology and Pragmatism in Nigerian-Soviet Relations, 1960–1991* (Trenton, NJ: Africa World Press, 2003).

5. Michael David-Fox's seminal study, "The Fellow-Travelers Revisited: The 'Cultured West' through Soviet Eyes," *Journal of Modern History* 75, no. 2 (June 2003): 300–335, constituted a major source of inspiration for this essay.

6. Vladislav Zubok, *A Failed Empire: The Soviet Union in the Cold War from Stalin to Gorbachev* (Chapel Hill: University of North Carolina Press, 2007), 38–39, 44–45.

7. Jerry Hough, *The Struggle for the Third World: Soviet Debates and American Options* (Washington, DC: Brookings Institution, 1986), 113–14, 227–28.

8. See Mark Philip Bradley, "Decolonization, the Global South, and the Cold War, 1919–1962," in *The Cambridge History of the Cold War,* ed. Melvyn P. Leffler and Odd Arne Westad (Cambridge: Cambridge University Press, 2010), 1:473.

9. Potekhin's analysis, dated April 20, 1951, under the title "Rost demokraticheskikh sil v angliiskikh koloniiakh Vostochnoi Afriki," was submitted to the Foreign Policy Commission of the Central Committee of the CPSU. Russian State Archive of Social and Political History (hereafter RGASPI), f. 17, op. 137, d. 581, ll. 18–24.

10. Evgenii Primakov, *Strany Aravii i kolonializm* (Moscow: Gosudarstevennaia Izdatel'stvo Politicheskoi Literatury, 1956), 81–93.

11. Eric Karpelson, president of the Central Committee of the Trade Unions of Workers in the Tanning Industry of Algeria, to the All-Union Central Council of Trade Unions of the USSR (VTsSPS). Algiers, September 18, 1944, State Archive of the Russian Federation (hereafter GARF), f. R-5451, op. 45, d. 25, l. 10.

12. GARF, f. R-5283, op. 22, d. 68, l. 7.

13. GARF, f. R-5283, op. 8, d. 334, ll. 143–47.

14. Bachir Merad and Mohamed Boualem to the VOKS, October 31, 1950, GARF, f. R-5283, op. 16, d. 571, l. 13.

15. Both the poem and the account are republished in Kateb Yacine, *Minuit passé de douze heures. Ecrits journalistiques, 1947–1989* (Paris: Editions du Seuil, 1999), 102–104.

16. André Lenormand, member of the executive committee of the France-USSR Friendship Society, discussed this issue with the Soviet Consul General in Algiers on April 21, 1947. GARF, f. R-5283, op. 22, d. 68, l. 14.

17. See the preface of Samir Amin in Amady Aly Dieng, *Les premiers pas de la Fédération des Etudiants d'Afrique Noire en France (FEANF), 1950–1955, de l'Union Française à Bandoung* (Paris: L'Harmattan, 2003), 23. Also see Guy Pervillé, "Anticommunisme et décolonisation" *Communisme* 62–63 (2000): 115–35. On the "mediation" of the PCF in Africa, see the reflections of Jean-Pierre Dozon, *Frères et sujets. La France et l'Afrique en perspective* (Paris: Flammarion, 2003), 333–34.

18. Frederick Cooper has demonstrated that top political actors from French West Africa had struggled to find a compromise solution, such as a confederation, allowing them both to be independent and to benefit from the resources of the Union. Yet such a mutually advantageous and sustainable agreement proved impossible to find. See his article "Alternatives to Nationalism in French Africa, 1945–1960," in *Elites and Decolonization in the Twentieth Century*, ed. Jost Dülffer and Marc Frey (Basingstoke: Palgrave Macmillan, 2011), 110–36. In the Maghreb, however, the vicious circle of violence and nationalism left little space for the search of any compromise.

19. GARF, f. R-7928, op. 3, d. 96, ll. 7–12.

20. Jacques N'Gom was among the foremost trade unionists in Cameroon and in French Equatorial Africa. Latyr Camara was a Senegalese trade unionist. Their speeches at the Congress are in GARF, f. R-9539, op. 1, d. 179, ll. 171–79 and 138–50 respectively.

21. Ibid.

22. Report on the World Peace Movement for the period 1952–54, GARF, f. R-9539, d. 152, l. 116.

23. The Soviet hosts inserted in the schedule a visit to a Catholic church after the demand of trade unionists from Lebanon, Cameroon, and Madagascar. They also organized a visit to a mosque at the request of Muslim delegates. The delegation of African and Arab trade unionists was invited for the thirty-sixth anniversary of the October Revolution in 1953. GARF, f. R-5451, op. 52, d. 214, ll. 42–51.

24. The trade unionist in question was Charles Richard Edison. GARF, f. R-5451, op. 52, d. 249, l. 46.

25. GARF, f. R-5451, op. 52, d. 373, ll. 112–21.

26. George Padmore, *Panafricanisme ou Communisme? La prochaine lutte pour l'Afrique,* trans. Thomas Diop (Paris: Présence Africaine, 1960), 24, 346–73.

27. Russian State Archive of Literature and Arts (hereafter RGALI), f. 631, op. 26, d. 4820, l. 4.

28. Submitted to the Politburo by Mikhail Suslov on November 10, 1957, this draft of the "Common declaration" "prepared by the CPSU and the CPC" undoubtedly had the imprint of the Chinese world view. See the text in Aleksander A. Fursenko, ed., *Presidium TsK KPSS, Postanovleniia 1954–1964* (Moscow: ROSSPEN, 2006), 2:723.

29. Aimé Césaire, *Lettre à Maurice Thorez* (Paris: Présence Africaine, 1956).

30. The president of the Madagascar-USSR friendship association, Paul Razafiharison, had visited the Soviet Union in 1955 as a member of a delegation of trade unionists from the French colonies. GARF, f. R-5451, op. 52, d. 301, ll. 1–2. A delegation of the Cultural Association Tunisia-USSR had also visited the USSR in August 1956. See GARF, f. R-5283, op. 16, d. 581, ll. 32–35.

31. Letter from Paul Razafiharison, entitled "Evénements de Hongrie," to the VOKS, February 28, 1957. Razafiharison underscores the influence that the position of French intellectuals and European communists had over the members of the association. At the end of his letter he nevertheless states that there had been "not one dissident following those events" in the association. GARF, f. R-5283, op. 16, d. 576, ll. 58–59.

32. Moncef Ben Abda, vice president of the Association Tunisia-USSR, to the VOKS, November 19, 1956, GARF, f. R-5283, op. 16, d. 581, ll. 60a–60b.

33. The enthusiastic African students were members of the Fédération des étudiants d'Afrique noire en France (FEANF) and arrived in Moscow from France. GARF, f. R-8581, op. 2, d. 457, ll. 20–22.

34. For the creation of the Soviet Society for Friendship and Cultural Exchange with the Countries of the Arab East and of the Soviet Association for Friendship with African Peoples, see respectively GARF, f. R-9576, op. 2, d. 61 and d. 94.

35. From the speech of Nikita Khrushchev at the twenty-second congress of the CPSU, October 18, 1961. *SSSR i Strany Afriki, 1946–1962 gg. Dokumenty i materialy* (Moscow: Gosudarstvennoe Izdatel'stvo Politicheskoi Literatury, 1963), 1: 50.

36. Ibid., 51.

37. David Kimche, *The Afro-Asian Movement: Ideology and Foreign Policy of the Third World* (Jerusalem: Israel University Press, 1973).

38. Constantin Katsakioris, "L'Union soviétique et les intellectuels africains. Internationalisme, panafricanisme et négritude pendant les années de décolonisation, 1954–1964," *Cahiers du Monde Russe* 47, nos. 1–2 (2006): 15–32.

39. Founded in 1956, the SAC was an organization with the aim to rehabilitate black African culture. Prominent black intellectuals were grouped around the SAC. See "Deuxième congrès des écrivains et des artistes noirs," *Présence Africaine* nos. 24–25 (1959): 1:431.

40. Ivan Potekhin's intervention in a discussion that took place on January 15, 1959, in the African Commission of the Soviet Afro-Asian Solidarity Committee (SKSSAA). GARF, f. R-9540, op. 1, d. 34, ll. 12–13.

41. Transcript of a meeting of the SKSSAA Presidium, April 25, 1960. GARF, f. R-9540, op. 1, d. 60, ll. 114–15.

42. Transcript of a meeting of the SKSSAA Presidium, August 20, 1962. GARF, f. R-9540, op. 1, d. 110, ll. 81–82.

43. Mohammed Harbi, *Une vie débout. Mémoires politiques, 1945–1962* (Paris: La Découverte, 2001), 350. Even if Moscow refrained from recognizing the GPRA, Soviet and especially Czech arms were sent to the Algerian insurgents through Egypt, Tunisia, and Morocco. See Mathew Connelly, *A Diplomatic Revolution: Algeria's Fight for Independence and the Origins of the Post–Cold War Era* (New York: Oxford University Press,

2002), 256; also Thomas Gomart, "Gêner sans pénaliser. L'utilisation du dossier algérien par la diplomatie soviétique," *Communisme* nos. 74–75 (2003): 134–35. Other forms of Soviet support were shipments of provisions, medicines, and clothing, the treatment of Algerian fighters in Soviet hospitals, and the admission of students in Soviet universities. Soviet "nongovernmental" organizations undertook the mission to provide humanitarian aid. Their action is summarized in two reports of the Soviet Ministry of Foreign Affairs, the first one of December 20, 1958, and the second of October 13, 1959. See respectively Archive of Foreign Policy of the Russian Federation (hereafter AVPRF), f. Referantura po Alzhiru, op. 2, papka 1, d. 110, l. 8, and op. 3, papka 1, d. 5, ll. 23–25.

44. For the account of the Soviet delegation, headed by Alim Keshokov, poet from the Republic of Kabardino-Balkaria, see RGALI, f. 631, op. 26, d. 4827, ll. 1–9. Boris Pasternak had been forced by the Soviet authorities to reject the Nobel Prize for his *Doctor Zhivago.* However, Zahouane's optimism concerning the freedom of expression in Algeria was proved to be terribly wrong. Three months after his discussion with the Soviets the military coup of Houari Boumedienne took place, following which Zahouane was immediately imprisoned.

45. Ivan Potekhin's letter was addressed to Senghor on November 3, 1959. GARF, f. R-9576, op. 12, d. 40, ll. 176–77.

46. Copy in Russian of Senghor's letter to Potekhin, January 18, 1961, GARF, f. R-9576, op. 14, d. 1, ll. 112–13.

47. Senghor's remark is quoted in the report of the delegation. GARF, f. R-9518, op. 1, d. 585, ll. 275.

48. For quotations from Senghor's letter to Evtushenko, written in French on March 5, 1963, see RGALI, f. 631, op. 26, d. 6376, ll. 1–3.

49. Copies in Russian of Senghor's letters to Evtushenko and Voznesenskii, January 7, 1966, GARF, f. R-9518, op. 1, d. 1136, ll. 25–26.

50. GARF, f. R-9518, op. 1, d. 1136, l. 103.

51. Maxim Matusevich, "Journeys of Hope: African Diaspora and the Soviet Society," *African Diaspora* 1 (2008): 74–75.

52. Recent studies on the reception of Third World students in the Soviet Union: Andreas Hilger, "Building a Socialist Elite? Khrushchev's Soviet Union and Elite Formation in India," in Dülffer and Frey, *Elites and Decolonization,* 262–86; Tobias Rupprecht, "Gestrandetes Flaggschiff. Die Moskauer Universität der Völkerfreundschaft," *Osteuropa* 60, no. 1 (2010): 95–114; Rossen Djagalov and Christine Evans, "Moskau, 1960: Wie man sich eine sowjetische Freundschaft mit der Dritten Welt vorstellte," in *Die Sowjetunion und die Dritte Welt. UdSSR, Staatssozialismus und Antikolonialismus im Kalten Krieg,* ed. Andreas Hilger (Munich: Oldenbourg, 2009), 83–106; Hessler, "Death of an African Student"; and Sergei V. Mazov, "Afrikanskie studenty v Moskve v god Afriki (po arkhivnym materialam)," *Vostok* 3 (1999): 89–103. The numbers of students cited are drawn from Constantin Katsakioris, "Sowjetische Bildungsförderung für afrikanische und asiatische Länder," in *Macht und Geist im Kalten Krieg,* ed. Bernd Greiner, Tim B. Müller, and Claudia Weber (Hamburg: Hamburger Edition, 2011), 396–415; Patrice Yengo, "Jalons pour une historiographie des élites africaines formées dans le Bloc soviétique," in Michèle Leclerc-Olive, Grazia Scarfo Ghellab, and Anne-Catherine Wagner, eds., *Les mondes universitaires face au marché. Circulation des savoirs et pratiques des acteurs* (Paris: Karthala, 2011), 135–48.

53. RGASPI, f. M-1, op. 46, d. 354, l. 107.

54. Ibid., d. 353, l. 65.

55. Ibid., d. 293, l. 35.

56. This took place while the students were resting at a nearby vacation camp. Ibid., d. 310, l. 107.

57. GARF, f. R-5451, op. 43, d. 1463, l. 1. The complaints of the students and of the trade unionists were cited in a "secret" report, which A. Bulgakov, secretary of the Central

Council of Trade Unions, sent to the Minister of Higher and Specialized Secondary Education, Viacheslav Eliutin.

58. RGALI, f. 631, op. 26, d. 4822, ll. 1–2. The student affirmed that he was treated as a "beast" and a "Tarzan." He protested to the Union of Writers on December 11, 1963.

59. The delegate asked the Soviet authorities to make an inquiry into the death of Liphapang Molapo. In the meantime, the anti-Soviet mood of the students was evidenced by the fact that they considered his death an assassination. The tragic event also nurtured the anti-Soviet critique in Basutoland. See GARF, f. R-9540, op. 1, d. 137, ll. 24–27, 35–35, 41–44, and 60.

60. The students were convinced that the deceased Edmund Assare-Addo had been assassinated. See Hessler, "Death of an African Student."

61. According to the Komsomol, twenty-nine students from Kenya left the USSR. RGASPI, f. M-3, op. 3, d. 33, l. 139. See also an interview of the Associated Press correspondent with one of those students: RGASPI, f. M-3, op. 3, d. 39, ll. 31–35.

62. RGASPI, f. M-1, op. 46, d. 337, l. 65.

63. See, for instance, the case of a student from Panama and of another from Basutoland, both beaten and robbed: RGASPI, f. M-1, op. 46, d. 354, l. 108, and GARF, f. R-9540, op. 1, d. 137, l. 51 respectively. One other report admits that in many residences for foreign students "stealing is flourishing": RGASPI, f. M-1, op. 46, d. 310, l. 108. If asking a foreign student to sell his watch, his pair of blue jeans, or other clothes was commonplace, stealing such items from foreigners was also motivated by the same desire: many Soviets wanted to acquire precious (for them) modern Western goods. In possession of such goods, the Third World students were hardly seen by the Soviets as needing aid and solidarity.

64. RGASPI, f. M-1, op. 46, d. 310, ll. 103–104.

65. Throughout the 1960s male students made up approximately 90 percent of all Third World students in the USSR. See GARF, f. R-9606, op. 1, d. 3532, ll. 1–2.

66. RGASPI, f. M-1, op. 46, d. 293, l. 164, and d. 339, l. 21.

67. RGASPI, f. M-1, op. 46, d. 337, l. 74.

68. RGASPI, f. M-1, op. 46, d. 310, l. 66.

69. RGASPI, f. M-1, op. 39, d. 129, l. 167.

70. Such organizations were the Soviet Afro-Asian Solidarity Committee, the Committee of Youth Organizations, the All-Union Central Council of Trade Unions, and the Committee of Soviet Women.

71. From 1964 to 1966 the Ghanaians received thirty-seven rubles more per month. RGASPI, f. M-3, op. 3, d. 338, l. 125.

72. The situation was tactfully denounced even by the vice minister of higher and specialized secondary education, Mikhail Prokopev. RGASPI, f. M-1, op. 46, d. 339, l. 23.

73. RGASPI, f. M-1, op. 46, d. 403, l. 123.

74. According an official survey conducted in 1962 at the MGU, among 292 African students, 47 of them apparently belonged to big landholder families and 41 to families of merchants. In 120 cases the students' parents were civil servants and employees, while 33 students were the offspring of workers and 71 of small peasants. See RGASPI, f. M-1, op. 46, d. 403, l. 98. There was, however, a constant tendency to exaggerate the percentage of wealthy African and Arab students.

75. RGASPI, f. M-1, op. 46, d. 310, l. 120.

76. This evolution of the Soviet policy was notably a consequence of the collapse of pro-Soviet regimes in Western Africa. See Robert Legvold, *Soviet Policy in West Africa* (Cambridge MA: Harvard University Press, 1970), 275–344; and Bruce Porter, *The USSR in Third World Conflicts: Soviet Arms and Diplomacy in Local Wars 1945–1980* (Cambridge: Cambridge University Press, 1986), 27–30.

77. It should, however, be noted that during the 1960s the Peoples' Friendship Uni-

versity acquired a rather negative reputation abroad, especially in noncommunist, moderate, and conservative countries, a reputation that in fact it did not deserve.

78. Hough, *Struggle for the Third World,* 97–103. The author convincingly argues that, through the example of capitalist Third World countries, the scholars were implicitly sending messages for the Soviet economy.

79. Amandine Regamay, *Prolétaires de tous pays, excusez-moi! Dérision et politique dans le monde soviétique* (Paris: Buchet Chastel, 2007), 174.

6

MEETING AT A FAR MERIDIAN

US-Soviet Cultural Diplomacy on Film in the Early Cold War

Marsha Siefert

"A few minutes later . . . he realized that he couldn't remember whether he had spoken in Russian or English. It was a startling experience; and for a moment . . . he tried to concentrate on his memory. . . . Then he gave it up because suddenly, and this was equally startling, it made no difference out here. This far from the world below, this far from boundaries, nationalities, governments, from men and women, all that mattered was that they understood each other as human beings."[1] The American physicist Nick Rennet has this epiphany high in the Caucasus Mountains where he and Soviet physicist Dmitri Petrovich Goncharoff have finally come together—and alone—to test which of their cosmic ray theories is correct. This "meeting at a far meridian" is the climax of the 1961 novel by Mitchell Wilson, published simultaneously in both the United States and the Soviet Union. The novel, *Meeting at a Far Meridian,* is the story of two physicists who visit each other's country and who learn from each other and the women who

---

The author would like to thank Sergei Dobrynin, Oleg Minin, Victor Taki, and Elena Vasilyeva for their invaluable research assistance. Sergei Kapterev and Yulia Karpova helped to obtain essential documents from the Russian archives. Others who aided this effort include Tighe Zimmers, Rene Corcoran and Kathy Weiner at the Nebraska Jewish Museum, Kimberly Brownlee at the Canaday Center, University of Toledo Library, Barbara Hall, Jenny Romero, and Clare Denk at the Margaret Herrick Library, the Academy of Motion Picture Arts and Sciences, Robert Parnica at the Open Society Archives, Eric R. Cuellar at the Lyndon B. Johnson Library and Museum, and the staff of the National Archives and Records Administration in Washington, DC. The author benefited from a Mellon Research Fellowship from the Harry Ransom Center, University of Texas, Austin, and the assistance of Richard Workman.

love them. Their relationships are played out against the background of the newly initiated US-Soviet cultural exchange program, which also facilitated the writing of the novel. Adapting this novel as a "joint film" began under the umbrella of the cultural exchange agreement. However, the *Far Meridian* film project was unique, something new—a cinematic collaboration to mutually represent opposing ideological systems in a feature film acceptable to both. It required portraying—and filming in—both countries, striving for an artistic product that would be politically acceptable and economically viable as well as cinematically compelling. Each side already had represented the other in early Cold War films like *Meeting at the Elbe* (*Vstrecha na El'be,* 1949) and *The Iron Curtain* (1948) as allies turned adversaries.[2] Such indelible images of black-and-white conflict were a dramatic norm and dependable repertoire. To what extent could a group of filmmakers fashion a more nuanced script, offer more positive portrayals, and still please the guardians of cultural orthodoxy on both sides? These were the challenges faced by the filmmakers of *Far Meridian.*

Both the novel and the story of its filming take place in the early 1960s when, after a flurry of visits and delegations, exports and exhibitions, the potential and limitations of cultural exchange were beginning to be understood. The crises in US-Soviet foreign relations intruded into *Far Meridian* script conferences and site location visits, and the filmmakers were drawn into the biannual diplomatic negotiations for renewing the cultural exchange agreement. However, the *Far Meridian* project went beyond chaperoned meetings and ritualized formalities. American and Soviet filmmakers spoke one-on-one through interpreters and, not unlike at the Pugwash conference and other citizen-initiated projects in this period, the Americans involved in *Far Meridian* came to see the film as important on the world stage. The filmmakers' efforts to work with each other recapitulated the novel's hopes, rivalries, and disappointments as they sought common ground through professionalism in negotiating the stars, sites, and screenplay for *Far Meridian.* This project, concretized in abundant documentation, is also a synecdoche for larger efforts at Cold War cultural negotiation, an interactive model for using a common project to overcome radically polarized systems of cultural production and ideological belief. Its ultimate value may lie not in its unrealized dream but in the distances willingly traveled by the participants to meet at a meridian that was perhaps just too far away.

"CULTURAL DIPLOMACY" AND THE US-USSR CULTURAL EXCHANGE (1955–60)

The US-USSR Exchange Agreement in Cultural, Technical, and Educational Fields represented the outcome of several years of negotiations initiated in the 1955 spirit of Geneva, accelerated after Khrushchev's not-so-secret speech on February 25, 1956, hindered by reaction to the October 1956 Hungarian Revolution but finally signed on January 27, 1958, by William S. B. Lacy, Eisenhower's Assistant on East-West Exchanges, and Georgii Z. Zarubin, Soviet ambassador to the United States.[3] The cultural exchange was one of several types of government and institutional agreements negotiated during the Cold War. In contrast to other Cold War institutions criticized for disingenuousness or subterfuge,[4] activities sponsored under the exchange agreement have been used as positive examples for modeling successful cultural diplomacy. For example, one influential description of "informal" or "multitrack" diplomacy emphasizes equality in the exchange definitions, e.g., citizen to citizen, media to media. The Cold War examples cite the US initiatives, e.g., Armand Hammer's USSR visits or a CNN special broadcast to Moscow,[5] but without the reciprocal Soviet component. Reciprocity was essential to the US-USSR agreement, however. If there were discrete units—for example, performing artists, scientists, scholars, or films, books, magazines—then equality was defined in numbers. Maintaining parity became more problematic when the results, such as the circulation of each others' magazines or purchase of each others' films, were unequal for whatever reasons, whether disinterest or disrespect. When monies—whether salaries, royalties, concert fees, or purchase prices—were added to the exchange, fundamental contrasts between the two modes of finance in capitalism and communism made effecting reciprocity as prescribed by the agreement even more difficult. These unequal outcomes plagued the film exchange, adding to continued Soviet insistence on exchange as a guarantee of Soviet film screenings in the United States and upon making a "joint film" as evidence of good faith.

Furthermore, extrapolating Cold War exchange experiences to more general theories of cultural diplomacy requires careful assessment of three factors: the context of reception, the contributions of particular individuals, and the scale of the effort.[6] Reception is central to discussions of the winners and losers in the cultural Cold War, which granted superiority to American "soft power" in popular culture and consumer goods, from kitchens to cola.[7] In comparison the Soviet Union was recognized in classical music, athletics, and science—whose representatives participated in the cultural exchange—while failing to gain a mass audience for their domestically produced films.[8] If the effectiveness of "soft power" depends upon "willing interpreters and receivers,"[9] what exactly is meant by a "willing interpreter" or "willing receiver?" What are the contributions of these particular individuals? Who might be willing and why? Anecdotal evidence suggests that many in Soviet society, especially among the young, were "willing receivers" of the varieties of American popular culture that were imported or otherwise made their way into the Soviet Union. A "willing interpreter," however, implies something more subtle—a person who is willing to listen to the language of the other, to understand the culture of the other, in order to move toward common ground. Such interpretation required the skills and willingness of particular individuals. The American author of *Far Meridian* was popular in the Soviet Union before visiting or writing about the country. How he and his colleagues became "willing interpreters" and how far the Soviet filmmakers were able to reciprocate shows in their intense interaction on the *Far Meridian* project. The third factor, the scale of the effort, may seem to marginalize *Far Meridian* as just one film project. However, the perceived value of its potential success would have responded to all of these concerns, multiplying a product of popular culture for positive reception in both contexts and combining the creative contribution of individuals from both sides, hence *Far Meridian*'s importance as an experiment in cultural diplomacy.

Far Meridian was conceived not only under the umbrella of cultural exchange but also as a commercial venture.[10] Economics mattered to both sides. Movie theaters throughout the USSR had to contribute a portion of their receipts to the government to finance future films, so they programmed films that the audience would pay to see. Often these were foreign imports or genre films that were not so highly regarded by the Soviet film bureaucracy, with Hollywood films among the most popular. With the exception of trophy films captured during the war and prewar imports, Hollywood films had been absent from Soviet screens since the Cold War began. The cultural agreement was to provide terms for "exchange" so that the Soviets could barter with the studios for their expensive purchase price. In return they hoped to find a way to ensure commercial distribution of their own films in the lucrative American market. A joint film like *Meeting at a Far Meridian* would presumably further open the American market to Soviet films and perhaps Hollywood-style economic success, an uncomfortable but acknowledged contradiction.[11] Hollywood also was interested. The onset of the Cold War coincided with hard times. Faced with stiff competition from television, a loss of necessary profits from all-but-destroyed European markets, and the legal dismemberment of its oligopoly of production and distribution, postwar Hollywood began to produce films in Europe and elsewhere, while European film industries turned to film coproduction as a way to boost productivity, to share production costs, and to increase the number of cinema-goers. By the time of the cultural exchange agreement, European film industries had coproduced over 1,000 films.[12] Thus, although Western skeptics recognized film coproductions as "one of the propaganda vehicles used by the Communists for some time," they also confirmed Hollywood's interest in the large and virtually untapped Soviet market and the success of other Western countries in realizing film coproductions, even with the Soviets.[13]

The *Far Meridian* negotiations took place in an era of expanding trade between East and West, with the Kennedy administration working toward its liberalization throughout the early 1960s.[14] The Soviet Union was already evolving a discourse of "doing business" in March of 1959, when Khrushchev introduced himself as "a representative of the business circles of the USSR"[15] and Anastas Mikoyan reported to a meeting of importers and exporters that once the Soviets sign a contract, "they perform it with accuracy,"[16] a claim supported by subsequent trade agreements.[17] Although "*biznes*" was discursively located in the "capitalist camp," "business talk" (*delovoi razgovor*) permeated the written correspondence and frequently revised protocols of *Far Meridian.* The Soviet filmmakers were incredulous about decentralized Hollywood film finance and grew impatient with American assertions of "entertainment" values as plot devices, while American filmmakers became frustrated by what they perceived as disorganization and even anarchy in the Soviet bureaucratic decision making. But each side spoke through the language of contracts and commitments.

In other East-West trade agreements requiring the selection of cocontractors for individual transactions, "state-trading entities [had] more freedom to bargain over arrangements with Western firms than could ever be imagined in a wholly collective environment."[18] To what extent there was relative freedom in the negotiations on *Far Meridian* is a difficult question. The meetings, visits, and arguments documented in internal memos and stenographic reports suggest a less scripted outcome of the negotiations than of the film itself. As is well known, Soviet bureaucrats had authority over the entire film through the centralized system of film financing, production, and distribution.[19] During this period the US State Department, which from the beginning had been "the least enthusiastic and most threatened by the proposal to increase informational and cultural ties" with the USSR,[20] also screened all potential films for sale to the USSR and required screenplay approval for any joint film with the USSR. In practice, then, either side could withhold script approval for *Far Meridian* and, by prolonging negotiations. keep the project alive without committing a single frame of film. The American financial partners also claimed the right to script approval, complicating the process even further. In sum, the filmmakers might share professional skills making a film together and might demonstrate "businesslike cooperation" through assertions of mutual respect, collective public statements, strategic press conferences, and ritualized meetings of small steps, but official oversight was always a script change away.

Overall, the *Far Meridian* project must be interpreted within the ideological paradoxes of the cultural Cold War. Its uniqueness might be located in its attempt to realize the Soviet formulation of "peaceful coexistence" through cinematic coproduction. Even though the American author of *Far Meridian* was careful not to use the phrase, and the phrase did not find its way into the multiple script revisions, "coexistence" was nonetheless embedded in the language in which the Soviet filmmakers explained the film when in the United States and appeared in various guises in correspondence. The Russian crew even referred to the American producer's office at Mosfilm as "the co-existence room."[21] At its most idealistic, the *Far Meridian* storyline about competition between a Soviet and American scientist could "tame" the Cold War, subsuming the implications of the nuclear arms race by personalizing a more abstract scientific rivalry.[22] But even if neither side anticipated a clear-cut ideological resolution in the plot, fears of ideological cooptation remained and intensified through agonizing and frustrating negotiations about every aspect of the film. A joint venture in symbolic cultural politics, even with willing interpreters, was still a contest in which everyone could lose.[23]

This contentiousness about joint film was present from the start of negotiations for the 1958 US-USSR Cultural Exchange Agreement. At Soviet insistence the Americans included a general provision on joint films: "To recognize the desirability and usefulness of organizing joint production of artistic, popular science and documentary films and of the conducting, not later than May, 1958, of concrete negotiations between Soviet Union film organizations and US film companies on this subject. . . . The subject matter of the films will be mutually agreed upon by the two parties."[24] In negotiating the supplementary agreement on film, the US ambassador to the Soviet Union, Llewellyn E. Thompson, complained in a telegram to Senator William S. B. Lacy that the chief Soviet negotiator from the Ministry of Culture (and future head of Mosfilm), Vladimir Surin, proposed several provisions that ran counter to US interests. One would grant Sovexportfilm the right "to contact any American firm to carry on direct contact and make direct deals regarding purchase and sale of films without reference to provisions of [the] cultural agreement." This was described as "an obvious plot . . . to obtain 'blanket approval' in advance . . . to make direct contacts with US concerns without any reference to protective clauses set up in [the] cultural agreement."[25] Another Soviet proposal provided for "wide joint production of feature, popular science and documentary films which named many strongly political film stories and requested names of US companies prepared to engage in joint production." The State Department affirmed: "These efforts will be resisted."[26]

In spite of a well-publicized contract for ten American and seven Soviet films to be exchanged via Sovexport and the Motiòn Picture Association of America (MPAA), the supplementary agreement on film exchange, eventually signed on October 9, 1958, remained vague about both joint films and the procedure for selling and purchasing films. The film exchange agreement applied only to members of the MPAA and did not apply to independent studios, which were free to deal with the Soviets outside the agreement.[27] Changes in how Hollywood did business also contributed to the gray areas of cooperation. In the 1950s the Hollywood studio system, admired by the Soviet Union in the 1930s, was stripped of its distribution networks, challenged by television, and beholden to the entrepreneurial film producer.[28] By 1957, independent film producers, who formed companies on a film-by-film basis and made individual deals for financing, accounted for 58 percent of all distributed films.[29] Moreover, the independent film producer assumed the burden of putting together a film package—obtaining financial backing, commissioning the script, and hiring the stars—and therefore the bulk of the commercial risk. A producer without a studio reinforced the definition of a film as "a wager, a bet, a gamble," "the funding of hope over experience,"[30] hardly the profile of an attractive partner for a Soviet state film studio.

Soviet filmmakers took note of these changes when they visited Hollywood in June 1960 at the invitation of the president of United Artists. As film director Sergei Gerasimov reported in *Izvestiia,*[31] the official Hollywood reception took on the character of an improvised meeting, chaired by Hollywood director Frank Capra.[32] What interested their "American friends" most of all was who initiated films in the Soviet system. "The writer and the film director," the Soviet filmmakers replied. "Next comes the studio and finally the state which finances the production of films. This did not make sense to [the Americans]." "Didn't we have any producers?" they asked. "The whole of their amazement was expressed in this question." Gerasimov went on to explain that there was no such designation in the Soviet film industry and that their films were made by "creative collectives invested with the trust of the studio and the State Film Board." After discussing various American films, "the talk kept reverting to collective productions. Everybody agreed that such productions demand determination, a keen sense of novelty; . . . that films must deal with new, original ideas, new observations and newly born images; that businesslike cooperation should begin with the creative cooperation of the artists themselves."[33]

Gerasimov's statement that businesslike cooperation began with the creative cooperation of the artists themselves is central to the unfolding of the *Far Meridian* story. Gerasimov himself was later appointed to the *Far Meridian* film team. He had been a veteran of USSR delegations to the United States since the 1949 "Waldorf Conference" in New York and was known for his successful cinematic adaptations of socialist realist novels, and he frequently wrote about American films. Vladimir Surin was involved from the beginning, first as a deputy minister of culture who visited the United States in 1956,[34] then as negotiator on the exchange agreement, and finally as head of Mosfilm. In contrast, before *Far Meridian* neither the American author Mitchell Wilson nor Lester Cowan, the American independent film producer who became the entrepreneurial energy behind the project, expressed any interest in the Soviet Union or exhibited any political leanings that would have predicted their involvement. Unlike some of the well-known Western cultural brokers in the cultural Cold War, such as Sol Hurok or Nicholas Nabokov, none of the

American protagonists in the *Far Meridian* story had Russian antecedents or government connections.[35] For Wilson and Cowan, as has been said of other individuals involved in informal cultural diplomacy, "the desires, the lines of policy, the targets, and the very definition of state interests become blurred and multiply." In fact, at times they competed with each other by communicating independently with their Soviet counterparts, assuming "a responsibility and an agenda of their own."[36]

The *Far Meridian* story opens with a small Soviet initiative. Among the first Soviet delegations to visit the United States in the fall of 1955 was a group of seven journalists and writers led by Boris Polevoi, *Pravda* correspondent and head of the international department of the Soviet Writers Union.[37] In a confidential sixteen-page report for the Central Committee offering advice on how to better communicate the socialist message to Americans,[38] he responded to complaints by "progressive American writers" whose works were translated and published in Russian without being paid royalties. Polevoi commented critically on the perceived discrimination these authors received "due to their political convictions and their friendship with the Soviet Union." He also pointed out that "the royalties from the Soviet Union usually arrive after a series of humiliating requests and reminders, and sometimes do not arrive at all." He mentioned specifically translations published in *Inostrannaia Literatura* by Howard Fast,[39] Lloyd Brown, Leon Feuchtwanger, and [Ethel] Lilian Voynich.[40] The question of royalties for translation into Russian also sparked the interest of a New York writer by the name of Mitchell Wilson.

THE NOVEL (1958–61)

"In a way, my passport is unique. . . . Out of ten pages, seven bear the hammer-and-sickle emblem of the Soviet Union. Yet I am neither diplomat, international correspondent nor secret agent. I am, I suppose, simply a commuter."[41] Mitchell Wilson wrote these lines in the first year of negotiations on the film version of his novel, *Meeting at a Far Meridian.* Before World War II, he had studied physics at Columbia University in Enrico Fermi's laboratory. According to the recollections of one of his fellow graduate students, Wilson hated Columbia and disliked the people, so he turned to writing. Following a "typical physicist's pattern . . . [Wilson] statistically analyzed a large number of published stories for the number of words in the opening, the development, love interest and denouement," and began writing titles like *Footsteps Behind Her* and *Stalk the Hunter.* He soon graduated from the "pulps" to the "slicks" like *Collier's,* abandoning science for fiction. His 1949 novel *Live with Lightning* was "an interesting semi-fictionalized account of events, primarily at Columbia, that led up to the development of the A-bomb. . . . It was not a flattering picture of Columbia. To protect himself [Wilson] reassembled accurate personality traits into individuals so that they could not be specifically identified."[42] To Soviet critics of the early 1950s, this verisimilitude fit neatly into a socialist-realist approach. Wilson "is well acquainted with the environment of the physicists described in the book," a Soviet reviewer noted, which gives the book "the value of being the true testimony of an eyewitness." A Russian translation was published in 1952.[43] Two years later Wilson heard that his novel was popular in Russia, so he sent a letter requesting royalties to the US State Department, which passed him on to the Soviet Embassy, which gave him an address in Moscow. He received no reply.[44] A year later he received a cable from Moscow, asking him to write an article about how he came to write his next book, *My Brother, My Enemy,* then being serialized in a Soviet literary magazine.[45] He replied, "Delighted to write article if paid for (1) article; (2) serial, and (3) previous novel." After a prolonged silence, his bank "telephoned excitedly: 'The Russians have just deposited $6,253 to your account!'"[46] By 1961 he had accumulated about $15,000,[47] a fact cited by almost any American publication that bothered to mention Wilson.

Getting royalties from the USSR was one thing, but, for Wilson, going there was something else. "Others may admire Soviet ballet or Soviet science. What I admired about the Soviet Union was that the Soviet Union admired me. Russians like my novels. To me, this was irresistible."[48] Still, Mitchell claimed he had to be both persuaded by his publisher and invited by the Soviets to visit for two weeks as part of a delegation in October of 1957. Once there, "instead of being on the moon or in funny-funny land," he found the country "full of vital people living lives of fascinating complexity." He officially asked the Soviet Writers Union if he could return later "on his own," to go where he wanted and to see whom he pleased, even work in a physics lab not covered by security restrictions—in order to write a novel. Two days before leaving, he received permission. After a crash course in Russian and several weeks in the MIT cosmic ray lab, a security-free field, he returned to Moscow in the spring of 1958.

For five months he lived in the Rossiya Hotel on rubles earned from royalties and from writing nonpolitical articles for Moscow magazines, eschewed an interpreter, and saw foreigners very rarely. After a time he was "unofficially assigned to a research group at the Lebedev Institute of Physics," and he accepted several personal invitations, including to Dubna, the atomic research center, and to a mountaintop laboratory in Armenia,[49] all of which featured in *Meeting at a Far Meridian.* The "semi-fictional" style of the novel is reflected in Wilson's recollections—of dacha visits, formal receptions, and mistakes made by his protagonist. In trying to find "the truth" about the Soviet Union, between "a prison and a paradise," he eventually agreed with a young scientist who said, "How can I make you understand: it was both!"[50] So it came to pass that *Meeting at a Far Meridian* was published simultaneously in New York, in London, and in issues 1–4 of *Inostrannaia literatura* (Foreign literature) in the early months of 1961.[51]

For US reviewers, Wilson's books were a publishing curiosity. Prior to *Far Meridian,* American visitors to the USSR found Wilson's fame a cause for consternation, assuming he was probably "un-American."[52] Scholars inaccurately described him as a "relatively unknown Russophile writer" and "specialist in science fiction."[53] *Far Meridian,* with blurbs in publications from *Science* to *Mademoiselle,*[54] and even an ad in the *Bulletin of Atomic Scientists,*[55] brought a bit more notoriety. Still, noted one contemporary scholar, his "novels about scientists might be considered distant cousins of science fiction."[56] *Time* was even less charitable—"written at too much length and with too little imagination, [the book] intermingles scientific razzle-dazzle, political flimflam, and wishy-washy sex"—but admits that "with the exception of several vague references to the peaceful universality of science, *Far Meridian* is nonideological."[57]

Wilson's Soviet popularity has been attributed by American scholars to his "critical realism" detailing scientific laboratory research. In his early works obstacles like bureaucratic difficulties, collegial rivalries, and public indifference clothed the scientists' "frustrations in capitalist conditions" while ethical conflicts and crises of conscience among scientists especially related to the atomic bomb added drama to the novels and value to the Soviet translations.[58] In reviewing *Far Meridian,* a Soviet critic recognized that Mitchell was not an adherent of socialism but thought the novel's protagonist "lived among people with faith in the future." Interestingly, he commented that due to Wilson's honesty and lack of prejudice, "the conclusion about the advantage of peaceful coexistence and the conclusion about the merits of the system of socialism force their way into his book independently of the author's will, and even against it."[59]

Wilson was also friends with Soviet writers. None other than Boris Polevoi wrote to "Mitch" in April of 1961: "I am not quite the swine you may imagine I am, considering my delay in responding to your present, the book *Meeting at a Far Meridian,* that you have sent me with such a friendly dedication. It is just that I wanted to have read the book first, and I was impatiently awaiting the fourth issue of *Inostrannaia Literatura* magazine which would publish the ending of the novel." Regretting that they failed to meet in New York to raise a glass to their "literary friendship," Polevoi was "awfully happy" when Wilson telephoned him at the Commodore Hotel, "speaking the same charming Russian as [his] character Nick." Comparing *Far Meridian* to *My Brother, My Enemy* ("one of the most interesting books I have had the opportunity to read in the last fifteen years"), *Far Meridian* "is a pioneering book . . . on the great subject of coexistence, which, in my opinion, is one of the greatest ideas of the century . . . an interesting book which will, I believe, find the friendliest response from a wide spectrum of readers."[60]

The "friendliest response" resonated with an ongoing discussion among Soviet intellectuals about the relevance of poetry in the scientific age. Named the "physicists and lyricists debate" after the eponymous 1959 poem by Boris Slutskii, the discussion and valorization of the scientist, especially the physicist, was carried on not only in prose but also during the gestation, filming, validation and eventual release of the dramatic Soviet film *Nine Days in One Year* (*9 dney odnogo goda*).[61] The several versions of the script begun during the summer of 1960 epitomized the physicist as hero whose sacrifice was questioned by the more "cosmopolitan" physicist, played by Innokentii Smoktunovskii. The film's recreation of the hitherto secret world of the physics lab created problems for the authorities but also contributed to its popularity with Soviet viewers.[62] Its criticism of American physicists' nuclear success was matter-of-fact, and the Soviet protagonist expressed regrets about having participated in making the bomb, not dissimilar to Wilson's main character. And along with a few other Soviet films in this period, *Nine Days in One Year* also showed interest in private emotions and critical reflection.[63] The film was released on March 5, 1962, just two days before Mosfilm announced its newest venture with Mitchell Wilson in Moscow—a joint US-Soviet film version of *Meeting at a Far Meridian.*[64]

THE JOINT FILM IDEA (1962)

The simplicity of this announcement belies its significance. In spite of well-publicized visits of American film personnel and senior Soviet film officials both before and after the exchange agreement was signed, representatives from both countries found it difficult even to agree on films to be exchanged, much less a mutually agreeable story for a joint film. In 1956 Mike Todd had suggested *War and Peace,* not a work for which the Soviet film establishment felt they needed American aid.[65] As Turner B. Shelton, a member of the Soviet and East European Exchanges staff at the US State Department, wrote in an April 1960 telegram to the Moscow Embassy, a procedure needed to be "worked out concerning 'joint production' which several U.S. producers have proposed so far unsuccessfully."[66] In a May 1960 visit to Mosfilm, Samuel Goldwyn Jr. also commented on the challenge of finding a story that met the demands of each country in equal measure. He declined some subjects predictably suggested by the Mosfilm administration, such as the "struggle for peace" or "a call to ban nuclear weapons." Goldwyn suggested a literary adaptation (Dreiser's *An American Tragedy* was offered by Mosfilm) or a musical comedy about guest performances of a Soviet entertainment ensemble in the United States; the necessary love story did not even have to end happily, conceded Goldwyn.[67] In the end he showed his film *Huckleberry Finn* in Moscow.[68] During the 1961 meeting of the Standing Committee on Film, set up by the exchange agreement, Soviet director Lev Arnshtam[69] informally discussed the problems concerning joint production with Shelton for several hours, with the Soviets proposing a film on American sailors rescuing four Soviet sailors. They were advised that the US side was interested in seeing the completed script, which they promised,[70] but the film was made later by Mosfilm alone.[71] Thus the prospect of a story that was in effect already copublished in the United States and the Soviet Union presented an opportunity that both governments were prepared to pursue.

Before departing for Moscow in January 1962 Wilson told the press that Mosfilm had approached him sometime in 1960 and, after the US State Department gave tentative approval for the project, he had selected Lester Cowan as the producer.[72] Cowan had spent several years in the formative period of the Academy of Motion Picture Arts and Sciences, including the first five Academy Award ceremonies and the Technical

Bureau,[73] later producing comedies with W. C. Fields (*You Can't Cheat an Honest Man,* 1939), May West (*My Little Chickadee,* 1940), and the Marx Brothers (*Love Happy,* 1949). He became an independent producer in 1941 and was experienced at making deals in Hollywood. His most successful film, *The Story of G.I. Joe,* documented the role of the war journalist Ernie Pyle and was released in 1945 after Pyle's death on the battlefield. William Wellman, *G.I. Joe*'s director, said of Cowan, "When Cowan started talking, all you could do was 'just sit and listen.'" Even when Wellman rejected his offer twice, Cowan returned with presents for his five children. He was "a persistent bastard."[74] This quality would serve him well in pursuing this coproduction.

Cowan may not have been Wilson's personal choice, although this formulation would have been important for introducing him into the world of Soviet cinema. Cowan's wife, Ann Ronell, who would later join the production team as its music director, offers a different version of their partnership. In early May of 1961, she wrote that Cowan had obtained the rights to Wilson's book and had "done a miraculous job in clearing it for filming in Russia! . . . The project is viewed optimistically in Washington and seems to have gotten to the President's attention." Cowan, who "tackles the most challenging projects—he just can't settle for less," spoke daily by telephone with Wilson—"tall, handsome remote in a certain way . . . smart and somehow intercontinental, lord knows what that means." This prescient description identified the disparity between the two men that was to play a role in Mosfilm's relations with both. As Ronell wrote then, "It's all very confidential, so just cross your fingers."[75]

Announcing the film together in New York on January 23, 1962, Cowan and Wilson envisaged the production as a high-budget color film, with each side paying for the production costs of the scenes shot in each country. They expressed interest in selecting a young Soviet director like Grigori Chukhrai of the well-received *Ballad of a Soldier* (1959) and the Russian female star of *The Cranes Are Flying* (1957) for the role of a Russian woman in love with the American scientist. Their announcement was made on the eve of their departure for Moscow to begin negotiations. Their visit was approved by the State Department on January 11, prior to their public announcement, but, as a telegram to the US Embassy in Moscow stressed, "DEPT [of State] has not repeat not approved this coproduction proposal under Exchange Agreement, but has agreed to interpose no objection to investigation by Cowan of possibility of specific arrangements he can make. These arrangements, plus script, subject approval by DEPT."[76]

Vladimir Surin, now director of Mosfilm, and Cowan announced the signing of the preliminary agreement in Moscow on March 9. The plans represented the parity demanded of all such joint projects. If the producer was American, the director would be Soviet, to "provide an element of Soviet control over the production," according to the *New York Times*.[77] The starring roles would be played by two Americans and two Russians. The American protagonist should be "a tall, dark, thoughtful character," as often portrayed by Gregory Peck or Henry Fonda.[78] One-fourth to one-third of the scenes would be filmed at a university laboratory in California and in New York, using the Soviet director, camera crew, and actors, to enable the Soviet viewer "to get a glimpse of the real United States,"[79] according to Cowan, rather than the issues of unemployment, juvenile delinquency, and race problems which characterized America more often in Soviet prose. The film would be made in the Soviet wide-screen process similar to Todd-AO.[80] The US company Continental Distributing was also investing in the film and would be responsible for distribution in the Western Hemisphere while the Soviets would handle distribution of the Russian-language version in the USSR and bloc countries. Wilson meanwhile gave interviews to *Pravda* and *Izvestiia.*

To the Hollywood film community Cowan hinted at a tantalizing opening of the Soviet market for film export. "Soviets 'Need' Comedy," Cowan told the *Motion Picture Daily,* and they are aware that "to reach an international market a picture must have entertainment values." Cowan sent nine of his own films for potential Soviet screening in return for selecting three of theirs. Expressing "great satisfaction" with his "thorough producer control over the actual making of the film," Cowan also praised the Soviet representatives who helped set up the deal, including Surin and the minister of culture, Ekaterina Furtseva, for their "cordiality, efficiency and fairness."[81] The future influential *New York Times* critic Vincent Canby, then writing for *Variety,* gave an upbeat front-page analysis of the "Hollywood-on-the-Volga Deal." "Don't you come over here to make 'Anna Karenina' and we won't go to the United States and do 'Huckleberry Finn,'" said the Russians, according to Cowan. Rather, the "Soviets are interested in stories in which Americans and Russians would figure naturally, and which, at the same time, would contribute to mutual understanding." "Despite the fact that there was no previous blueprint for the agreement, [Cowan] and the Russians were able to negotiate it in just eight days. It could set the blueprint for the future."[82] Others in the film trade were more cautious. "Cowan was said to have been cleared to discuss but not contract for the deal," as under the cultural exchange agreement just renewed in 1960, "talks by one government with individuals, lacking clearance, of the other nation are banned. State was said to have so advised the Soviet Union." Reportedly Cowan traveled at his own expense and was to report to the State Department upon his return about details and eventually script approval.[83]

That he did just days after his press conference, in two visits to Turner B. Shelton at the US State Department. In a three-page summary of his conversations with Cowan, shared with a range of government agencies including the USIA and the Justice and Commerce Departments, Shelton reviewed Cowan's "preliminary agreement" with Mosfilm. After confirming that he wanted to work closely with the State Department and had kept the US Embassy "fully informed at all times" while in Moscow, Cowan then requested State Department approval for the entire project on the basis of a screen treatment rather than wait for the screenplay, which was extremely expensive to commission. Shelton responded that such an agreement was "impossible." The State Department could give informal views but "could not definitely state that this project was under the 'umbrella of protection' of the Exchange Agreement until the Department had an opportunity to review the script." After "considerable discussion" and Cowan's concurrence, Shelton also cautioned Cowan about making statements to the press that could seem to present the State Department's approval. On the second day Cowan expressed his concern about how the Soviets could be "forced to live up to the agreement they entered into." Shelton responded that Cowan should include as many self-enforcing provisions as possible. "In effect," he said, Cowan was "dealing with a sovereign country and that the Soviet Union does not have an outstanding reputation for living up to agreements with which they are not satisfied."[84] To what extent "doing business" with Mosfilm meant dealing with Soviet government officials became clearer in subsequent visits.

Meanwhile, Cowan continued building his relationship with Mosfilm. Although he sent his comedy films, it was *G.I. Joe* that made an impression on Surin and the two young Russian directors, Alexander Alov and Vladimir Naumov, who had been chosen to work with Wilson on the screenplay for *Far Meridian.*[85] Alov and Naumov, whose World War II film *Peace to Who Enters* (*Mir vkhodiashchemu*), portraying three Soviet soldiers who attempt to rescue a trapped pregnant German woman, won a special jury prize at the 1961 Venice Film Festival,[86] were formally named by TASS in May.[87] Cowan also appeared to keep his bargain with the State Department. Even though the July *New York Times* headline trumpeted that the "Draft Script of '*Far Meridian*' Gets U.S. and Soviet Approval," the article correctly stated that it was just the "initial screen treatment" that was endorsed by the State Department under the terms of the cultural exchange agreement as well as being approved by Soviet officials.[88] In State Department language, "on a tentative and preliminary basis . . . the present treatment constitutes an acceptable basis for further development."[89]

In August, when Wilson and Cowan returned to Moscow to work on the screenplay, Wilson appeared on Soviet television, along with the family of the two cosmonauts who had just returned safely from their space mission, and reported on his visit in both the *Nation* and the *London Observer.*[90] Cowan's wife, Ann Ronell, a Broadway and Hollywood composer as well as longtime Cowan collaborator, was welcomed by the Soviet musical establishment in her own right. During the last week of August 1962 she was also a guest of Mosfilm, the "first American lady to be taken on a set."[91] There she played tape recordings of several American film scores and had preliminary discussions about music for *Far Meridian.* She also took part in several music-related occasions in Moscow, including a reception in her honor at the US Embassy. One of the most celebratory was a party after the Mosfilm private screening of the new film musical *Ballad of a Hussar,* where she met the director Eldar Riazanov and Alexander Gladkov, author of the original theatrical play.[92] Present at all these events was Tikhon Khrennikov, the Soviet Composers Union's powerful secretary since 1948 who also happened to be the composer for the film. Khrennikov had visited the United States as head of the first delegation of Soviet composers for a month in the autumn of 1959. Described as "cold and officious" in politically sensitive situations, he was said to be "friendly and co-operative" in personal dealings.[93]

Ronell responded in kind when she was invited by Khrennikov to visit the Composers Union. When asked about her famous song, "Who's Afraid of the Big Bad Wolf?" she enjoyed the surprise that it was not a folk song and was written by a woman. She also assented to requests to play and sing it for them—with the Russian lyrics she had learned. A top musicologist assured her that the song's "gaiety and laughing at fear" had endeared the song to Russians when they badly needed it. After her reception at the US Embassy she was asked to perform on Soviet television during her next trip. In the spirit of the *Far Meridian* enterprise, Ronell collaborated with Khrennikov. After he played his own tune "Moscow Windows" for her, they both thought it might do well in the United States with English lyrics, which she supplied. He immediately called a mutual friend "to announce the first musical coproduction between the United States and the Soviet Union, with music by Khrennikov and Ronellova."[94] All in all, the summer 1962 trip seemed to augur success for the joint film.

Behind the scenes, however, problems were emerging. In a dense August memo to Surin, Cowan complained that Wilson was unwilling to work with Alov and Naumov except as consultants and was unwilling to work on the screenplay in Moscow, as specified in his contract. More crucially, Cowan expressed his concern that, judging by the overly literary treatment, Wilson "has not yet revealed himself as a screenwriter." In spite of Surin's belief that Wilson could solve these problems with broad help, Cowan said he was sufficiently unsure to talk to other screenwriters—with Wilson's knowledge. Concluding the memo, Cowan vowed that, for his part, he would "spare no effort or expense to achieve the best results" and said he knew that he and Surin were united in this goal. Surin responded tersely that the literary treatment constituted an acceptable basis for continuing.[95]

THE NEGOTIATION (1962–63)

In early September 1962 Cowan announced from Moscow that Soviet cultural officials agreed to a "realistic treatment" of the Cold War, with the two scientists working together shown "as achieving more than they could separately." The film contract "provides for safeguards against any propaganda distortions," and the Soviet government agreed to a single release of the film.[96] This announcement did not go unnoticed in the United States. *Human Events*, a conservative Washington weekly, had published an account of the film agreement referring to the US State Department approval, and a concerned St. Louis citizen sent a letter to US senator Stuart Symington, who in turn queried the State Department about the film, which was said to be "sympathetic to communism." The State Department reply, which went through at least one draft, reassured Senator Symington that if they had any basis to believe that the screenplay would be "sympathetic toward communism," their approval would not be granted. Still, the State Department also reaffirmed that any proposals that might come from private citizens under the US-USSR Exchanges Agreement would be examined on their merits.[97] Similarly, in mid-October the US ambassador in Moscow, Foy D. Kohler, asked the State Department for a status report on the film exchanges, both documentary and commercial, as official callers, including Minister of Culture Furtseva, had complained that film was the least satisfactory area of exchanges.[98]

Late October brought a different kind of realism to Soviet-American relations, however, with the US president's revelation that Soviet missiles were found on Cuban soil.[99] This "October surprise" had been preceded just the day before by a culturally daring act—Khrushchev's agreement to publish Solzhenitsyn's *One Day in the Life of Ivan Denisovich,* which resonated in both countries.[100] Within months two different English translations of the book were released in the United States, and in December of 1962 variations of its title had been registered with the Motion Picture Association of America's Title Registration Bureau by two Hollywood producers—Clarence Greene and Russell Rouse.[101] On January 23, 1963, they made bold public statements to the film community in *Variety:* they expected to involve Columbia Pictures; they would contact both the author and Premier Khrushchev; they might use Russian locations, seeking distribution rights and possibly a dual-language production. The news story lead boasted about "production plans that, *for the first time,* could involve Russian cooperation."[102]

The announcement did not go unnoticed. Two weeks later, Lester Cowan called upon Soviet ambassador Anatoly Dobrynin in Washington. In a polite letter written to Minister of Culture Furtseva on February 8, Cowan affirmed that Wilson's screenplay was on schedule and, with a growing understanding of cinematic possibilities, "his work constantly improves." He also mentioned that this letter, and one to Surin, would be personally delivered by Evgenii Bugrov, a Soviet Embassy counselor who was present at the meeting with Ambassador Dobrynin and who would "report to you on this meeting personally."[103] Presumably he did, for on

March 6, 1963, Furtseva wrote a memorandum to the Central Committee of the CPSU ominously titled "On Countermeasures to the intentions to adapt for the screen in the US the Aleksandr Solzhenitsyn novella 'One Day in the Life of Ivan Denisovich.'" In this memo she interpreted Cowan's visit as a warning about the planned Solzhenitsyn adaptation. Given his familiarity with the people (presumably Greene and Rouse) who intended to adapt the novella, Cowan told her that "it would be advisable to study the opportunities to influence the content of the film so it could not be used in hostile ways." Cowan wanted to present his own suggestions on this issue when he next visited Moscow to discuss the *Far Meridian* screenplay. Furtseva then suggested, representing the USSR Ministry of Culture, that it would be appropriate for the Central Committee to send a directive to the Soviet Embassy to take every step possible to prevent such a film adaptation. Cowan was included in this admonition, and Furtseva outlined the reasons that the Soviet Union was not interested in making a film of this novella "on any cooperative basis whatsoever."[104] However well intentioned Cowan's back-channel communication to Furtseva,[105] the message gathered more sinister connotations as it progressed through the Soviet bureaucracy.

Just a few weeks after her memorandum and Khrushchev's seminal March 8 speech to the Central Committee declaring there could be no peaceful coexistence in ideology,[106] Furtseva's oversight of cinema was seriously undermined when Alexei K. Romanov from the Central Committee's Department of Propaganda and Agitation[107] was dramatically named head of a new Cinematography Committee at the USSR Council of Ministers on March 23, 1963.[108] Romanov brought strong ideological expectations for Soviet film as "the political enlightenment and aesthetic education of the people" in accordance with "the interests of communist construction and the Soviet nation,"[109] and he represented a drive toward greater control in the arts that had spread to the film industry by the spring of 1963.[110] Cowan was back in the USSR in early May to protect his production, and on May 19 he announced from Moscow that both Furtseva and Romanov had "assured him that any changes in the domestic ideological line would have no bearing on Moscow's determination to continue its expanding cultural contacts with the United States."[111]

This public reassurance belied the problems that continued and multiplied. Although friendly cables had been exchanged between Wilson,

Cowan, Surin, and Alov and Naumov, in his note to Furtseva Surin had privately criticized Wilson's lack of dramatic form and cinematic means in the literary scenario, which by March had grown to over 360 pages.[112] Alov and Naumov's contribution to the screenplay also became an issue when Cowan spoke for ninety minutes to the Filmmakers' Union early in his May 1963 visit before he talked to Romanov. He openly stated that he considered the completed *Far Meridian* screenplay to be weak and therefore requiring the right director. He punctuated his entire talk with his doubts about Alov and Naumov, "good guys" whom he "liked a lot," but who were lacking in stature and appropriate style, adding that their most recent film (*The Coin/Moneta,* 1962), based on three Albert Maltz stories, was "anti-American." Cowan used most of his time at the Filmmakers' Union to propose a number of other coproductions, offering a specific screenplay based on a US visit of the Moiseev Ensemble when an American and Russian trade places, both roles to be played by Tony Curtis. At the end of the talk he asked how he could invite a number of Soviet filmmakers to dinner and was told that invitations had to go through Surin. The Soviet report on his visit concluded with the impression "that Cowan's visit to the Union was aimed at somehow circumventing the official state organizations, and that he wanted through the Union to enter into contact with, and receive some information about, other creative artists who could be interested in taking part in American-Soviet co-productions."[113] Cowan may not have intended his dinner invitations to circumvent state organizations, but his pitch was received with suspicion. His pursuit of other coproduction ideas and scripts with "entertainment value" became a theme of most all his subsequent meetings with Soviet film personnel.

Another high-level US visit was also offered, and Surin, unaccompanied by Alov and Naumbov, came to the United States for several days in May. Cowan insisted that the Soviet side sign a protocol approving Wilson's screenplay to show the bankers and public some "real progress," but at Surin's request they agreed to postpone signing the protocol until later in Moscow,[114] and proposed several changes to the screenplay, with Mitchell Wilson included.[115] In New York Surin met with the presidents of United Artists and of ABC Television and Paramount Theaters. In Washington he lunched with Senator William J. Fulbright, who expressed support for the project.[116] Surin also spoke with Ambassador Llewellyn Thompson, who stated for the record that the State Department had no position on *Far Meridian* since its content was unknown—but he wished them well. In interviews with the *New York Times* and the trade press, Surin avoided committing to similar ventures but said he was trying "to improve contacts in general." Cowan added, "When you work with Russians you need time to get acquainted and dispel prejudices and doubts."[117] Cowan later wrote Cinematography Minister Romanov, complimenting him on his "alert and decisive action" in supporting Surin's visit to the United States and extended a similar invitation to Romanov for November meetings with equally prominent persons, like Franklin D. Roosevelt Jr., who saw *Far Meridian* as a "pioneering example of good and successful business relations."[118]

The Moscow summer of 1963 was again a time of contrasts in politics and culture. The last-minute aversion of scandal at the Moscow Film Festival (July 7–21) by awarding the grand prize to Fellini's *8½* overlapped with an easing of political relations, when discussions for a partial test ban treaty culminated in its approval on August 5.[119] In Moscow Cowan managed to make use of these events. Senator Fulbright, in Moscow for the treaty signing with Khrushchev, visited Cowan's personal Mosfilm office—the "co-existence room"—and had photos taken with Russian film artists.[120] At the State Committee for Cinematography, Cowan again proposed three new coproductions corresponding to his assessment of American public interests—the Bolshoi Ballet, the Moiseev Ensemble, and the Soviet circus, films that would be easier to make than *Far Meridian.* Asking the committee members to pass these ideas along to Minister Romanov, Cowan concluded by agreeing with Romanov's speech at the Moscow Film Festival, confirming that he was "far from alone in his opinion that cinema is a mass art" and predicted a very small audience for *8½* in America.[121]

With *Far Meridian* still without an assigned director or stars from either side, talks resumed in Moscow in November. Cowan presented an ambitious proposal for a co-advertising campaign, name-dropping more American stars and mapping out publicity and cohosted film premiers complete with ambassadors from both sides.[122] Less than a week later, the cultural exchange agreement was to come up for renewal and difficulties were expected in the negotiations, which perhaps accounted for Cowan's energetic suggestions linking government officials and *Far Meridian.*[123]

The shock of the assassination of President Kennedy on November 22, 1963, brought an outpouring of grief from Soviet citizens and a strong response from Cowan. In a revealing set of personally typed numbered points later titled by hand "Notes on Kennedy Death, etc.," Cowan proposed a letter to "Sr." (Joseph P. Kennedy) "with copy to fulbright to show to johnson" and "copy to furtseva to show Mr. K., etc." that would be signed by Russians, members of the ministry, "who have come to know lester cowan in connection with coproduction and to whom we have expressed our grief etc. . . ."[124] Writing on the train to Leningrad he had "to pour out heart someone and you are the one . . . not only because will make you proud but also because you better than anyone understand and appreciate the importance of the mission in which we are engaged." He claimed he was not writing from a personal standpoint but only as a person "here on mission." Nevertheless Cowan's tone is more understandable given that, as an active member of the Los Angeles Academy of Motion Pictures who was instrumental in setting up academic film studies, he undoubtedly had dealings with Joseph P. Kennedy during the latter's Hollywood years.[125] Cowan described how someone he didn't know and didn't know English learned two sentences and telephoned him because "they all knew that [I] intended [to] send script which has been approved and that the president would read it."[126]

In the midst of his "writing points" Cowan "confess[ed] my attitude from start has been one of deliberate and calculated optimism . . . but had skepticism and private reservations because knew that things don't change that fast and knew we had to practice what we preach in the film . . . But this experience settled things for me . . . I can afford not being in politics to speak out . . . whereas before made it policy to let picture speak for itself . . . there is something great and wonderful between our peoples which cold wars and ideological differences cann [?] down . . . maybe its revolutionastary[*sic*] instincts, maybe its our ppr tuan[*sic*], certainly is more than self interest in peace. . . ." Remembering a similar shock when Ernie Pyle died before Cowan finished *G.I. Joe* and his renewed sense of work on the film, it "suddenly occurred to [him] that this was the president['s] picture inspired somewhat by his speech at american university and senators fullbright [*sic*] speech. . . . both of which were referred to constantly in my work here . . . then I began to wonder whether film could be good enough to be dedicated to him."[127] "[E]ven the possibility has given us the necessary purpose." Cowan proposed to screen the film privately for the Kennedy family and "if you think worthy we will dedicate and inasmuch as may open in capitals with joint invitation. .fitting to set memorial with the receipts." "You know first that I know how to make the picture," Cowan wrote, and "now that we have the extra sipiration[*sic*] we will make it . . . ." "Not publicity . . . you know me better. .work speaks for itself. .will mention this only to Pierre [Salinger] and you can to family. .and they say nothing about it until we show you the picture." "We in the picture industry have always consider[ed] you on[e] of your fan [?] you know that because you were. .therefore felt free in writing you this way. . . ."[128] After these numbered points and a set of dashes, Cowan stated what might be considered his "conversion" to the "mission":

> lost my skepticism . . . never again will I doubt the instincts or motives of the Russian people . . . their leaders may err . . . but the people are good. . . . as far as ideology is concerned the reality is different . . . their living ideology is what counts what they do and not what their own propaganda or ours . . . The president tried to do something. . . . And the Russians are earnestly trying to do something . . . we must keep the word HOPE in biggest headlines before us.[129]

This sense of purpose, affirmed aboard a Leningrad train, can be witnessed in the vigor with which Cowan tackled the considerable problems awaiting the coproduction of *Meeting at a Far Meridian* as it became tangled with the renewal negotiations for the cultural exchange agreement. Cowan had become a "willing interpreter."

THE PUSH (1964)

In less than a month a new Soviet film team was in place. Meeting with leading Soviet film directors in Moscow and Leningrad about both *Far Meridian* problems and a continuing coproduction program, Cowan received enthusiasm and "constructive understanding" of his "mission."[130] Igor Talankin had been agreed upon as the film's director,[131] and Sergei Gerasimov had been designated by Romanov to work on the coproduction, welcomed by Cowan as "a professional."[132] Even though Gerasimov had been criticized in Khrushchev's March 8, 1963, speech for not having sufficiently "supervised" his protégé's film, *Ilich's Gate* (*Zastava Il'icha,* 1961, rel. 1965),[133] Gerasimov had also just coproduced a war film with the GDR film studio DEFA (Deutsche Film-Aktiengesellschaft) in the spirit of the thaw but critical of capitalism (*Men and Beasts*/*Liudi i zveri,* October 1962). Gerasimov was referred to as the "coproducer" in subsequent negotiations. Cowan also apprised the US State Department of the new arrangements, selection of Soviet actors, including Innokentii Smoktunovskii and Nikolai Cherkasov, plus, as a concession to entertainment values, special appearances by a Soviet ballerina and a Soviet clown.[134]

Cowan and Gerasimov affirmed their joint efforts at a meeting with Ambassador Kohler, who was heading the US delegation and who, according to Cowan's *aide memoire* addressed to Chairman Romanov, copied to Ambassador Kohler and cosigned by Gerasimov, assured them of his "full support." Although the diplomatic equality of coproducers and officials was maintained in the *aide memoir,* Ambassador Kohler also "pointed out the difference in the conditions under which the Soviet and American parties commence the coproduction. The Soviet side participates in it through state organizations while the American side must depend on the initiative and patriotism of independent entrepreneurs like Mr. Cowan."[135] Kohler's remarks on the eventual signing of the "continuance and expansion" of the US-Soviet exchanges reiterates these differences: "The very length of the negotiations—46 days—reflects the complexity of the problems[136] considered in the various fields of exchanges, as well as the differences in systems and methods in carrying out exchanges and visits between the two countries."[137]

For *Far Meridian* "the screenplay approved by both sides . . . will be further improved in accordance with suggestions already mutually agreed upon."[138] This improvement was undertaken in June of 1964 when Gerasimov, Talankin, and the Soviet cinematographer and production designer visited New York, San Francisco, and Hollywood for a month. In an extensive report on the trip for *Izvestiia,* Gerasimov described the difficulties of joint efforts by two countries that differ in their ideological and economic system, and explained why every word in the screenplay needed to be weighed as not only "a fact of art, but a fact of economics." He discussed the paradox that, compared with admiration for the Soviet ballet and circus, Americans they spoke with knew little about either Soviet contemporary literature or film, which confirmed the importance of *Far Meridian.* Mitchell Wilson introduced them to his fellow scientists at Stanford in the university cafeteria and told them about the film. "A great idea. . . . We should wish you good luck," the scientists replied.[139] The Soviet filmmakers' impressions at meeting "representative American people as well as scientists" also resulted in an agreed reconceptualization of the American section of the screenplay.[140] "As a result of mutual familiarization," Gerasimov concluded, we hope to "create a truthful and humanistic film capable of bringing closer together our two nations, which have been entrusted by history with the responsibility of preserving peace on earth."[141]

Not all Hollywood responded positively to the Russian visit. Local writer Abe Greenberg asked, is the "U.S. to be Patsy in Russian Film Deal?" "It seems strange and oddly significant," wrote Greenberg, "that we must rely on a film company, rather than our State Department, to keep abreast of startling developments in what seems to be a growing entente cordial between the United States and Soviet Russia." Greenberg worried that "this all sounds awfully brotherly, or comradely, on the surface . . . but our State Department, methinks, must be frightfully naïve if they believe that the Marxis[t]-oriented Russians won't be doing their darndest in the way of subtle espionage in behalf of the Soviet cause." Greenberg concluded, "This could be the greatest sucker deal since somebody sold the Brooklyn Bridge."[142] Other troubles were brewing. American writer Fay Kanin had been added to the team to improve the script,[143] while Wilson complained by letter to Romanov, Talankin, and Gerasimov independently about being sidelined from the film.[144] At the same time in New York, Cowan announced yet another spin-off project from the film—a Broadway musical entitled "Spasso House," the love story between an American journalist and a Soviet ballerina—with music by Ann Ronell.[145] He was already hedging his bets.

Whether or not the ouster of Khrushchev on October 14 affected his decision,[146] Cowan did not arrive back in Moscow until over a month later, when he, Gerasimov, Talankin, and Kanin "reconstructed" the screenplay between November 20 and December 14, both improving Smoktunovskii's role as the Soviet scientist and adding the scenes at the circus and with the Soviet puppeteer.[147] A reference memo in Cowan's files on using multiple communication channels in both government hierarchies showed his very broad understanding of his role as a private businessman and "interpreter" in cultural diplomacy. "The protocol might well be entitled 'Twenty Steps to Licking the Bureaucracy.'" Cowan aimed to assemble "all the top officials concerned with the film," getting them to sign the protocol and "set down in writing the conditions that—hopefully—will govern operations during the next few months." He offered a few points "that should be made clear to the Soviets." First, "Gerasimov must be able to wield effectively the authority implied in his title of 'co-producer.'" Cowan obviously took that title seriously, citing "much evidence of bureaucratic undercutting of his position." Second, Romanov "will be kept fully informed of decision and activities by memos from Cowan in the future. This will prevent his underlings from playing on a lack of information on his part." And third, "Ambassador Dobrynin and the Foreign Office will continue to be channels which the Americans will use for contacts when it seems appropriate."[148]

The bureaucracy fought back. Having assembled everyone involved in the film but Surin, Romanov opened the meeting by stating his expectation that work on *Far Meridian* was nearing its end. Cowan replied that both sides had new leaders and asked Gerasimov and Talankin to describe the work they did on the film. "Mr. Cowan wants to shift the responsibility to us. Why such modesty?" Gerasimov responded, listing the deadlines broken by the Americans. Mitchell Wilson's complaints were again raised, and Romanov pronounced twice, "I am not at all interested in the relations between the Americans," but asserted that Wilson's name must be in the credits in order for the film to be successful. Gerasimov complained twice that Cowan had brought no American star for the leading role. Cowan's response was procedural and potentially far-reaching in its implications: as a result of several meetings in Washington, he said, *Far Meridian* would be considered within the framework of the cultural exchange agreement. Furthermore, the source of American oversight had shifted; Cowan said that Fulbright and other government officials regarded *Far Meridian* primarily "as a business venture," so he did not have to submit the screenplay to the State Department for approval. Instead he would report to a subcommittee that reported to the president on the fulfillment of the cultural agreement. Additionally, Cowan told them, according to Franklin Roosevelt Jr., the film would be given the same guarantee as the business people who sold wheat to the USSR. Romanov responded, "I can neither condemn nor approve the American way of doing things." After further discussion and some conciliatory remarks Romanov wished them "full speed ahead."[149] This positive spirit was reflected in Mosfilm's 1965 thematic plan announcing that "the [*Far Meridian*] screenplay is ready"[150] and in a feature of the December 1964 issue of the Soviet export magazine *Soviet Film*.[151] The accompanying photo of Mitchell Wilson and Igor Talankin, glasses in hand, discussing their impressions, represented the partnership they desired, but the champagne was poured too soon.

THE RESCUE ATTEMPT (1965)

Moscow meetings on *Far Meridian* resumed in March of 1965. By then the US bombing of North Vietnam and the beginning of the ground war in South Vietnam had strained the relations between the two countries. On a much smaller scale the *Far Meridian* relations were being undermined by the separate story lines reaching Surin and Gerasimov from the American partners. Surin received a surprising letter from Walter Reade of Continental Distributing, saying he had stopped the US financing of *Far Meridian,* but not to worry, MGM was involved. Surin demanded answers from Cowan. He wrote Reade that "we are business people [*delovye liudi*]. . . . According to our production agreement . . . neither side can transfer its privileges without the agreement of the other."[152] Wilson meanwhile wrote Gerasimov and Talankin that Reade had withdrawn his support because of Cowan's tricks and that MGM had not signed on to the project.[153] Cowan later responded to these charges, but critical here is that the Soviet filmmakers were directly involved with the individual American disputes, both on business and artistic grounds. Not surprisingly, this information rose to the top of the Soviet film bureaucracy, with the complaint that MGM had previously rejected the purchase of Soviet films.[154] The fact that MGM was known to be the company financing and distributing the US screen version of *Doctor Zhivago* probably did not help.

This was the atmosphere when Surin announced to Cowan and the other eleven film personnel involved in *Far Meridian* at Mosfilm that the purpose of the March 9 meeting was to decide whether they would work together or not. He gave Cowan a memo of complaint and asked sarcastically whether Cowan was surprised that movies could be made in such a "semi-savage country." In the past three years Mosfilm has made over 120 films, including coproductions, while Cowan was just procrastinating, Surin declared. Cowan argued that he did not want to make a bad film, because there would not be another chance and all depended upon whether the two sides trusted each other. Surin replied that the Soviet side was in the position of a "disrespected partner." Each argued about their investments, with Cowan claiming $250,000 and Surin lamenting 15,000 rubles per month of delay, plus the lost year for their team. At the mention of MGM, Surin stated that the Soviet side was "not indifferent" to the source of funding. Two hours of heated accusations later, Gerasimov declared that if there was no screenplay by March 20, he would no longer be responsible for the film to Surin and Romanov.[155] This time it was Cowan who claimed that the American actor was the most important.

Six days later Surin and Cowan went head to head at the Hotel Metropole, with only an interpreter. Each accused the other of being responsible for the delays and for disorganization. Surin complained that Cowan wrote to everyone at the same time, showing a lack of organization, while Cowan complained that if Surin had three more subordinates, Cowan could not make the film at all. Surin received an apology from Cowan for improper behavior in the discussions with Reade without informing the Soviet side and was promised another invitation to Washington.[156] Two weeks later the financial issue exploded in another collective meeting at Mosfilm when in front of assembled staff Surin demanded to see Cowan's contract with MGM, which Cowan refused on the basis of its other confidential clauses. Surin persisted, citing his positive correspondence with Reade. We invited Reade five times, said Surin, and would be happy for his return. Otherwise Surin demanded that they sign a protocol with MGM about financing before the Soviet side would continue. After yet another debate about screenplay credit for Mitchell Wilson, whom Cowan accused of having fooled both sides, Surin stated that they were both "business people" but that he had made a mistake by not demanding to see the conditions of Cowan's agreements with Wilson, Reade, or MGM. "You are dealing with an honest partner," Surin declared.[157]

Back in New York, Ann Ronell tried to keep the project alive by speaking to the press. She planned to return to Moscow on the "newly expanded exchange" to sing and play on Russian TV and to write the story for an hour-long television film, *Warm Sounds in a Cold War,* to be codirected by King Vidor and Sergei Gerasimov. "It's to be all about the cultural agreement,"[158] "to dramatize music's immunity to the US-USSR cold warfare." *Far Meridian* remained "very much active," she said.[159] Active was the right word, as Moscow meetings multiplied. "Even though I said nothing at the time," wrote Cowan to Talankin on April 9, "I want you to know that I was deeply moved by your expressions of personal respect at our meeting yesterday. I hope to earn and continue to deserve such expressions from you." Formally speaking of business matters, he signed his letter "With good wishes for all, I am your Angel *iz ada* [from hell]." At his April 10 meeting with Vladimir Baskakov, the deputy chairman of the State Committee of Cinematography, Cowan promised to resolve the remaining problems by having the scenario reworked again by another writer like Irwin Shaw and to get the confirmation by a large firm that was willing to finance the American part of the production.[160] From New York Cowan promised financing not only from MGM but also United Artists, with another invitation to Washington. Surin responded that MGM and United Artists had to write to Mosfilm to confirm. All deadlines had passed. If there were any more delays, "we will have to cancel our agreement since the further exchange of words in meaningless." Executives from both United Artists and MGM sent telegrams to Surin, but both were conditional on the final screenplay, with MGM specifying further development of the "American section . . . from a dramatic and entertainment standpoint."

At the end of June two letters crossed, one of expansion and another of closure on the coproduction project. On June 21 Cowan wrote to Edwin L. Weisl, President Johnson's close friend for over twenty-five years. "The subject is again the Cold War," he began, arguing for an overhaul of the cultural exchange agreement when negotiations for renewal begin in the fall of 1965. The American objectives, in spite of the work of "our information agency, our diplomats and press representatives" were not being fulfilled and "we are not reaching the Russian people." Citing *Meeting at a Far Meridian* as the "first example of reciprocity in films, the key medium in people-to-people communication," Cowan recounted his initial dealing with A. V. Romanov, "the big Party man," and his discussions with Minister of Culture Furtseva, "which were both frank and private (only her personal interpreter was present)" about her frustrations with the US State Department bureaucracy.[161] The outcome was what he called the "Cowan-Fursteva Plan,"[162] an ambitious and elaborated structure for film cooperation that he would like to have incorporated into the negotiations for renewing the cultural exchange agreement in 1966. The plan was discussed before "Vietnam which precipitated a temporary freeze on new ideas while the Soviets grapple with some of their own dilemmas." But he felt that Senator Fulbright's statement and the president's support may have "rounded the corner" in rebuilding the relationship. Many of those mentioned as potential board members were Cowan's friends, already drawn into the *Far Meridian* project and slated to maintain contacts with the State Department, the Senate Foreign Relations Committee, and the White House. He suggested four familiar coproduced film projects—The Last Battle,[163] an American Girl in the Bolshoi, an astronaut-cosmonaut film dramatizing a future flight together, and a comedy "so that the peoples of both countries can enjoy some laughs together"—as extensions of the present coproduction agreement.[164]

Significantly, Cowan enunciated the flexibility of his own role in this cultural exchange: "In writing you, I am for the first time putting on paper some of the things which I have learned. I am trying to suggest that a new US position is emerging, that of the individual US businessman who can make decisions on the spot, who can make proposals without alternatives, and who can always pack up and go home—a power and privilege not shared by bureaucrats. Furthermore," he added, "I have found that success on the part of a US entrepreneur in doing business with the Soviets is not interpreted to mean that he has been brainwashed." In fact, he added in a postscript, "the profit motive is understood and respected by the Soviet side. To admit to any other motive would make them suspicious and apprehensive." Cowan concluded with President Johnson's emphasis on the desirability of trade with the USSR on several occasions and the starting point as "leadership by the President."[165]

That same week Surin sent Cowan a five-page letter postmarked June 25, 1965, and received July 19 by Cowan. Surin summarized Mosfilm's activities over the three years since the preliminary agreement, emphasizing not only the prestige of the film workers involved, but also the heavy financial investment. He then outlined the endless delays and nonfulfillment of deadlines: "Consequently, today June 18, 1965, we have at our disposal neither a completed literary scenario on the basis of which the work could be carried out, nor an American actor to fill the role of Nick or your contract with him, nor an American firm that would be willing to finance the American part of the film." As a result, he said, he and his team "have lost all hope that the production of the film *Meeting at a Far Meridian* has any practical likelihood of every being realized." The director and the film team demanded to be given the opportunity to work on other films, and Mosfilm believed themselves to be released from all contractual obligations regarding the joint production of *Far Meridian.*[166] Undated and unsent draft documents from Romanov and others involved in the Cinematography Ministry discussed and approved the cancellation of the contract with Cowan, including an unsent letter to Ambassador Dobrynin, but a handwritten annotation stated that Surin's letter was sent instead.[167]

Of course, Cowan did not interpret that letter as the end of the relationship or the film. In telegrams sent to both Romanov and Surin at the end of July, Cowan stressed the strained relations between both countries as "causing hesitations." While assuring Surin that he would honor his commitment to reimburse Mosfilm for expenses, he posed a starker question to Romanov: "We are confronted as patriotic citizens—you of your country and I of mine—with the serious responsibility of making a choice. We can believe that time will restore the good recent atmosphere and intent of your governments[*sic*] co existence policy or we can add fuel to the flames by taking thoughtless hasty action based on pessimism." He promised to write frankly of his hopes, which he was confident would be shared.[168]

In the coming months Cowan wrote to political figures and film personnel from both the US and the USSR. In addition to writing Senator Fulbright, he appealed to Harry McPherson, appointed special council to President Johnson in August of 1965, citing President Kennedy's personal encouragement, and assured McPherson that "he made it a point to keep in close touch—every step of the way—with Ambassador Thompson, Senator Fulbright, Franklin D Roosevelt Jr. and . . . Pierre Salinger."[169] In late November he wrote long and elaborate letters to all who had been involved on the Soviet side—Romanov, Surin, Baskakov, Gerasimov, and Furtseva. Once again he was optimistic. "Good relations and understanding between our peoples is there for the asking. All we have to do is multiply the personal contacts," he told Furtseva. To Romanov he praised the "discretion and calm restraint of Soviet leaders during the period of crisis" that commanded respect in the United States as well as complimenting him on his "prompt and constructive decisions." To both Romanov and the Mosfilm group he spoke of the "entirely positive" tone of ads for the December opening of MGM's *Dr. Zhivago,* predicting they would be able to judge for themselves whether the film would "bring additional understanding and good will for the Soviet people." He even provided the Mosfilm group with a copy of the latest *Far Meridian* screenplay and offered Richard Burton as the American star. He closed with a handwritten New Year's greetings in Russian.[170] On January 19, 1966, he received the following telegram: "Your letters received and studied. In connection with the fact that work on the picture has been terminated your trip to Moscow not necessary.[171]

THE DENOUEMENT (1966)

In the tense political atmosphere the cultural exchange agreement expired at the end of December 1965 without approval for renewal. Still, American film executives expressed hope in late February of 1966 that it would be renewed, based on the increased prices that each side would pay for individual films. For *Far Meridian,* the same newspaper article characterized both sides as "hesitant to proceed because of its obvious political implications." That disclaimer was preceded by the announcement of a new US-Soviet coproduction agreement: a life of Tchaikovsky, to be produced by the Russian émigré and Hollywood composer Dmitri Tiomkin, in cooperation with Warner Brothers and Mosfilm. On April 4 the director and cast of *Tchaikovsky* were announced with the same creative team—Talankin and Smoktunovskii—and the cooperation of the same Soviet cultural leaders—Surin and Furtseva—as *Meeting at a Far Meridian.* Obviously the Soviet film team had also been hedging their bets by developing a second film coproduction project with American participation. Even though Warner Brothers pulled out at the last minute, the Russian version of *Tchaikovsky* appeared in 1969 and the English-language version, under the same title, in 1971.[172] In London, Smoktunovskii attributed the failure of *Far Meridian* to the politics of Vietnam.[173]

Other more far-reaching changes were instituted in the Soviet film bureaucracy after the organizational difficulties experienced during the *Far Meridian* project. In 1967 Cinematography Minister Romanov sent a memo to the CPSU Central Committee requesting the creation of "a special creative artistic unit that would centralize work on co-productions with foreign countries, as well as production services to foreign film companies." "The Soviet cinema at present is not fully prepared to conduct broad-based joint film cooperation with foreign countries." Romanov enumerated the challenges in practical terms, from how to get sufficiently quick decisions from the authorities when negotiating with foreign film companies to how to pay for visiting foreign film dignitaries to the fact that Soviet studio representatives arrive for business meetings "later than scheduled." He even ventured economic comparisons like the difference in the costs of film production and its organization, as well as in the salaries of actors and film personnel in the studios of the USSR and other socialist countries. Although the memo was withdrawn at that time, the All-Union Corporation of Joint Productions and Production Services for Foreign

Film Organizations, or Sovinfilm, was later established in December of 1968. The most important projects were those "in which our film studios participate as equal partners."[174] By 1970 the number of Soviet coproductions had almost doubled. The Soviet filmmakers also learned from the specific failures with *Far Meridian.* When negotiating for the first—and only—completed US-Soviet coproduced film, *The Blue Bird* (1976), the Soviet filmmakers insisted up front on a famous American director and the biggest American stars.

None of Cowan's other projects ever materialized. In a letter drafted in 1984, Cowan explained his view of what happened. After the production had commenced, his Russian friends began asking, "What are you doing in Vietnam?" And he was unable to answer. "We reached a point," he wrote, "when the Minister of Culture, Madame Furtseva, and I decided that it would be better to suspend production until 'a better time.' Shortly thereafter Khrushchev was ousted and Furtseva died, and I was left along with my broken dream." Still he was upbeat, misremembering that the screenplay was approved by both sides, which represented "an ideological agreement between our people and the Russian people, dramatizing the fact that our common interests and beliefs far exceed the differences."[175] In 1977 Belarussian television made a solo, darker version of *Meeting at a Far Meridian*—without an American partner.

CLOSING CREDITS

As Wilson intended, the meeting at a "far meridian" served as a metaphor for the distance to be traveled in seeking Cold War cooperation, often beginning as a one-to-one relationship. Film coproduction provided a location where the lines between the cultural and political were continually crossed, even transgressed, in the goal of making things happen, doing business, getting the job done. The role and understanding of business on both sides, in structurally such different systems, nonetheless revealed the stakes and pitfalls in using film in the cultural Cold War. The importance of personal relations, of establishing trust, at least in this instance, seemed to rest more easily in reciprocal artistic or professional relations that were less colored by business associations. The equivocal figure of the film producer, here represented by Cowan, was not only nonequivalent in the Soviet system in spite of attempts to name a counterpart. It was also tainted with the financial responsibilities and capitalist overtones that were more tenuous than the "artist" connotations lent to Wilson or Ronell. In fact the *Far Meridian* character of the capitalist who tried to enlist the troubled scientist-hero in seeming political intrigues might foreshadow interpretations of Cowan and his motives, even his relation with Wilson. Cowan's grand plan, viewed suspiciously at the Filmmakers' Union, and Furtseva's demotion in the film hierarchy suggested that private conversations and relationships are never just private. Yet the longevity of the attempt to make this film, the gradual education of the various personae on both sides in how and how not to conduct cultural diplomacy, and the seemingly willing move of the Soviet personnel to the new film coproduction of *Tchaikovsky*, showed a learning curve about which stories can be told and which motives matter. Thus content mattered, and people mattered in forging transnational relationships. Coproduced films were made one film at a time.

Talankin ended his 1964 film script for *Meeting at a Far Meridian* with a fitting epitaph. The American and Soviet scientists have returned to the mountain camp and are standing outside in the snow. The Soviet scientist places his hand on the American's shoulder and asks, "Whenever are we going to see each other again?" The American replies, "A conference next year in Washington?" "Perhaps." They stand embracing. They are so different and yet so close to each other. They are silent, each thinking his own thoughts.[176]

NOTES

1. Mitchell Wilson, *Meeting at a Far Meridian,* 1st ed. (London: Secker and Warburg, 1961), 360.

2. Sergei Dobrynin, "The Silver Curtain: Representations of the West in the Soviet Cold War Films," *History Compass* 7, no. 3 (2009): 862–78.

3. On the American-Soviet cultural exchange see J. D. Parks, *Culture, Conflict, and Coexistence: American-Soviet Cultural Relations, 1917–1958* (Jefferson, NC: McFarland, 1983); Yale Richmond, *Cultural Exchange and the Cold War: Raising the Iron Curtain* (University Park: Pennsylvania State University Press, 2003); Victor Rosenberg, *Soviet-American Relations, 1953–1960: Diplomacy and Cultural Exchange during the Eisenhower Presidency* (Jefferson, NC: McFarland, 2005).

4. Frances Stonor Saunders, *The Cultural Cold War: The CIA and the World of Arts and Letters* (New York: New Press, 1999); Hugh Wilford, *The Mighty Wurlitzer: How the CIA Played America* (Cambridge, MA: Harvard University Press, 2008).

5. John W. McDonald, "Further Exploration of Track-Two Diplomacy," in *Timing the De-Escalation of International Conflicts,* ed. Louis Kriesberg and Stuart J. Thorson (Syracuse: Syracuse University Press, 1991), 201–20, as summarized by Cosima Krueger, Con-

flict Research Consortium, http://www.colorado.edu/conflict/peace/example/mcd03682.htm (accessed September 1, 2012).

6. These three variables come from the excellent analysis of exchange programs in Giles Scott-Smith, "Mapping the Undefinable: Some Thoughts on the Relevance of Exchange Programs within International Relations Theory," *ANNALS of the American Academy of Political and Social Science* 616, no. 1 (March 1, 2008): 173–95.

7. Victoria De Grazia, *Irresistible Empire: America's Advance through Twentieth-Century Europe* (Cambridge, MA: Belknap Press of Harvard University Press, 2005); David W. Ellwood, *The Shock of America: Europe and the Challenge of the Century* (Oxford: Oxford University Press, 2012).

8. David Caute, *The Dancer Defects: The Struggle for Cultural Supremacy during the Cold War* (New York: Oxford University Press, 2003); Joseph S. Nye, *Soft Power: The Means to Success in World Politics,* 1st ed. (New York: Public Affairs, 2004), 75; Marsha Siefert, "From Cold War to Wary Peace: American Culture in the USSR and Russia," in *The Americanization of Europe: Culture, Diplomacy, and Anti-Americanization after 1945,* ed. Alexander Stephan (New York: Berghahn Books, 2005), 185–217.

9. Nye, *Soft Power,* 16.

10. Yale Richmond, *U.S.-Soviet Cultural Exchanges, 1958–1986: Who Wins?,* Westview Special Studies on the Soviet Union and Eastern Europe (Boulder, CO: Westview Press, 1987), 63–64.

11. Siefert, "From Cold War to Wary Peace"; Sudha Rajagopalan, *Indian Films in Soviet Cinemas: The Culture of Movie-Going after Stalin* (Bloomington: Indiana University Press, 2009); Kristin Roth-Ey, *Moscow Prime Time: How the Soviet Union Built the Media Empire That Lost the Cultural Cold War* (Ithaca, NY: Cornell University Press, 2011), ch. 2.

12. Anne Jäckel, *European Film Industries* (London: British Film Institute, 2003); Marsha Siefert, "Twentieth-Century Culture, 'Americanization,' and European Audiovisual Space," in *Conflicted Memories: Europeanizing Contemporary Histories,* ed. Konrad Hugo Jarausch, Thomas Lindenberger, and Annelie Ramsbrock (New York: Berghahn Books, 2007), 164–93.

13. R.r.g., "Films and 'Guided Creativity," Office of the Political Advisor, Radio Free Europe/Munich, Background Information USSR (August 8, 1958), Open Society Archives, Budapest, 19–21.

14. Philip J. Funigiello, *American-Soviet Trade in the Cold War* (Chapel Hill: University of North Carolina Press, 1988), 128–30; Milton Kovner, *The Challenge of Coexistence: A Study of Soviet Economic Diplomacy* (Washington, DC: Public Affairs Press, 1961).

15. Quoted in Samuel Pisar, *Coexistence and Commerce: Guidelines for Transactions between East and West,* 1st ed. (New York: McGraw-Hill, 1970), 35.

16. A. I. Mikoyan, "We Are for Trade That Is Equal and Mutually Profitable," speech at National Association of Importers and Exporters of Mexico, *Pravda,* November 30, 1959, 3; translated in *Current Digest of the Soviet Press* [hereafter *CDSP*] 11, no. 48 (December 30, 1959): 22–23.

17. Pisar, *Coexistence and Commerce,* 286.

18. Ibid., 294.

19. For an analysis of Soviet aims leading to the creation of a bureau for coproductions, see Marsha Siefert, "Co-Producing Cold War Culture: East-West Film-Making and Cultural Diplomacy," in *Divided Dreamworlds? The Cultural Cold War in East and West,* ed. Peter Romijn, Giles Scott-Smith, and Joes Segal (Amsterdam: Amsterdam University Press, 2012), 73–94.

20. Walter L Hixson, *Parting the Curtain: Propaganda, Culture, and the Cold War* (New York: St. Martin's Press, 1996), 105.

21. Cowan to Leonard [Goldenson] of ABC Television, undated draft, 1984), with

reference to the contracted ABC television coverage of the Moscow Olympics, Ann Ronell Collection, Carl Frohm Archival Center, Nebraska Jewish Historical Society, Omaha [hereafter Ann Ronell Collection].

22. V. M. Zubok and Konstantin Pleshakov, *Inside the Kremlin's Cold War: From Stalin to Khrushchev* (Cambridge, MA: Harvard University Press, 1996), 187, 271.

23. Ibid., 165.

24. Sec. VII, item 5, in the cultural exchange agreement, reprinted in United States and U.S.S.R. Sign Agreement on East-West Exchanges," [US] *Department of State Bulletin,* February 17, 1958, 243–47, quotation on 245.

25. For a description of US State Department oversight of Hollywood exports, see Tony Shaw, *Hollywood's Cold War* (Edinburgh: Edinburgh University Press, 2007).

26. Confidential cable from Moscow (Ambassador Thompson) to Lacy from Shelton (signed by Ambassador Thompson), September 29, 1958, National Archives Record Administration [hereafter NARA], RG 59, 511.615/9–2958.

27. Hans N. Tuch, *Communicating with the World: U.S. Public Diplomacy Overseas* (New York: St. Martin's Press, 1990), 134; "United States and U.S.S.R. Agree on Films to Be Exchanged," [US] *Department of State Bulletin,* November 3, 1958, 696–98; Richmond, *U.S.-Soviet Cultural Exchanges,* 64.

28. Richard Dyer MacCann, "Independence, with a Vengeance," *Film Quarterly* 15, no. 4 (July 1, 1962): 18; Drew Casper, *Postwar Hollywood, 1946–1962* (Malden, MA: Blackwell, 2007).

29. Tino Balio, *United Artists: The Company That Changed the Film Industry* (Madison: University of Wisconsin Press, 1987), 87.

30. Alexander Walker, *Icons in the Fire: The Decline and Fall of Almost Everybody in the British Film Industry,* illus. ed. (London: Orion, 2005), 205.

31. Sergei Gerasimov, "Film Trends: East and West," *Russian Social Science Review* 1, no. 5 (1960): 45–55, quotation on 47; translated from "Films and Man in the 1960s," *Izvestiia,* August 12–13, 1960.

32. For a discussion of the Soviet relations with Capra and his films, see Marsha Siefert, "Allies on Film: US-USSR Filmmakers and the Battle for Russia," in *Extending the Borders of Russian History: Essays in Honor of Alfred J. Rieber,* ed. Marsha Siefert (Budapest: Central European University Press, 2003), 373–400.

33. Gerasimov, "Film Trends," 48.

34. In August of 1956, Surin, then Soviet deputy minister of culture in charge of film—"the highest-ranking cultural emissary to visit the United States in the last decade"—stated in an interview that his ministry was "open minded" about "barter" in the entertainment field for reciprocal film festivals, the exchange of actresses and actors to star in each other's films, and joint production by both motion picture industries. "Russia Ready for Talks on Film 'Barter,'" *Chicago Daily Tribune,* August 27, 1956, 16.

35. Cowan's *The Story of G.I. Joe* (1945), "the ultimate example of World War II combat films," has no records at the Office of War Information. Cowan corresponded with the US Army to obtain Italian soldiers for the film. Clayton R. Koppes and Gregory D. Black, *Hollywood Goes to War: How Politics, Profits, and Propaganda Shaped World War II Movies* (Berkeley: University of California Press, 1987), 304–307.

36. Jessica C. E. Gienow-Hecht, "What Are We Searching For? Culture, Diplomacy, Agents, and the State," in *Searching for a Cultural Diplomacy,* ed. Jessica C. E Gienow-Hecht and Mark C. Donfried, Explorations in Culture and International History, vol. 6 (New York: Berghahn Books, 2010), 10.

37. Vladislav Zubok, *Zhivago's Children: The Last Russian Intelligentsia* (Cambridge, MA: Belknap Press of Harvard University Press, 2009), 91–92. For a critical evaluation of this visit see Frederick Charles Barghoorn, *The Soviet Cultural Offensive: The Role of Cultural Diplomacy in Soviet Foreign Policy* (Westport, CT: Greenwood Press, 1976), 294–300.

38. Rossiskii gosudarstvennyi arkhiv noveishei istorii [hereafter RGANI], f. 5, op. 15, d. 734, ll. 131–45, quotation on ll. 140–41. Polevoi also recommended the idea of reciprocal film festivals, "ardently supported by filmmakers, by studio executives, and by the so-called Hollywood 'tycoons'." This meaning of this trip for cultural diplomacy is nicely elaborated by Rósa Magnúsdóttir, "Mission Impossible? Selling Soviet Socialism to Americans, 1955–1958," in Gienow-Hecht and Donfried, *Searching for a Cultural Diplomacy,* 50–74. I thank her for sharing this document with me.

39. Polevoi's personal correspondence with Howard Fast came to the attention of the Soviet authorities when he left the party in 1957. See Harrison E. Salisbury, "Writers in the Shadow of Communism," *New York Times Magazine,* June 9, 1957, 10.

40. RGANI f. 5, op. 15, d. 734, ll. 143–44. "It is also advisable to transfer some funds to the dramatist Lillian Hellman, who is so outraged at the absence of royalties from the Soviet Union that she refused to meet with the Soviet delegation, and we barely talked her out of her intention to immediately address the press regarding this issue and make a scandal."

41. Mitchell Wilson, "Russia's Social Elite," *The Nation,* August 26, 1961, reprinted in Radio Free Europe / Munich Research and Evaluation Department, *Background Information USSR,* September 20, 1961, 7–18; quote on 7. Also reprinted in the *Observer Weekend Review* (London) as "How Rich Are the Richest Russians?," August 12, 1962, 15.

42. Interview of William A. Nierenberg by Finn Aaserud on February 6, 1986, Niels Bohr Library & Archives, Center for History of Physics, American Institute of Physics, College Park, MD, www.aip.org/history/ohilist/4797_1.html (accessed November 20, 2010). Nierenberg states that the account may have "some minor errors" because "he obtained almost all the information from Wilson himself and had no way to check it."

43. V. Galanov, "Power of a Truthful Book," *Pravda,* November 25, 1952, 3; translated in *CDSP* 47 (January 3, 1953): 39. The book was published as *Life in a Fog* by the Foreign Literature Publishing House.

44. John Brooks, "Best-Seller," *New Yorker,* January 6, 1962, 19.

45. *My Brother, My Enemy* sold over 750,000 copies in the USSR between 1954 and 1964. Maurice Friedberg, *A Decade of Euphoria: Western Literature in Post-Stalin Russia, 1954–64* (Bloomington: Indiana University Press, 1977), 133.

46. Polevoi's 1955 advice could have been heeded, given his acquaintance with Wilson, as discussed below. In a November 28, 1958, letter to Lillian Hellman, Adlai E. Stevenson, then a Chicago lawyer, wrote of his efforts to negotiate on behalf of seventy-nine authors and dramatists to obtain royalties from the USSR during his July and August visit. Although unsuccessful for Hellman, he does note that later royalties were paid to William Saroyan, Somerset Maugham, Harlow Shapley, and seven other American scientists, all with the exception of Saroyan's, unsolicited. Harry Ransom Center, Lillian Hellman Papers, box 86, folder 6.

47. Wilson, "Russia's Social Elite."

48. Ibid.

49. Even recently, an assessment of the centenary of the birth of Academy of Sciences corresponding member A. I. Alikhan'ian's achievements uses Wilson's description in *Far Meridian* to describe his initiation of a high-altitude station in 1960, the scene of the novel's climax. G. A. Mesiats and G. M. Asatrian, "His Scientific Achievements: On the Centenary of the Birth of Corresponding Member of the USSR Academy of Sciences A. I. Alikhan'yan," *Herald of the Russian Academy of Sciences* 78, no. 6 (2008): 522–26, reprinted from *Vestnik Rossiiskoi Akademii Nauk* 78, no. 11 (2008): 1039–43.

50. Wilson, "Russia's Social Elite."

51. In a 1968 survey, although this journal ranked lower than others, nearly three times as many engineers and technicians, compared with workers, named it as their favorite literary periodical. Friedberg, *A Decade of Euphoria,* 63–64.

52. Bridget Ashbourne, "The Fame of Mitchell Wilson," *The Nation,* September 10, 1960: 134–35.

53. Barghoorn, *The Soviet Cultural Offensive,* 117, 67; Friedberg, *A Decade of Euphoria.*

54. "Big in Russia," *Time,* March 10, 1961; J.[oseph] T[urner]., "Say Comrade," *Science* June 15, 1962; *Mademoiselle,* April 1961, 154.

55. Ad in Bulletin of Atomic Scientists, May 1961, 252.

56. Melville J. Ruggles, "American Books in Soviet Publishing," *Slavic Review* 20, no. 3 (October 1, 1961): 429.

57. "Big in Russia," 100.

58. Deming Brown, *Soviet Attitudes toward American Writing* (Princeton, NJ: Princeton University Press, 1962), 183–88.

59. R. Samarin, "Wilson Writes about Us," *Izvestiia,* June 21, 1961, 4; translated in *CDSP* 13 (July 19, 1961): 29.

60. Boris Polevoi to Mitchell Wilson, April 27, 1961, RGALI, f. 631, op. 26, ed. khr. 4126, ll. 20–21.

61. For a discussion of the importance of the scientist, especially the physicist, as an emblem of this period, see Zubok, *Zhivago's Children,* ch. 4; Rosalind J. Marsh, *Soviet Fiction since Stalin: Science, Politics, and Literature* (London: Croom Helm, 1986), 214–15.

62. Zubok, *Zhivago's Children,* 183–84. Alexei Adzhubei, the editor of *Izvestiia* and Khrushchev's son-in-law, interceded to save the film from the shelf. He had also visited the United States with the 1955 Soviet writers delegation. Ibid., 400, n. 62.

63. Tony Shaw and Denise J. Youngblood, *Cinematic Cold War: The American and Soviet Struggle for Hearts and Minds* (Lawrence: University Press of Kansas, 2010), 127–42, 156–57; see also Josephine Woll, *Real Images: Soviet Cinema and the Thaw,* KINO, the Russian Cinema Series (London: St. Martin's Press, 2000).

64. Eugene Archer, "U.S.-Soviet Film under Discussion: Co-Production of Novel by Mitchell Wilson Weighed," *New York Times,* January 24, 1962, 23.

65. "Todd Seen Shooting 'War and Peace' in Russia as Co-Production," *Variety,* April 11, 1956.

66. Department of State to American Embassy in Moscow (telegram), April 7, 1960, NARA, RG 59, 511.615/4–760.

67. RGALI, f. 107, op. 1, d. 16, ll. 66–67.

68. Ambassador Thompson to State Department (telegram), May 3, 1960, NARA, RG 59, 511.615/5–360.

69. Arnshtam had already directed two Soviet joint productions, *History Lesson* (1956) with Bulgaria and *Five Days, Five Nights* (1960) with the GDR.

70. T. B. Shelton to State Department (telegram), October 6, 1961, NARA, RG 59, 511.615.

71. *Forty-Nine Days* (1964) was described by *Time* magazine as a "Russian movie that is warmly and explicitly pro-American—and just possibly critical of Communism too." "Cinema: Mother Russia & Uncle Sam," *Time,* February 14, 1964.

72. Archer, "U.S.-Soviet Film Under Discussion," 23.

73. Robert Cowan, Oral History Interview by Barbara Hall, Margaret Herrick Library, Academy of Motion Picture Arts and Sciences, 1992–93.

74. Quoted in Lawrence H. Suid, *Guts & Glory: The Making of the American Military Image in Film* (Lexington: University Press of Kentucky, 2002).

75. Ann Ronell to Lou Applebaum, May 6, 1961. Ann Ronell Collection.

76. Turner B. Shelton, US Department of State, to the American Embassy, Moscow (telegram), February 19, 1962, NARA, RG 59, 511.615/2–1962.

77. Theodore Shabad, "Joint Film Is Planned," *New York Times,* March 9, 1962, 1.

78. Cowan's letter to "Greg" on May 11, 1962, indicated he had already discussed

the "values" and "shortcomings" of Wilson's novel and appreciated Peck's expressions of personal confidence. A copy of this letter in English is found in RGALI, f. 2944, op. 13, d. 550, l. 1.

79. Shabad, "Joint Film," 2.

80. For a history of cinematic technical competition see James H. Krukones, "Peacefully Coexisting on a Wide Screen: Kinopanorama vs. Cinerama, 1952–66," *Studies in Russian and Soviet Cinema* 4, no. 3 (2010): 283–305.

81. Sidney Rechetnik, "Says Soviets 'Need' Comedy," *Motion Picture Daily*, March 14, 1962), 1, 5. The other Russian representatives were A. Danilov, deputy minister of culture, and N. Davydov, chief of Sovexportfilm.

82. Vincent Canby, "Hollywood-on-the-Volga Deal: Cowan Move Key to Coexistence?" *Variety*, March 14, 1962, 1–2.

83. "Soviet Co-Prod. Deal Waits Govt. Approval," *Film Daily*, March 12, 1962, 1, 3.

84. Department of State Memorandum, "Proposed Co-Production of Film with Soviet Motion Picture Industry of '*Meeting at a Far Meridian*,'" NARA, RG 59, 511.615/3–2162.

85. V[adim] Murashko, Mosfilm, to Cowan, April 6, 1962, Lester Cowan Papers, Margaret Herrick Library, Academy of Motion Picture Arts and Sciences, Beverly Hills [hereafter Cowan Papers]. As the collection has not yet been fully cataloged, no file numbers are given.

86. Their film caused outrage from Ministry of Culture bureaucrats, but was eventually supported by Furtseva, who personally took the film to Venice. Woll, *Real Images*, 121–24.

87. "2 Directors Named for U.S.-Soviet Film," *New York Times* , May 18, 1962, 36.

88. Eugene Archer, "Draft Script of '*Far Meridian*' Gets U.S. and Soviet Approval," *New York Times*, July 11, 1962, 28.

89. Frank G. Siscoe, Director, Soviet and Eastern European Exchanges Staff, Department of State, to Lester Cowan, July 13, 1962, RGALI, f. 2944, op. 13, ed. khr. 550, l. 6.

90. Mitchell Wilson, "Space Week in Moscow," *Observer Weekend Review* (London), August 19, 1962, 15.

91. Ronell to Herman Finkelstein, August 26, 1962, 3, Ann Ronell Collection.

92. Documented by photographs in the Ann Ronell Collection.

93. Boris Schwarz, *Music and Musical Life in Soviet Russia 1917–1970* (London: Barrie and Jenkins, 1972), 317–18. In late 1962 the Composers Union was at the "height of its power," as showcased in its Third Composers' Congress, with members of forty-two nationalities and foreign guests, including the United States. Khrennikov was reelected first secretary. Ibid., 348–49, 360.

94. "Little Lady of Song: An Interview with Composer Ann Ronell," interview by the USIA staff, Washington, DC, for their magazine *Amerika*, n.d. (presumably late 1964 or early 1965), Ann Ronell Collection. She also wrote a new section for a longer version with the title "Take Me, Take Me to the Moon," anticipating its use in *Meeting at a Far Meridian*. Thanks to Tighe Zimmers for providing the sheet music.

95. RGALI, f. 2944, op. 13, ed. khr. 550, ll. 47–50.

96. "U.S.-Soviet Film to Treat 'Cold War' Realistically: '*Far Meridian*' to Show How Two Scientists Overcome Ideological Barriers," *New York Times* (dateline: Moscow), September 6, 1962.

97. Correspondence between Senator Stuart Symington and Frederick G. Dutton, Assistant Secretary of State, September 25, 1962, and November 7, 1962, NARA, RG 59, 511.615/92562.

98. Foy D. Kohler, US Ambassador in Moscow, to Secretary of State (telegram), October 19, 1962, NARA, RG 59, 511.615/10–1962.

99. Amid the large literature on the Cuban Missile Crisis, see A. A. Fursenko and

Timothy J Naftali, *One Hell of a Gamble: Khrushchev, Castro, and Kennedy, 1958–1964* (London: Pimlico, 1999).

100. On the decision to publish *One Day,* see William Taubman, *Khrushchev: The Man and His Era,* 1st ed. (New York: W. W. Norton, 2003), 525–28.

101. Although they were known for film noir like *D.O.A.,* their most recent success had been the Academy Award for the romantic comedy *Pillow Talk* (1959) with Doris Day. The translation they intended to use was yet a third one by the same Boris Leven who was also consulted on the *Far Meridian* project.

102. "Greene-Rouse Envision Soviet Aid in Filming K-Okayed Book," *Variety,* January 23, 1963, emphasis added. According to his first wife, Natalia Reshetovskaia, Solzhenitsyn turned down several offers to "turn it into a film in the Soviet Union" because he believed that every work of art had an optimal form of expression. Cited in Ben Hellman and Andrei Rogachevskii, *Filming the Unfilmable: Casper Wrede's "One Day in the Life of Ivan Denisovich"* (Stuttgart: Ibidem-Verlag, 2010), 11.

103. "*Far Meridian,*" Cowan to Furtseva, February 8, 1963 (reverse translation from Russian), RGALI, f. 2453, op. 4, ed. khr. 1305, l. 25. The Cowan Papers as currently cataloged lack correspondence from 1962 to 1964. This letter was found in the official Soviet translator's file for the project.

104. RGANI, f. 5, op. 55, d. 52, l. 36. Reprinted in *Kinematograf ottepeli: Dokumenty i Svidetel'stva* (Moscow: Materik, 1998), but with incorrect date. David Caute, *The Dancer Defects,* 238, cites this document with the correct date but lacks the context of the *Far Meridian* story.

105. As is well known, from his appointment to the post in mid-1962, Ambassador Dobrynin recognized the use of "confidential channels" in negotiating with Americans. Anatoly Fedorovich Dobrynin, *In Confidence: Moscow's Ambassador to America's Six Cold War Presidents (1962–1986),* (New York: Times Books, 1995), 52–55.

106. Nancy Condee, "Cultural Codes of the Thaw," in *Nikita Khrushchev,* ed. William Taubman, Sergei Khrushchev, and Abbot Gleason (New Haven: Yale University Press, 2000), 164.

107. Valery S. Golovskoy, with John Rimberg, *Behind the Soviet Screen,* trans. Steven Hill (Ann Arbor: Ardis, 1986), 13–14.

108. Peter Johnson (Reuters), "New Film 'Czar' Named in Red Cultural Shakeup," *Washington Post,* March 24, 1963.

109. Quoted in Woll, *Real Images,* 225.

110. Priscilla Johnson, *Khrushchev and the Arts: The Politics of Soviet Culture, 1962–1964* (Cambridge, MA: MIT Press, 1965), 95–101; Woll, *Real Images,* 103–111.

111. Theodore Shabad, "Soviet Arts Shift Spares Joint Film: Culture Chief Assures U.S. Producer Plan Is Safe," *New York Times,* May 19, 1963.

112. Surin to Furtseva, January 29, 1963, RGALI, f. 2453, op. 4, ed. khr. 1306, l. 5; various telegrams, ibid., ll. 13, 23, 24, 26, 27; Cowan to Surin, January 25 and February 19, 1963, ibid., ll. 14, 15.

113. Conversation with Lester Cowan at the USSR Union of Cinema Workers, May 9, 1963, RGALI, f. 2944, op. 13, ed. khr. 89, ll. 18–21. Valerii Fomin, a senior film scholar, notes that the report on Cowan was the first of a new genre defined as "the record of the talk with" that he compares to writing familiar from KGB agents. "The Year 1963," http://www.film.ru/article.asp?ID=2210 (accessed March 2011).

114. From the diary of the adviser to the Soviet ambassador, E V. Bugrov, Report on the Trip to New York City, May 21–24, 1963, RGALI, f. 2944, op. 13, ed. khr. 550, ll. 61–63.

115. "Memorandum of Suggestions for Improvement of Screenplay as discussed and agreed upon by Lester Cowan, Vladimir Surin and Mitchell Wilson (28–29 May 1963) New York," Cowan Papers.

116. Bugrov diary, RGALI, f. 244, op. 13, ed. khr. 550, ll. 61–63.

117. "Ready Plans for Joint U.S.-Russian Film," *Motion Picture Daily,* May 29, 1963, 1, 3.

118. Cowan to Romanov, August 13, 1963, RGALI, f. 2944, op. 13, ed. khr. 550, l. 76.

119. Funigiello, *American-Soviet Trade in the Cold War,* 142–52.

120. Cowan to Leonard [Goldenson] of ABC Television, 1984. Ann Ronell Collection.

121. RGALI, f. 2944, op. 13, ed. khr. 550, ll. 141–42.

122. RGALI, f. 2453, op. 4, ed. khr. 1306, ll. 2–3. This practice inaugurated the film exchange with the November 1959 film premiers of *Marty* in Moscow and *The Cranes Are Flying* [*Letiat zhuravli,* 1957] a few weeks later in Washington, DC. Gary Cooper and the American delegates were introduced by the Soviet minister of culture and the Washington premiere, was attended by the US Secretary of State. B. Galanov, "Premiere of American Film," *Izvestiia,* November 11, 1959, 6; *CDSP* 45, no. 11 (December 9, 1959); Bosley Crowther, "Screen: Exchange Film: The Cranes are Flying Bows Here," *New York Times,* March 22, 1960.

123. Max Frankel, "U.S., Soviet to Tackle Cultural Exchange," *New York Times,* November 12, 1963, 6.

124. Lester Cowan, "Notes on Kennedy Death, etc.," n.d., Cowan Papers. Typed by Cowan with only rare capital letters and many ellipses. Spacing typos, misspellings, and type-overs are not reproduced in the quotations unless judged meaningful.

125. Dana Polan, *Scenes of Instruction: The Beginnings of the U.S. Study of Film,* 1st ed. (Berkeley: University of California Press, 2007), 175–93.

126. Cowan, "Notes on Kennedy Death, etc."

127. Khrushchev told his staff that Kennedy's speech was the best given by any US president since Roosevelt. Taubman, *Khrushchev,* 602.

128. Cowan, "Notes on Kennedy Death, etc."

129. Ibid.

130. Cowan to Romanov, November 28, 1963, RGALI, f. 2944, op. 13, ed. khr. 550, l. 81.

131. In Cowan's later account, Romanov was responsible for removing Alov and Naumov from *Far Meridian,* which was first attributed to the "moral issue" created by *The Coin,* but then the Writers Union became involved. "Romanov at one point refuted his firing of them, but when Cowan requested other directors, they were 'busy.' Eventually Romanov 'repudiated his repudiation' and allowed Talankin to become director after Cowan threatened to appoint an American." "Reference Memo: Background Reasons for Presentation of Protocol Demands on Tuesday, December 15," December 10, 1964, Cowan Papers.

132. Cowan to Romanov , December 20, 1963, RGALI, f. 2944, op. 13, ed. khr. 550, ll. 85–87. A large portion of this letter argued for a mutual guarantee of completion required by the US investors. In lieu of dollars, at Surin's request, Cowan proposed bartering release prints for the film. He describes the relationship between himself as a US businessman who invested "brave money" without assurance that the screenplay would be accepted and the "unlimited resources" of the Soviet state.

133. Furtseva was also instrumental in this film's completion. Woll, *Real Images,* 109, 145.

134. Cowan to Siscoe, January 7, 1964, RGALI, f. 2944, op. 13, ed. khr. 551, ll. 119–21.

135. Cowan to Romanov *aide memoire* (with copy to Kohler), January 13, 1964, RGALI, f. 2944, op. 13, ed. khr. 551, ll. 16–17; also found as enclosure in a letter to the White House, August 25, 1965, in S. Douglass Cater, White House Aides Collection, Lyndon Baines Johnson Library, Austin, Texas.

136. Kohler recounts that Russians would often come ask him to include one of their

proposals in the American negotiations for the renewal of the exchange agreements because the Soviet authorities would not. "Naturally, I obliged." Foy D. Kohler, *Understanding the Russians: A Citizen's Primer,* 1st ed. (New York: Harper & Row, 1970), 128.

137. Remarks by Ambassador Kohler, press release 76, dated February 22, reprinted in [US] *Department of State Bulletin,* March 23, 1964: 451–52.

138. Cowan to Romanov *aide memoire.* Two scripts can be identified in the first part of 1964. An English-language script was sent to Harrison Salisbury, former Moscow bureau chief for the *New York Times,* who remarks in a February 19 letter to Cowan that the proposed script has a "substantial degree of realism" and that it "would be most difficult for anyone on either side to claim a propaganda advantage." His only objection was that in his own experience it would be rare for a Russian waitress to refuse a tip. Harrison E. Salibury, Director of National Correspondence for the New York Times, to Cowan, February 19, 1964, Cowan Papers. A second literary scenario—in Russian and uncut—by Igor Talankin and dated March 1964 (in Cowan Papers) was still not seen by Cowan as of his April 9, 1965, letter to Talankin.

139. Sergei Gerasimov, "Meetings at a *Far Meridian,*" *Izvestiia,* July 5, 1964.

140. "Screenplay changes and improvements agreed upon as a result of meetings in New York and California between Fay Kanin and Messrs. Gerassimov [*sic*], Talankin and Cowan," July 1, 1964, Cowan Papers.

141. Gerasimov, "Meetings at a *Far Meridian.*"

142. Abe Greenberg, "U.S. to Be Patsy in Russ Film Deal?" *Citizen News,* n.d.[ca. May 29, 1964].

143. "Three in Hollywood Signed for American-Soviet Film," *New York Times,* July 4, 1964.

144. Wilson to Romanov. July 21, 1964; Gerasimov and Talankin to Wilson, August 26, 1964; Gerasimov and Talankin to Cowan, n.d., Cowan to Gerasimov, September, 26, 1964, RGALI, f. 2944, op. 13, ed. khr. 551, ll. 29–37.

145. Louis Calta, "News of the Rialto: Lester Cowan Readies New Musical with Soviet Setting," *New York Post,* July 19, 1964.

146. "Program and Schedule of Work in the USSR," October 2, 1964, Cowan Papers. This document, which appears to be written for Surin, does not seem either to have been sent or to have reached him, since it discusses new arrangements with MGM studios as a partner to Walter Reade.

147. "Reconstruction of Screenplay (Cowan, Kanin, Gersimov & Talankin), Nov. 20-Dec. 14, 1964," Cowan Papers.

148. "Reference Memo: Background Reasons." He also expects to get a completion guarantee from the Export-Import Bank.

149. Minutes of the talk with the chairman of the USSR State Committee for Cinematography, Comrade A. V. Romanov, with American producer Lester Cowan, December 14, 1964, RGALI, f. 2944, op. 13, ed. khr. 551, ll. 42–46.

150. "Meeting at a Far Meridian," RGALI, f. 2453, op. 4, ed. khr. 75, ll. 2–3.

151. "The First Joint U.S.S.R.-U.S.A. Film," *Soviet Film* 91 (December 1964): 13.

152. Surin to Reade, n.d., RGALI, f. 2944, op. 13, ed. khr. 552, ll. 13–14.

153. Wilson to Talankin and Gersimov (Russian translation), February 13, 1965, RGALI, F. 2944, op. 13, ed. khr. 552, ll. 24–25.

154. A. Slavnov to Romanov, February 27, 1965, RGALI, f. 2944, op. 13, ed. khr. 552, l. 26.

155. Record of Conversation with Lester Cowan at Mosfilm, March 3, 1965, RGALI, f. 2944, op. 13, ed. khr. 552, ll. 35–39.

156. Record of Conversation between Surin and Cowan (and the interpreter Anashenkova), Hotel Metropole, March 9, 1965, RGALI, f. 2944, op. 13, ed. khr. 552, ll. 53–57.

157. Record of Conversation with Lester Cowan at Mosfilm, March 24, 1964,

RGALI, f. 2944, op. 13, ed. khr. 552, ll. 68–75. At this meeting Cowan says he is embarrassed by the fact that notes are taken on the conversation.

158. Sally Hammond, "A Veteran of Cultural Exchange Will Write It into a Film Script," *New York Post,* March 17, 1965.

159. Jack Pitman, "With Joint U.S.-USSR Pic Still Pending, Cowan-Ronell Try TV Cold War Thaw," *Variety,* March 17, 1965.

160. Cited in the translation of Vladimir Surin's letter to Lester Cowan, postmarked June 25, 1965, received on July 19; Cowan telegram to V. Surin, Cowan Papers.

161. Ambassador Kohler to Secretary of State, October 19, 1962, NARA, RG 59, 511.615/10–1962.

162. Although no copy of this plan has yet turned up in the Soviet archive, the plan is not inconsistent with Furtseva's interest in coproductions. Woll states that while generous to younger directors, she became more dogmatic after Khrushchev's ouster. But Ambassador Kohler notes that his "old friend Furtseva" concluded her attack on America at the Twenty-Third Party Congress with the affirmation "After all, we have to be willing and able to compete." She also supported the coproduced biopic on Tchaikovsky in the United States in 1972. Marsha Siefert, "Russische Leben, Sowjetische Filme: Die Filmbiographie, Tchaikovsky und der Kalte Krieg," in *Leinwand zwischen Tauwetter und Frost: Der osteuropäische Spiel- und Dokumentarfilm im Kalten Krieg,* ed. Lars Karl (Berlin: Metropol, 2007), 133–70; Foy D. Kohler, "Trends and Prospects of U.S.-Soviet Relations," speech presented at the National War College, Washington, DC, January 25, 1967, 13–14, Foy Kohler Papers, Canaday Center, University of Toledo Libraries, box 16, MSS-036; Woll, *Real Images,* 145.

163. *The Last Battle* was the title of a book by Cornelius Ryan, author of *The Longest Day,* and portrayed the battle of Berlin; the movie was to reenact the part played by Soviet troops and the meeting at the River Elbe. This MGM project was still being discussed by Cowan in a letter to Romanov in November of 1965. Cowan to Romanov, November 23, 1965, Cowan Papers.

164. Cowan to Edwin L. Weisl, June 21, 1965, S. Douglass Cater, White House Aides Collection, Lyndon Baines Johnson Library.

165. Ibid.

166. Surin to Cowan, postmarked June 25, 1965, stamped received July 19, 1925, English translation in Cowan Papers.

167. Romanov to Ambassador Dobrynin, draft, n.d. RGALI, f. 2944, op. 3, ed. khr. 551, ll. 55–57.

168. Cowan to Surin, Cowan to Romanov, July 1965, Cowan Papers.

169. Cowan to McPherson, August 23, 1965, S. Douglass Cater, White House Aides Collection.

170. Cowan to Romanov, Cowan to Furtseva, Cowan to Boskakov [*sic*], Surin, and Gerasimov, November 23, 1965, Cowan Papers.

171. Surin to Cowan, January 19, 1966, Cowan Papers.

172. Vincent Canby, "U.S.-Soviet Deals on Films Pending," *New York Times,* February 26, 1966, 14. "Life of Tschaikovsky [*sic*] Will Be U.S.-Russ Film," *Los Angeles Times,* April 4, 1966, C27; Siefert, "Russische Leben, Sowjetische Filme."

173. "Much More Tiring," *Evening Standard* (London), May 7, 1966.

174. Siefert, "Co-Producing Cold War Culture," 87.

175. Cowan to Leonard [Goldenson], draft ca. 1984. There is as yet no evidence that the letter, found in the Ann Ronell Collection, was ever sent. Of course, Furtseva remained in office almost another ten years after *Far Meridian* was suspended.

176. "Takie raznye i v to zhe vremia udivitel'no blizkie drug drugu. Oni molchat, kazhdyi dumaia o svoëm." Talankin script, "*Meeting at a Far Meridian,*" Cowan Papers.

CONTRIBUTORS

Patryk Babiracki is an assistant professor in Russian and East European history at the University of Texas-Arlington and Volkswagen-Andrew W. Mellon Post-doctoral Fellow at the Zentrum für Zeithistorische Forschung in Potsdam. He is completing his first monograph *Soviet Soft Power and the Poles: The Battle for Hearts and Minds in Stalin's New Empire, 1943–1957.* His current research concentrates on transnational dimensions of Soviet and East European communisms during the Cold War.

Michael David-Fox holds a joint appointment in the Edmund A. Walsh School of Foreign Service and the Department of History at Georgetown University. He has published widely on the political, cultural, and intellectual history of late imperial Russia and the early Soviet Union. He is author of *Revolution of the Mind: Higher Learning among the Bolsheviks, 1917–1929* and *Showcasing the Great Experiment: Cultural Diplomacy and Western Visitors to the Soviet Union, 1921–1941* (Oxford, 2011), and the forthcoming *Crossing Borders: Modernity, Ideology, and Culture in Soviet Russia.* He is currently conducting research for a book entitled "Smolensk under Nazi and Soviet Rule." David-Fox is founding and executive editor of the journal *Kritika: Explorations in Russian and Eurasian History.*

Constantin Katsakioris is a historian whose research concentrates on the relations between the Soviet Union and the Third World. He is currently completing his PhD thesis at the Ecole des Hautes Etudes en Sciences Sociales in Paris. He has published articles in the *Cahiers du Monde Russe,* the *Journal of Modern European History,* the *Ezhegodnik sotsial'noi istorii,* as well as various reviews and essays in several edited volumes.

Elidor Mëhilli teaches in the history department at Hunter College of the City University of New York. Previously, he held fellowships at Columbia University and the University of Pennsylvania. He is working on a book on socialist globalization through the angle of Albania under Yugoslav, Soviet, Eastern bloc, and Chinese patronage, based on archival research in Tirana, Berlin, London, Moscow, Rome, and Washington.

Nick Rutter received his PhD in history from Yale in 2013 and is currently revising his dissertation for publication as a book, tentatively titled, *Communism's Party: The World Youth Festivals, 1945–1989.* He is the author of, "Look Left, Drive Right: Internationalisms at the 1968 World Youth Festival," in Diane P. Koenker and Anne E. Gorsuch (eds.), *The Socialist Sixties: Crossing Borders in the Second World* (Indiana, 2013).

Marsha Siefert teaches cultural and communications history at Central European University, Budapest. Her edited books include *Mass Culture and Perestroika in the Soviet Union* and *Extending the Borders of Russian History,* along with books on world communication and the history of technology. Recent publications include book chapters on film co-productions and cultural diplomacy in the USSR and Eastern Europe, the subject of her current book project, and on nineteenth-century telegraph systems in the Russian and Ottoman Empires. She was for many years the editor of the *Journal of Communication* at the University of Pennsylvania and co-edited two book series with Longman Publishers and Oxford University Press. She is currently co-editing the book series *Historical Studies in Eastern Europe and Eurasia,* for Central European University Press.

Kenyon Zimmer is an assistant professor of history at the University of Texas at Arlington. His research focuses on the intersections between migration and political radicalism, and has appeared in *Labor: Studies in Working-Class History of the Americas, The International Encyclopedia of Revolution and Protest, 1500-Present* (Blackwell, 2010), and *The Encyclopedia of Global Human Migration* (Wiley-Blackwell, 2013). He is the author (with Mario Gianfrate) of *Michele Centrone, tra vecchio e nuovo mondo: Anarchici Pugliesi in difesa della libertá spagnola* (SUMA Editore, 2012), and is currently completing a book on Jewish and Italian anarchists in the United States.

Vladislav M. Zubokis is chair of International History, Department of History, London School of Economics. His numerous publications include *Inside the Kremlin's Cold War: From Stalin to Khrushchev* with C. Pleshakov (Harvard University Press, 1996), *A Failed Empire: the Soviet Union in the Cold War from Stalin to Gorbachev* (University of North Carolina Press, 2007), and *Zhivago's Children: The Last Russian Intelligentsia* (Belknap Press, 2009). He is a recipient of numerous fellowships and professional awards, including the Lionel Gelber and Marshall Schulman prizes; the W. Glenn Campbell and Rita Riccardo-Campbell National Fellowship at the Hoover Institution, Stanford University; fellowships at the George Washington University's National Security Archive; and the Cold War International History Project at the Woodrow Wilson International Center for Scholars. In 1995–98, Zubok was one of the principal consultants of the CNN 24-part series "Cold War." In 2007–12, he was director of the Carnegie Corporation's International Summer School Project for Social Sciences and Humanities for the young educators of the post-Soviet space. Zubok is currently finishing a book on life and works of Dmitry Likhachev, and is starting a new project about the collapse of the USSR.

INDEX

Selected Titles in the Walter Prescott Webb Memorial Lecture Series

The African Diaspora, Alusine Jalloh and Stephen E. Maizlish

Manifest Destiny and Empire, Sam W. Haynes and Christopher M. Morris

Creolization in the Americas, David Buisseret and Steven G. Reinhardt

Women and the Unstable State in Nineteenth-Century America, Alison M. Parker and Stephanie Cole

Sacrifice and National Belonging in Twentieth-Century Germany, Gregg Eghigian and Matthew Paul Berg

Beyond Black and White: Race, Ethnicity, and Gender in the U.S. South and Southwest, Stephanie Cole and Alison M. Parker

Traveling between Worlds: German-American Encounters, Thomas Adam and Ruth Gross

Transatlantic History, Steven G. Reinhardt and Dennis Reinhartz

Lights, Camera, History: Portraying the Past in Film, Richard V. Francaviglia and Jerry Rodnitsky

Catholicism in the American West, Roberto R. Treviño and Richard V. Francaviglia

Baseball in America and America in Baseball, Donald G. Kyle and Robert B. Fairbanks

Assumed Identities: The Meanings of Race in the Atlantic World, John D. Garrigus and Christopher Morris

Crossing the Atlantic: Travel and Travel Writing in Modern Times, Thomas Adam and Nils H. Roemer

The Folly of Jim Crow: Rethinking the Segregated South, Stephanie Cole and Natalie J. Ring

The Mexican Revolution: Conflict and Consolidation, 1910–1940, Douglas W. Richmond and Sam W. Haynes